# A Brief History of Theology

# A Brief History of Theology

## From the New Testament to Feminist Theology

Derek Johnston

continuum

**Continuum International Publishing Group**

The Tower Building
11 York Road
London SE1 7NX

80 Maiden Lane
Suite 704, New York
NY 10038

www.continuumbooks.com



**British Library Cataloguing-in-Publication Data**

A catalogue record for this book is available from the British Library.

ISBN-10: HB: 1-8470-6090-0
PB: 1-8470-6091-9
ISBN-13: HB: 978-1-8470-6090-7
PB: 978-1-8470-6091-4

**Library of Congress Cataloging-in-Publication Data**

A catalog record for this book is available from the Library of Congress.

Typeset by Newgen Imaging Systems Pvt Ltd, Chennai, India
Printed and bound in Great Britain by MPG Books Ltd, Bodmin, Cornwall

For

Penny, Caroline, Hugh and Keith

# Contents

# Introduction

Some people think that Theology is a body of knowledge given to some and held back from others. It seems to me, however, that Theology is a process; one never comes to a finished state of theological insight and one can never say, 'I know it all, now!' Theology is a struggle between a sense of summons and the world in which we live. That summons is the uncomfortable, persistent nagging of a value that surpasses us.

The purpose of this book is not to write History and not to write Theology. It is aimed at the first-time reader of Theology, the person who wonders what it is all about. So, hopefully, you will be introduced here to the sort of ideas that have occupied the attention of theologians, and more importantly, to the sort of language that theologians use. This little volume will not answer all your questions. My hope, however, is that it will answer some and provide the foundations from which you may continue to think theologically.

The fact that you have picked up this book is already an indication that you are interested in 'doing' Theology. In fact we all ask the sort of questions Theology struggles with. Here are a few of them: Does God exist? How do we know? How can I come to know God? Where have we come from? Who are we? What is our ultimate purpose? If you are asking such questions (you do not have to be answering them), then you are already 'doing' Theology. Most people do Theology and never realize it.

In a work of this size, one could never cover everything that theologians have wrestled with during the two millennia of Christian speculation. So, inevitably, people will ask questions such as 'why did you put in so and so?' and 'why did you leave such and such a person out?' The second aim of the book is, therefore, to allow you to become familiar with a broad range of theological styles, rather than with everything.

It has never been my purpose to confine myself to academic Theology. It seems to me to be much more interesting to examine how a wide variety of individuals, from a broad diversity of backgrounds, have allowed that mysterious sense of summons to rub up against the contexts in which they found themselves. What most of them do is illustrate a style of doing Theology that has been influential over generations; the more recent ones offer possibilities which people may, or may not, run with. I have thought it important to devote about half the work to twentieth century figures: Theology is actuality!

Thirdly, I thought it better not to deal too much with abstractions. This may seem a strange idea for a subject as rarefied as Theology, but people may be interested in ideas while finding abstract discourse difficult. Consequently I have tried to tie different ways of doing Theology to a person, hoping that the concreteness of the person will carry along the abstractness of the thinking.

Finally, I am convinced that Theology is not something that belongs exclusively within ivory towers and ivy-covered walls but is something that a great many people do in the concreteness of their daily lives and are frequently surprised to find that they are doing it.

But what do we mean by Theology? We may have to look at a wide variety of examples of theological thought, but let us see if we can get some basic notion of what is meant when we talk about both Philosophy and Theology.

Theology is an effort to organize the doctrines of religion in a systematic fashion. Religion is the expression of how we see the ultimate nature of Reality: some of its elements are rational; some of its elements are not. (This is not the same as saying they are irrational.)

The non-rational elements involve intuitions, emotions and the surrender of self to God in worship. Such elements depend on the content of the 'revelation' of religion. This 'revelation' includes information or knowledge considered to have come from a divine source.

The rational elements of religion are how people think about that revelation, work out values, give balanced importance to the teaching of holy books and holy teachers, judge questions of right and wrong, and plan and develop liturgy and worship in the light of what they have pondered.

Theology assumes that religion is a convincing and authentic human activity; its basic premises are those of faith (non-rational). Theology organizes the ideas involved in religion into a reasonable, logical and coherent system. Theology enquires into the implications of faith and sifts out what is not consistent with its truth and values.

Philosophy assumes only that all experience can be examined in a rational manner. It tries to give a coherent, consistent, comprehensive account of human experience and of our environment. This is done by means of reason, without revelation. There is a very clear tension between the two ways of thinking. While religion finds its most important expression in surrender to God, philosophy does not surrender itself to theory that cannot be proved.

The theologian argues that Spirit is the true source of all existence and that Spirit maintains a true fellowship with all who depend on it. The theologian must therefore distinguish carefully between all elements that have real spiritual importance and those elements which have merely traditional and emotional value. The philosopher accepts the methods of Science and notes that Science does not concern itself with values. A Philosophy of Religion is only possible when we accept the fact that intuition and a sense of values are part of the reality in which we live and which we are investigating.

Christian Theology is thinking about Christian faith. This suggests two things: our activity will use the tools of reason and our activity will be critical. That is to say, it will make judgements. But what about faith? Is that a critical and rational activity? Probably not, though it does not despise reason! Let us say simply that it has to do with belief concerning something of great value and that what is glimpsed here commits us to seeing everything – the world, our lives and those around us – under a certain light.

When theologians came to write their theology they were giving, in terms appropriate for their day, what they considered to be an appropriate way of stating the Christian Gospel.

Why then are there so many different ways of expressing that gospel? It all depends on what one's concerns are and what is considered to be most important. The early Christian writers were worried about death. The writers of the Middle Ages were concerned with guilt. By the time of the Reformation this had become an obsession. The Reformation writers may well have cleared the intellectual way for the modern world, but they were in many ways still medieval in their mindset. Is the dynamic of grace which they expressed so powerfully one of the obsessions of the modern age?

Post-Enlightenment thinkers are more worried about progress and scientific discovery. But does this allow them to escape from considerations about values? Has not the abuse of scientific and technological power (e.g. Holocaust, Gulag and industrial pollution) thrown us back in confusion to seek a sure base for ethical outlook and moral action?

And what preoccupies those who inhabit the world in the opening years of the twenty-first century? Would it be a sense of alienation? We experience alienation from our best selves by the demands of a market economy and alienation from community by the economic imperatives of affordable housing and long hours commuting. We are aware of alienation from family in the experience of the latchkey child with parents away from the home all day and in the practice of weekend marriage where marital partners must live the working week hundreds of miles apart and may only meet two days out of seven. We are coming to know alienation from the earth as we inhabit an increasingly polluted environment, which we have little time to repair or control. We feel alienated from power as unscrupulous operators manipulate the levers of power for their own ends or as faceless multinational companies manoeuvre, often clandestinely, to shape the economic climate to their best advantage.

That was a very negative list. What does talk of creation and redemption, of right and wrong, of ultimate concern or of God with us, mean in such contexts? This book will not necessarily answer all or any of these questions. But it seeks to give an insight as to what have been the questions of ultimate concern in a number of historical and social contexts of the past. It hopes to raise questions about these topics in the minds of its readers and to set them off on their own theological quest.

# 1 The First Christian Theologians: St Paul

We do not think of writers of the New Testament as theologians. We tend to think of them as the authors of the raw materials out of which later thinkers developed Theology.

The writings which we read in the New Testament are all about Jesus of Nazareth who was a popular and, at times, exasperating religious teacher in early first-century Palestine. His impact upon his followers was so great that they came to see him as the messenger of God, seeking out those who were in need of the comfort of God. This mission infuriated both the religious and civil powers and as a result they had him executed.

However, his followers were so convinced of the God-given quality of his message that they experienced it in renewed fashion, found it impossible to ignore and were conscious of the presence of Jesus with them as one raised by God from the dead. They conferred on Jesus a title: the Christ. This meant the 'Anointed One' or the 'One Sent by God'.

As you can see from the paragraph above, this is more than the telling of a story, this is thinking about a life and a message in a certain way and moulding that story to be significant for living. The early writers were not just telling a story, they were interpreting a life and a message, beginning to think systematically and critically.

## The world of the first Christians

The first Christians appeared in a tiny province of the Roman Empire. That huge empire stretched down from Northern Britain, covered much of western continental Europe, went around the eastern side of the Mediterranean and included the northern fertile lands of the African continent out as far as the Atlantic Ocean. Augustus had put an end to the long series of civil wars which had brought the proud Roman Republic to a whimpering end, and he had replaced it with a strong, central imperial government and competent administration. It was like a ring of well-governed territories around the Mediterranean Sea: 'Our Sea' as the Romans called it.

The Roman Empire was in transition and central authority was at its strongest, but traditional values were crumbling. There was a new interest in ethical philosophies, particularly ones claiming to have universal application. These were expected to provide comfort and reassurance for the deepest human longings.

The tiny province where Christianity emerged was Judea in the eastern part of the empire. It covered roughly the modern Israeli and Palestinian lands. This was ruled, on behalf of Rome, by puppet kings, sons of Herod the Great. There was a Roman governor in Jerusalem. Through this land ran the main land routes connecting the northern part of the empire (Europe and Asia Minor) and the southern part (Mediterranean Africa).

The Jewish religious situation was complex but might be stated very simply as follows. The Sadducees were religious conservatives who co-operated with the Romans and generally had control of the Temple. The Pharisees were religious modernists and rigorous upholders of the ritual law who taught a new doctrine of resurrection. This was the notion that, after death, God would raise up individuals for judgement. They would then be rejected or accepted as worthy of being, for ever, in the presence of God.

The third current involved religious ascetics, anxious to leave the corruption of civilization and to lead harsh and simple lives in religious communities in the desert, where they awaited the Day of the Lord. The Essenes are examples of this tendency. There were also political purists, physical-force nationalists, called Zealots, who brooded over the possibility of armed rebellion, the overthrow of Rome and the return to a pure Jewish lifestyle and government.

## What we know about the writers

What writings exist about Jesus? In the New Testament, the writings which Christians accept as having authority, there are four types. First, there are the gospels. 'Gospel' means good news, and is the name given to four texts telling the story of the life and ministry of Jesus. Then there is the Acts of the Apostles which is the story of the very early Christian church, later concentrating on the life, travels and witness of Paul. Thirdly, there are letters to churches in various parts of the eastern Roman Empire, all about living life as Jesus would have wished. Finally, there is a book of visions, called Revelation or the Apocalypse. We are just going to look at five writers or documents.

We really know very little about these writers. We can say with a high degree of probability that the first to write about Jesus Christ was Paul; later texts are named after Matthew, Luke and John. All are mentioned in the gospel writings as disciples of Jesus. Finally, there was Mark; is he the Mark mentioned in the Acts of the Apostles? We cannot be sure that these people all actually wrote the texts that are attributed to them. Some of the texts may have come from early church communities who particularly venerated the memory of one apostle or another. This rapid overview by no means covers all the texts of the New Testament nor does it do full justice to the complexities they reveal.

### Timeline

44 BCE Death of Julius Caesar
19 BCE Death of Virgil; the *Aeneid* published posthumously
5 BCE approx. Birth of Jesus
4 BCE Death of Herod the Great
26 CE Pontius Pilate becomes governor of Judea
27 CE approx. Baptism of Jesus by John the Baptist
30 CE approx. Crucifixion of Jesus
38 CE approx. Conversion of Paul
64 CE Nero becomes Emperor: first persecution of Christians
65 CE approx. Martyrdom of Peter and Paul
70 CE Destruction of Jerusalem by Titus
70–90 CE Writing of the gospel accounts named Matthew, Mark and Luke
70–82 CE Building of the Coliseum
85–100 CE Writing of the gospel account named John

## Life (died 65 CE)

This chapter will deal with just one of the New Testament writers: St Paul. Paul was a Jew who was born in Tarsus in modern Turkey. He was a cultivated man who had received both a Jewish and a Greek education. He had also acquired Roman citizenship. It was thanks to him that Christianity was first expressed in a way that could be understood by non-Jews. Jesus had used stories and images drawn from the countryside: the farmer sowing seed, the fig tree and the shepherd. Paul used the language of the cosmopolitan city: athletic contests, military service, slave-owning, the theatre and trade.

Though he was born in Tarsus, he appears to have grown up in Jerusalem and to have received an orthodox Jewish education. He himself names his principal teacher as Gamaliel, a well-known Pharisee of the early first century AD. He followed one of the strictest disciplines known in the Jewish world of his time. He was a Pharisee. Like the Pharisees, Jesus had been a believer in, and a teacher of, the doctrine of the resurrection. There is, however, no suggestion that Paul and Jesus ever met.

Paul was present, as a young man, on the occasion of the stoning of Stephen (Acts 7). He was active in persecuting the early Christian church, until he had a vision of the Risen Christ and experienced dramatic and sudden conversion while travelling to Damascus.

From now on he would be one of the most energetic supporters of the new faith, travelling far and wide to preach and gain converts to Christianity. He also became a prolific writer of early Christian texts. Much of the New Testament is attributed to him, although it is possible that not all the documents so described were actually written by Paul; they may be the work of pupils.

Paul did not, of course, receive a ready-made theology on his conversion; neither did those who had known Jesus personally. They were to spend the rest of their lives struggling to apply their insights about Jesus to the lives they now lived, following his departure from them.

After his conversion, Paul spent some years teaching in Arabia, followed by a further three years teaching in Damascus, but we know nothing of his life there. He returned to Jerusalem and met church leaders there. We have been given, in the Acts of the Apostles, an account of three missionary journeys undertaken by Paul. The first was to Antioch, Cyprus and Galatia (in modern Turkey).

Paul returned from this trip with gifts for the relief of hardship in the Jerusalem church. When in Jerusalem he was involved in controversy over whether non-Jewish converts to Christianity should be forced to accept Jewish ritual customs: circumcision, certain banned foods and so on. He was against such a restriction.

On the second missionary journey he revisited Galatia and then crossed to Greece, visiting Philippi, Thessalonica and Athens. He spent some time in Corinth, then via Ephesus and Antioch he returned for a short visit to Jerusalem.

The third journey was to Galatia and to Ephesus. Here he irritated the silversmiths of the city who made statuettes of the goddess Artemis. His preaching must have been bad for business because they rioted against him and he had to leave, moving on to Macedonia and eventually to the Peloponnesus in southern Greece.

After his return to Jerusalem he was praying in the Temple when he was accused of introducing Gentiles (non-Jews) into that part of the Temple reserved for Jews alone. This provoked a riot and he was rescued by being arrested and brought for trial before the Roman governor, Felix. Felix delayed pronouncing judgement, as he hoped Paul would bribe him. He was still in jail two years later when the new governor, Festus, heard his case. Paul appealed his case to the Emperor in Rome. This was his right as a Roman citizen and Festus had no option but to send him to Rome.

During the journey he was shipwrecked off Malta but eventually arrived at his destination. He was placed under house arrest but was free to preach and write. We know little of his death. He was probably executed under Nero.

**Resurrection** is the theological teaching that God would raise up each individual after death to stand in the divine presence and be judged fit for the company of heaven (or not). The early Christians believed that the experiences they had of the presence of Jesus after death were proof of resurrection teaching and a promise of such a hope and destiny for all committed to Jesus.

**Ascetics** are individuals who seek spiritual enlightenment by severely disciplining the body. They tend to shun comfort, luxury, fine clothes, good food and live very simply, even imposing harsh conditions upon themselves.

## Thought

### *The first Christian theologian*

At the beginning of Paul's mission, the fledgling Christian church was composed entirely of Jews who continued to worship in the traditional Jewish fashion, even though they were now followers of Jesus. By the time of Paul's death, those conditions had started to change and within one further generation the situation was totally reversed and the young Christian church was now almost entirely composed of Gentile (non-Jewish) converts. Between Christianity and Judaism a huge gulf had opened up.

Paul seems to have had a gift for abstract thought, even though some of his philosophical or theological concerns seem strange to the twenty-first century mindset. We must also remember that he started elaborating his Christian thought in a context of expectation and suspense; he was expecting Jesus to return soon!

Paul thought long and hard about his situation as a believer in Jesus Christ, about the religious tradition he had come from, what he had been seeking, his failure to find it and how his new faith supplied his need. What is more, he was not content to allow old habits to impose a straightjacket upon the way he thought but argued and fought for a new vision, stressing how different things were, now that he was a follower of Jesus. His thought is strongly marked by his struggle to understand the novelty of the gospel but also by the difficulty to integrate the former (Jewish) awareness of God into the new (Christian) theological vision.

We are now going to have a brief look at a small number of Paul's theological concerns.

### *The mystery of Christ*

Paul felt himself called to a special work in co-operation with God. Paul was convinced that he had a part to play in the mission that had started with the Creation and would eventually end when humanity at large would know the 'fullness of Christ'. Other stages on the road involve the calling, the election, of a holy people by God, the deliverance of the human family from the attachment to sin, their tendency to turn away from God and finally the adoption of the human race as children of God and inheritors of the eternal Son of God. All this is expressed in what we might think of as very fuzzy language.

**Election** is the idea that God in every age chooses a people, or an individual, in preference to others, to carry out some task. It often refers to those who do God's will and remain steadfast in times of trial.
**Sin** is a deliberate missing of the mark; the intentional disobedience to God's known desire; it is the state of humanity which, in its weakness, cannot attain divine perfection.

A further difficulty is that, with Paul, we are not dealing with normal speech. Paul is not setting out a reasoned exposé of new thinking about the human condition. Paul is trying to express, in systematic form, his thoughts about a personal experience and he must now make it understandable by all. He had had a vision of the Risen Christ; the mystery of Christ had been revealed to him by Christ himself in a devastating and earth-shattering experience. His rational mind and systematic education might allow him to dress and present it in a certain way, but the content is like being struck by lightning! Paul is convinced that he is not passing on his own ideas but the thought of Christ himself.

### *Creation and resurrection*

Paul saw the world as made in and through the Word of God. In Christian thought the Word is identified with the second person of the Trinity, the Son, present in the world and present to human persons in the person of Jesus of Nazareth. Christ is the very seed and fullness of all creation – alpha and omega, the beginning and the end.

Twenty-first century people know much about this long, creative process: the genesis of matter, the constitution of a cosmos, the emergence of life – plants, animal and finally reflective (human) life. What is more, human life is reflexive, the only form of creation capable of stepping aside from itself and considering itself at a reflective distance.

But this was not the end of creation; we pass from the stage of creation by God to the stage of co-creation of a universe by created beings, in co-operation with God. What is more, we are invited to become capable of participating in the life of God. Yet human creatures are not complete; they are radically unfinished creatures and also, at a very fundamental level, resist the destiny to which they are called.

Human persons are called, as created beings, to participate in creator–being, in Christ, through the Holy Spirit, the union of creature and creator, the reign of Love. We may not be able to measure the gap, but we may have a sense of its enormity. The death and resurrection of Christ do not create a new creature but they make a new creature possible.

This creation will only be finished, complete and perfected at the final resurrection. Paul starts with the resurrection of Jesus, which he sees as an actual and historical fact. But what does 'resurrection' mean? It originally meant that after death each individual would be raised to be in the presence of God and to be in the same mode as the being of God. It seems to have involved a notion of judgement.

The resurrection of Christ is a model for our resurrection – a 'glorious body' which is just impossible to conceptualize. This is nevertheless the fullness of our destiny. The old flaws are wiped away; what we are, have been and have done are all now made into a truly fulfilled mode, when Christ will 'transform our lowly bodies so that they will be like his glorious body'. (Phil. 3.20)

### *Servitude and freedom*

One of the great stories of the Jewish tradition is the experience of slavery, oppression and abandonment in Egypt, followed by the Exodus, or great escape, led by Moses, the Lawgiver. From it grew the notions of deliverance, redemption and salvation, which were seen as being constant throughout Jewish history and also in personal experience. In Paul's day a slave could 'buy back' (redeem) freedom. Paul used this notion as a theological term. The Jewish tradition often thought in terms of a hero, one who had the mind of God, coming to deliver God's people. From this we get the notion of a 'Saviour'. But note that the Deliverer in the old story was the Lawgiver; the price of being freed from oppression was the call to live as God demands. One could live in slavery to sin or one could live in freedom in accordance with the will of God.

Those who, during the course of Jewish history, were called to act as the leaders or deliverers of the people were seen as having the hand of God upon them. Later this position became formalized and both kings and priests were anointed. This anointing was seen as the sign of the mission conferred on them by God. 'Messiah' meant one who was anointed; the Greek term for anointed is 'Christ'.

As a devout Pharisee, Paul had believed that he must devote strenuous efforts to observing even the most trivial rules of the Law of Moses. In this way he would be justified by the Law; that is to say, he would receive the justice of God eternally because he had been a faithful observer of the Law.

But following his encounter with the Risen Christ he came to see a justification of this sort as impossible. He could never perfectly obey the Law; all such attempts were a type of unconscious slavery. He now saw that Jesus, in his sacrificial living and dying, had swept aside such petty concerns and that all believers were, from now on, justified, relieved of the burden of the Law, because they had turned to Christ. When we are justified by faith we have peace with God (Rom. 5.1); from now on death and sin in the believer are submerged by grace.

### *The Incarnation*

'When the time had fully come, God sent his Son, born of a woman . . . that we might receive the full rights of sons' (Gal. 4.4). The notion that the earth has been visited by God, so that humanity might be persuaded of the sheer enormity of the love of God for human beings, is called the 'Incarnation'. This implies both the action of God and the concrete physical presence of a human being who helps us to become aware of the power of God's love for us. The extremes to which God is prepared to go are exemplified by the crucifixion of Jesus.

What are the limits of the love of God? There are no limits! To what extremes is God prepared to go to bring about the salvation of the world? To every extreme! Paul saw the resurrection of Christ as showing the victory of Jesus; it demonstrated the failure of Jesus' execution. What appeared to be failure, in terms of human judgement and career considerations, was, in fact, the victory of the love of God.

*The Body of Christ*

Christianity is not a set of principles for private consumption. The Jewish tradition had seen the work of God as being demonstrated in a holy nation. In the same way, Christianity saw the fruit of the work of Christ, and the continuation of the work of Christ, being demonstrated in a special community of the resurrection. This community is participation in the life of Christ. Paul referred to it over and over again as 'the Body of Christ'.

When Paul used the word 'church', he could, depending on context, mean the local worshipping assembly or the totality of the members of those who believed in the Risen Christ. This Body of Christ is the Temple of the Holy Spirit. Paul often used images of the body and of building to emphasise that notion of community. He is thinking of something, created out of individual elements, which is, for him, the crucial place of God's action on earth. This Body of Christ offers itself to God as a living sacrifice. The individuals accept their own mortality, they have no hold on, or mastery over, their lives; this allows them to live by grace, through the mercy of God.

**Eucharist** The great Thanksgiving Liturgy of the Church as it celebrates the death and resurrection of Jesus in which believers eat a ritual meal in communion with the sacrifice of Christ; it is also called the Lord's Supper, the Holy Communion, The Mass or The Liturgy.

**Eschatological** Concerned with the last things: death, judgement, heaven and hell. It is concerned with the final destiny and hope, both of the individual and of humanity.

**Covenant** originally an agreement between two parties; it came to be seen as the faithfulness of God towards Israel in return for the inner righteousness of the people before God. Jesus restated it as humanity receiving a gracious gift from God by which their desire to serve God was made perfect. It has its highest expression in the example of the life and death of Jesus.

**Sacrifice** The offering of something costly (often an animal) to God in thanksgiving or to request a favour. Jesus appears to reinterpret the notion of sacrifice as a disposition of the heart in terms of mercy and justice, particularly a disposition to help and be of service to others. Jesus' own death was seen as a self-offering on behalf of all. Christian theology often sees the believer's conscious obedience to God as a sacrifice offered in union with the self-offering of Jesus.
**Apostle** is a title given to the original twelve disciples of Jesus, minus Judas Iscariot, plus Matthias, elected to replace him. An apostle was to be a witness to the resurrection and a member of the group who travelled with Jesus during his time on earth (Acts 1.21–22). Paul and Barnabas also claimed to be apostles. The word originally meant 'somebody sent (by God)'.

### *The Holy Spirit*

Paul constantly refers to the Holy Spirit as dwelling in us. The Spirit in us is the mark of our becoming children of God; it is also the transforming agent that will make us new individuals, spiritual beings. We know we are called to this state of adopted children of God by the witness of the Holy Spirit in us. It is by the power of the Spirit, and through the Spirit, that we pray to God.

This is the source from which we receive that perfected love that allows us to live lives of offering and sacrifice on behalf of others. This is God dwelling in a holy people, creating and strengthening the Body of Christ, through which God is an operative, active, inspiring and transforming presence in the world.

Human action is thus grafted onto divine action. This force does not take away our freedom; on the contrary it allows us to match our freedom with the will of God. The spirit sustains, encourages, cures and strengthens us. It is not a freedom that can either accept or refuse God. It is a freedom that allows us to appreciate where our greatest good lies and agree to it joyfully.

This freedom is a manner of living as Christians in the world. We do not automatically refuse everything the world proposes to us. Rather we are empowered to resist any other reality than God; any other thing which is suggested to us as capable of fulfilling our deepest desires can be refused.

### *Baptism*

For Paul, the event that makes any individual Christian is Baptism. He considers being baptised into Christ Jesus as a dying to sin and a rising with Christ to new life, deeply drawn in to the death and resurrection of Jesus Christ. He asks all Christians to look back to the event of their baptism, to live out the implications and duties of being Christians here in the present and to look forward in hope to being involved in the risen glory of Christ.

The action of asking for and accepting baptism represents and accomplishes a vital union with Christ in the saving events of Jesus' personal history. It is concerned with creating and developing a relationship with Christ and with becoming Christ's disciple. It is always set in the context of radical change (conversion), passing from the dominance of sin to the dominance of life and grace.

However, Christians still living on this earth have not yet come to the stage where God is 'all in all'. Therefore they are in a state of tension between this passing, temporary, at-risk state and the conclusiveness of the resurrection.

The resurrection of Jesus could not take place without his first passing through death so Jesus had to become like us – to empty, to humble himself, to take on the role of slave and to accept death. The believer who is 'in Christ' has also to follow this route; believers must also accept for themselves a 'theology of the cross' to come to a 'theology of resurrection'.

### *The Lord's Supper*

We have four sources for the institution of the Lord's Supper: Paul, Luke, Mark and Matthew. Paul's account (1 Cor. 11.23–25) is probably the earliest. Paul was not present at the institution of the Eucharist. He claimed that he received his information 'from the Lord'. It is often remarked that Paul's emphasis is eschatological, directed to the end of all time, rather than sacrificial. In Paul's understanding, we call the original last meal to memory, and, at the same time, look forward to the great feasting–rejoicing at the end of time.

In Paul's version the bread ritual and the cup ritual appear to be separated by the meal itself. Each is seen as a sign of the Lord's death, but the ritual over the cup is more developed – we come to a new covenant, we are now looking forward and beyond. Other early Eucharistic rituals are seen as beginning to suggest the notion of sacrifice; such a view may be a later development and it is absent from Paul.

Later outlooks would develop the ideas of covenant and sacrifice. 'Covenant' is a very powerful Jewish concept. As Christianity moved out beyond its original Jewish setting, it would find that the idea of 'sacrifice' already had very rich associations. For many, it was already making amends for wrong-doing – a 'getting the accounts straight'. For Judaism, it involved the deep sense of a personal relationship between God and a special people. So the Lord's Supper grew out of an experience of covenant and sacrifice which stretched beyond dependence but was experienced as a giving of self to God in deep communion.

Paul's account mentions first the idea of an offering on behalf of others, 'for you'. Secondly, we find the notion of covenant, but 'the new covenant', presumably arising out of the imminent offering. Thirdly, it states that it is 'in remembrance of me'. What 'remembrance' means would be much debated. It might mean a simple memorial, which is a statement of loss. Or it might mean a 'making present', which is a re-possession beyond what appears to be failure.

### *Paul's letters*

Paul did not write a gospel, in the sense of a life of Jesus. His letters are his writings about the Christian faith and his passionate attachment to the Risen Jesus. They constitute his gospel, and we repeat that this word originally meant 'good news'.

Paul's letters were attempts to work out what the good news of Jesus meant to the people he had met, in their concrete situations, as they went about their daily lives. Here also we have problems, not everybody is convinced that all the texts we possess, and which claim to be by Paul, were actually written by him. In those days it was not unusual for the disciple of a great teacher to write about how the teacher would have approached certain subjects and to write in his name.

In Paul's letters we can see his thought undergoing gradual changes and refinements. In early writings Paul expects the immediate return of Jesus. In other writings Paul is teasing out what it means to be considered 'just' in the eyes of God. In some writings Paul meditates on the role of Christ in creation and in history; in further writings he meditates on the work of Christ in his Church.

More writings are about the organization of the Church and how to keep the faith pure from the corruption of false teachers. These are called the Pastoral Epistles; many believe they are not by Paul but are the work of a follower.

Paul's concern in his letters is to urge believers to practise discernment in their daily Christian lives. His theology was concerned with ethical practice as well as metaphysics. He urged them to develop sharp Christian insights in order to know what is good, what is agreeable and what is perfect.

The Christ event had not just been a historic event but was also an eschatological event (turned towards the end and the fulfilment of time); it involved a new relationship with reality. Christians have a responsibility to show concretely in their lives that human existence can be freed from the fear of death; they must live joyfully and practise justice.

**Metaphysics** is the study of being as being; speculation about the meaning of what is; the study of first principles and first causes; the rational knowledge of those realities that go beyond us; the rational study of things in themselves.

## Appraisal

We talked of Paul trying to put the experience of being 'struck by lightning' into words. It is probably true that only Paul could have expressed a Christian experience in this way. He was, after all, the only highly educated, extremely literate apostle. But is it possible to separate away the content of thought from the way it is expressed? Is it not true that only a person who had had this sort of life experience and training could have expressed Christian faith in this way? Can a Christian theologian operate apart from a context? And when the context changes must the thought be expressed differently?

Paul's texts seem to express Christian teaching in the context of the life of Paul. Does this suggest that there must be, in Christian witness, a transfer of value from the context of the life of Jesus to the context of the life of the believer?

Is Paul the only person who could write in that way? Or are his writings normative for everybody?

# 2 The First Christian Theologians: the Gospel Writers

The New Testament is the collection of writings in Greek which form the second part of the Christian Bible. These texts give special witness to Jesus Christ and the early story of his Church. This collection of texts has four accounts of the life of Jesus which are called gospels. Gospel means 'good news'.

The texts are named after four people: Matthew, Mark, Luke and John. We do not know if any of these individuals had any hand in writing the texts named after them. Some of the texts are considered to be the product of early Christian communities which gathered around the memory of a particular disciple of Jesus. These texts show signs of later editing.

**Timeline**

44 BCE Death of Julius Caesar
5 BCE approx. Birth of Jesus
4 BCE Death of Herod the Great
11 CE Death of Caesar Augustus
26 CE Pontius Pilate becomes governor of Judea
27 CE approx. Baptism of Jesus by John the Baptist
30 CE approx. Crucifixion of Jesus
38 CE approx. Conversion of Paul
64 CE Nero becomes Emperor: first persecution of Christians
65 CE approx. Martyrdom of Peter and Paul
70 CE Destruction of Jerusalem by Titus
70–90 CE Writing of the gospel accounts of Matthew, Mark and Luke
70–82 CE Building of the Coliseum
85–100 CE Writing of the gospel account of John

Before turning to the four New Testament gospels, we must take brief note of the similarities and dissimilarities of three of them and of the problems they pose.

## The synoptic problem

Three of the four gospels (Matthew, Mark and Luke) are known as Synoptic Gospels. Their purpose was to give an outline of the life, teaching and work of Jesus. These three gospels have very obvious differences, but they also have major points of agreement. If one writes an outline of each gospel and lays them side by side so that they can be viewed together (*synopsis*), then we can see that they have more or less the same structure.

Here both the differences and the likenesses are interesting; every witness to an incident will later tell the story differently. There is by no means total agreement in the scholarly community, but a widely accepted theory of how they came to be written is sketched here.

Mark was the first Gospel to be written. The author was unaware of any stories about the birth of Jesus and did not include any in his story. He told the story of Jesus' public ministry, concentrating first, but by no means exclusively, on the works of Jesus – his miracles. He then told the story of Peter's confession of faith at Caesarea Philippi (8.27–30), this is followed by Jesus' speech about his future suffering and death (8.31–9.1) and this is followed by the story of the transfiguration (9.2–13).

The story of Jesus' ministry continued, this time with greater emphasis on the teaching of Jesus – his parables. Finally, we read Mark's version of the Passion: the arrest, trial, suffering and death of Jesus, which is followed by the resurrection and after-death appearances.

Matthew and Luke have exactly the same structure as Mark. The text is frequently the same or similar with only minor word changes. Matthew and Luke have in common another set of stories about Jesus, which do not appear in Mark. Finally, both Matthew and Luke have stories about Jesus which are unique to that one writer and found nowhere else.

This has led to speculation that the texts came into being something like this. Mark was the earliest writer and both Matthew and Luke had access to his manuscript while composing their own texts. There was another set of writings about Jesus which is now lost, but both Matthew and Luke had access to that also. This hypothetical source is known as *Q* (from the German word *Quelle*, meaning source). Both Matthew and Luke copied large chunks of both Mark and Q. Finally, both Matthew and Luke individually had access to different sets of stories about Jesus which nobody else has written down.

This, of course, throws doubt on the notion that any of these three gospels was written by an individual who was an actual eyewitness to the life and teaching of Jesus, though they may have, on occasion, met somebody who had known Jesus. Even though tradition and, sometimes, text suggest an author, this must be taken with reserve. Each writer probably received his information at second or third hand and all received and pondered it through the prism of the resurrection.

Each gospel is frequently approached as a tradition (something handed on from one generation to the next) about Jesus preserved, meditated on and prayed about over long years in a believing community. In those days communities were much more isolated from each other than they are today.

### *Matthew*

It was believed that this text was written by Matthew the tax gatherer. This is now thought unlikely. The text has a unique set of teachings by Jesus called the 'Sermon on the Mount'. It is thought to be a collection of teachings gathered from different sources, rather than the report of an actual occasion. The writer may have been an early Christian teacher; perhaps this individual was a rabbi or a scribe.

This text is anxious to preserve the notion that the old Jewish Law has value and it suggests how observance of the law might be pleasing to God in the light of the resurrection of Jesus. It is thought to come from a community of people who were originally Jews but who had converted to Christianity. However, some students feel that by the time the end of the text was being written the link with Jewish religious practice had been broken. The writing is often dated to between 80 and 90 CE.

Matthew urges us to distinguish in the whole body of traditional teaching those tendencies which have greatest weight. Love of neighbour is more important than remembering to carry out some minor duty in fussy detail. It constantly reminds us also that the original will of the creator is more important than later legally detailed regulations. Finally, in a series of contraries, 'you have heard it said . . . but I say unto you . . .' Matthew asks us to consider the Law in its deepest sense, rather than in its surface meaning.

At the very beginning of Christian history all believers were converts from Judaism, and while they adopted new forms of worship, prayers and breaking of bread, they also worshipped as Jews in both synagogue and Temple. Following the destruction of Jerusalem and of the Temple by the Roman Emperor Titus in 70 CE, Judaism was reformed and reorganized, possibly by the Pharisees. This new version of a fragile and brittle Judaism may not have been sympathetic to anyone lukewarm about the new party line.

There seems little doubt that, at some stage, there was a dramatic rupture and Christians may have been expelled from the synagogue. This may well be represented in the harsh judgements concerning the Pharisees placed in the mouth of Jesus. The community suggested by Matthew appears to have been open to Gentiles. What is more, the Gospel of Matthew is one of the two to include a birth narrative. Here, the visitors who were summoned by a miracle to visit the newborn child were outsiders: Gentile men of learning.

On the other hand, this is the most Jewish of the four gospels. It is a document concerned to proclaim Jesus as the Christ, that is the promised Messiah. Jesus is portrayed as the great healer and teacher – Wisdom herself. Another focus of the gospel is the nearness of the Kingdom of God which Jesus came to announce.

Matthew does not see the Kingdom of God as being embodied by the Church, but the Church is where the Kingdom can be most easily discerned. It is the great theme of hope in this gospel. It is both at hand and imperfectly realized. It involves a vision of a redeemed humanity, not just as individuals, but in social and political terms as well. Redemption is to be announced on earth as in heaven, here in time as well as in eternity. It has a strong moral content because of its concern with the law. There is an emphasis on justice which is the believer's response, in obedience, to the will of God.

Matthew has a constant desire to tell how, in Jesus Christ, the ancient prophecies of Israel have been fulfilled. Nevertheless Christian communities, as portrayed here, are a mixture of saint and sinner; Matthew is very realistic! Matthew stresses that Jesus 'came not to destroy, but to fulfil'.

Matthew was probably written in an early Christian community that had its own tensions about doctrine and discipleship, not at all the idealized vision of the Church many see in the Acts of the Apostles. Many consider this gospel to be an account of the Jesus of history, living beside the Galilean Sea in 30 CE, seen through the prism of the author's experience of the Lord, as he worked in a Church community in 85 CE. Moreover, many guess that this young Christian community may not have been in Palestine but possibly in Antioch.

The text of Matthew is riddled with turbulence, and the Church in Matthew will accordingly be battered throughout its existence.

### *Mark*

No claim is made here that the author was the Mark mentioned in Acts. That identification was added later. Some see this person as Paul's companion, John Mark; others claim he was a later collaborator of Peter's.

The text of Mark may well have been written in Rome shortly after 65 CE, the traditional date for the executions of both Peter and Paul in that city. A threat of persecution seems to hang over the text. Early preachers had used the word 'gospel' as an announcement of good news. Mark invented 'gospel' as a literary form – an account of the ministry of Jesus.

Mark has no birth narrative. It starts with a prophetic announcement from Isaiah, followed by one from John the Baptist. After a mere eight verses, Jesus comes to be baptized by John and his public ministry has begun. The order of the text follows some movement around Galilee and then becomes a steady progression to Jerusalem.

It may be that the text was written for a community dominated by Gentile converts to Christianity, rather than Jewish ones. This document takes trouble to translate and explain Jewish words and customs. In the early first century, Galilee was a place where members of many nations had settled. The religious authorities in Jerusalem considered it to be a place of outsiders. As against this, Jerusalem was the centre of rigid orthodoxy and religious certainty. From Galilee came a challenge to the religious establishment; from Jerusalem came the most virulent opposition to Jesus.

Mark declares without any doubt who Jesus is. Jesus is the Christ (the expected Messiah), the Son of God. The text focuses on the Kingdom of God and it opens with the declaration that the Kingdom of God is at hand and calls on hearers to repent and believe. It constantly emphasizes the paradox of how the crucified Jesus could be the son of God. The baptism, transfiguration and resurrection of Jesus all move in this way from the ordinary to the heavenly voice, to the 'letting see' of the mystery.

The people of Jesus' time understood the Kingdom of God to be a display of power. Jesus' preaching is not an attempt to underplay the power of God but to get people to understand that God does not use power in a forceful, dictatorial manner. The way of God is persuasion, an appeal to the heart. Thus the signs of the Kingdom are displays of power used to heal.

Jesus' life was, in itself, the illustration of how God sees the work of the Kingdom – the healer–teacher justified by God. The cross is the climax of this life of healing and teaching. The preacher of the Kingdom has now become the model for the Kingdom.

When Peter confesses that Jesus is the Messiah, the three Synoptic Gospels all portray Jesus as immediately speaking about his suffering and death. Only when this double aspect of Suffering Messiah is understood can the texts talk of transfiguration.

The gospel of Mark has a thread running through it whereby Jesus heals but then warns the healed person not to tell anybody. This is often referred to as the 'messianic secret'. It is difficult to know what was meant by this. It may be that the author of Mark did not understand Jesus' messianic role as a statement of wonder-working power but as something that could only be appreciated in terms of the crucifixion–resurrection event.

Mark is trying to draw out a very radical response to the story of Jesus, and that response is discipleship. The disciples of Jesus were called to share his preaching and healing, and they often misunderstood his mission. It has been suggested that the first half of the gospel portrays the disciples as role models, while the second half recommends that their behaviour be avoided. No doubt Mark is laying out not only the duties but also the failures and distortions of discipleship.

Christians in Mark have a double responsibility: they must persevere, no matter what temptations arise (4.16–19) and they must be of service to others (10.44). In the working out of Christian duty in daily life, Christians must fight against despair, fatalism and blindness, making obvious God's secret, but real, struggle among us.

Mark's Jesus is very much a human being, not the all-knowing Son of God: he makes mistakes; he does not know when the world will end and he is afraid of death. The most frequent title used for Jesus in Mark is Son of Man. At one level it simply means human being; in the Old Testament book of Daniel it means the one to whom God has given power to judge. It is a confusing title.

**Redemption** This is the act of freeing humanity from the power of sin and restoring the world and its inhabitants to communion with God. In Christianity, redemption became effective with the dwelling of Jesus on earth and his death on behalf of others.

**Messiah, Christ** A person given great power and special functions by God. The Jews expected such a figure, apparently to restore some form of national autonomy. Jesus was seen by early Christians as Messiah. The word means 'anointed' – a sign of special mission: kings and priests were anointed. 'Messiah' is a Hebrew word; the Greek equivalent is 'Christ'.

**Disciples, Discipleship** Disciples were and are the followers of Jesus; those who believe in and seek to follow his teaching. Discipleship is the willed attempt to be a disciple of Jesus in one's own historical and geographical setting.

**Transfiguration** A moment in the Synoptic Gospels when, at the top of a mountain, Jesus was seen by chosen disciples in the company of Moses (the great lawgiver) and Elijah (the great prophet) in the appearance of heavenly glory.

### *Luke*

Once again this gospel does not claim to be written by Luke, but there are reasonable grounds for accepting that a physician named Luke, who was a companion of Paul, wrote both it and the Acts of the Apostles. The two are frequently considered as a single literary unit – one work written in two volumes. This suggests that the author saw the work of Jesus continuing in the work of the Church. This writer was probably from Antioch. Luke is written in stylish Greek and has elegant literary devices to stress its theme; the three Gospel Canticles, the Songs of Zechariah, Mary and Simeon, are all found in Luke alone.

Scholars believe that the text shows little knowledge of Paul's later theology, or of his letters, so they believe that Luke's collaboration with

Paul was early in the latter's ministry. There seems to be internal evidence that Luke knew of the destruction of Jerusalem (21.5–6); therefore it was written after 70 CE. It does not seem to reflect the tensions between young church and synagogue and therefore probably written before 85 CE.

This text was probably written for Gentile believers, away from Palestine. Luke tends to use the word 'Lord', a Greek title, rather than 'Messiah', a Jewish one. This community sees the gifts of God as offered to all. This text seems to be addressed to a Gentile audience, aware that Christianity was living in a hostile environment. The Temple has been thrown down, the city destroyed and a totally pagan one is being built on the site.

The author of Luke seems to have a threefold vision of time. There was the time of Promise, when Moses and the prophets announced God's concern for the chosen people. There was the time of Presence, when Jesus was present on earth: 'he went about doing good'. There is the time of the Spirit; as the full impact of the message dawns: the message is announced beyond the confines of Israel and spreads out from Jerusalem.

The writer of Luke appears to have had three authoritative sources of inspiration: the Old Testament writings, Jesus himself and the early community of the founding apostles.

The purpose of Luke is to show that God is trustworthy, often in a way people did not expect. You might think that God has not been faithful to the promises made to the chosen people, but this is a misunderstanding and the new Christian people of God can rely on God's providence.

This new people is composed of the old elect who repented, but also of people who were frequently despised: Gentiles, the poor, lepers, tax collectors, women, Samaritans and other outcasts. Luke also tells stories about the birth of Jesus. In his account the baby is visited by Jewish shepherds. These people are outsiders also, because their work prevented them from being at all times ritually pure.

The vision of the early Church given in the Act of the Apostles is probably hopelessly idealistic, but the document urges believers to persevere in the teaching of the apostles, in brotherly love, in the breaking of bread (the Lord's Supper/Eucharist) and in prayer. These practices preserve the identity, unity and cohesiveness of the believing community. The message of Luke is not given in a series of exhortations, but the stories set examples before us.

The moral teaching in Luke stresses how important it is that Christians remain linked to each other, that they should be moved by each others' distress, that they undertake concrete and sensible actions to help each other, and that they should not place others under an obligation by making them indebted to generous givers: the Roman political system of gaining power by building up a grateful client base was out!

Luke's Jesus often lays aside the detail of the old Jewish Law, but he is nevertheless an upholder of the general thrust of the law and other Jewish traditions. There are many good things in the Pharisaic tradition of prayer; the Church is founded on the twelve disciples, as Israel is founded on the twelve tribes. The gospel begins in the Temple and the promise arises out of the Temple; after the final departure of Jesus the disciples return to the Temple. However, there are theological battles. In Luke, the Pharisees are opposed over strict dietary habits, over who has the right to be considered a child of Abraham and over notions of self-righteousness.

Jesus' mission is to all but particularly to the marginalized. Jesus himself is marginalized; his mission as a prophet is rejected by the religious establishment. The ideal in Luke's Christian community is the wounded and abandoned traveller in need of the other. Luke preaches a concrete ethic of perseverance. This is no longer an ideal of the seeker who leaves all to follow the truth; the Christian model has been transferred to an urban community where one cannot escape from the other.

The boyhood incident of learning and enquiring in the Temple (2.41–52) stresses that Jesus had much to learn from his native tradition and that his ministry was a lost opportunity for Judaism. However Luke portrays the ordinary people as having more shrewd insight than their leaders. The rejection of a prophet does not finally shut off the gift of God's mercy.

### *John*

The author of John was traditionally held to be the author of the three letters which bear his name and of the book of Revelation too. This common authorship is disputed.

This gospel was finally accepted into the approved list of writings which go to form the New Testament (the canon). But that approval was delayed. The text is very different from the other three gospels and it also appears that this gospel was popular with early heretical groups. Both these factors may have aroused suspicion about the orthodoxy of the teaching contained in it.

The literary style is quite characteristic; it involves repetition, antithesis and chiasmus. The author often interrupts the flow of the narrative to give explanations or to prevent misunderstandings. In fact, John's explanatory technique often involves structuring the text to allow Jesus' opponents to misunderstand him; that misunderstanding is then highlighted and corrected. It is often referred to as the spiritual gospel, being the result of long, prayerful meditation on the Christ-event, rather than a straightforward relating of it.

Peter plays a prominent role in this gospel; he is obviously considered to be the leader among the Twelve, although his faith and commitment are often portrayed as inferior to that of the Beloved Disciple who gets special mention in the text. This Beloved Disciple is often identified with John the son of Zebedee. The Beloved Disciple is identified as the author of the gospel.

Once again, many scholars feel that the final version of this text is the work of a community, possibly one founded by John. It may have been written at Ephesus in modern Turkey, where there was a Christian community claiming to be founded by a preacher named John.

**Heresy** Teachings which cast doubt on or deny the official doctrines of the Church.
**Incarnation** The Christian teaching that the Son of God became a human being as the historical Jesus, both fully God and fully man, without the integrity of the manhood or of the godhead being compromised.
**Gnostic** Gnosticism was a loose set of tendencies, seeing the world in terms of a conflict between two great powers of good and evil and seeking to develop a special relationship with God by means of one's favoured insight, study and knowledge.
**Transcendence** Above, independent of, surpassing the material universe.

Scholars now appreciate that first-century Judaism was more complex, rich and diverse than had previously been thought. Many attempts have been made to find the sources of John's gospel in this hotchpotch of slightly off-centre religious traditions. This gospel is very concerned about the expulsion of Christians from the synagogue. Three times in the text of John we find a word found nowhere else in the New Testament meaning 'a person expelled from the synagogue'.

John's text suggests that the community from which this document came needed to establish a separate identity from three other groups. Those were the followers of John the Baptist, the Jews who by now have probably expelled Christians from the synagogue and other Christians who have disagreed with this community, possibly over the divinity of Jesus.

This suggests that the document dates from after 85 CE. Since it appears to have been in circulation on papyrus, suggesting copies made in Egypt, by the very early second century, the latest date for composition is held to be 100 CE. The document also appears to reject Gnostic tendencies. This is a tradition which denied the Incarnation. Gnostics tended to believe that the soul alone was good while the body was evil. In addition, the Gnostics believed that salvation came to those with special knowledge, which they have acquired by discipline or by being found worthy. Christianity has always maintained that saving faith is within the reach of all, rich and poor, Jew and Gentile, male and female, clever and less gifted.

John's manner of presenting Jesus is quite different from that of the other three. Jesus frequently utters long figurative speeches; the miracles related here often provide an occasion to allow symbolic insights into Jesus' identity. He frequently refers to his relationship to the Father. Of course many of the incidents and sayings in John are also reported in the Synoptic Gospels.

The text refers to three journeys to Jerusalem to keep the Passover. Consequently people assume that Jesus taught and healed over a three-year period.

In the gospel of John there are no birth narratives and there is no narrative of the institution of the Lord's Supper. Instead it begins with an abstract and poetic theological prologue concerning the Word. 'Word' is a term which had been used in some pagan philosophy to denote the inherent divine, creative spirit and wisdom which orders the universe.

The theme of the victim also runs throughout John: somebody sacrificed on behalf of others. There is the ritual victim; an animal dies in the place of the sinner: John the Baptist early designates Jesus as the Lamb of

God (1.29–30). There is the victim of community, one holding divergent views from the group and expelled from the group; Jesus was at constant variance with the Jews over contrasting ideas of piety, the Sabbath, the spiritual food of his body, his daring to teach as one without formal education and his claiming identity with the Father. Instances abound in chapters 5, 6, 7, 8, 10, 11, 12, 17 and 19. Finally, there is the notion of triumphant victim – the one who has suffered and around whom a new community of salvation is gathered. There is even the notion of the new community of salvation as victim.

The gospel makes frequent reference to Jesus' 'hour' or his 'time', when he will be revealed for what he is. This appears to be the moment of leaving the world and passing to the Father. Nevertheless the gospel keeps giving us hints that the time is now. In one famous story, Jesus' mother tells him the wine has run out at a wedding feast. He protests, 'my time has not yet come'; nevertheless he changes water into wine.

This gospel proclaims that Jesus speaks for God and should be received as God, for a rich merchant's agent has the authority to make decisions as though he were the superior himself. This gospel points to faith in Jesus Christ as Son of God. It frequently calls on disciples to believe in Jesus. This is a definite qualification for salvation: 'no-one comes to the Father except through me' (14.6). The text seems to separate Jesus, as one from above, from those who are of this world. The second part of the gospel is concerned with the return of Jesus to the Father.

The writer of John often uses terms and images for Jesus which, up to now, had been considered suitable only for the transcendent reality of God. At first this must have appeared quite startling in a narrative devoted to the earthly career of a human being. On the other hand, what appears more startling to the Christian outlook today is those synoptic texts which describe Jesus' human flaws.

The preface to the text, the passage dealing with the *Logos* or Word (1.1–18), implies that Jesus had a pre-existence with the Father before his human birth. There are later references to his imminent return to that glory. These are found in the priestly prayer of the Word made flesh (ch. 17). John's Jesus has not come to allow us to make sense of human experience; he has come to reveal the Father.

The text seems to assume that the reader knows many of the facts concerning Jesus' life and work and does not speak about the Baptism, the

Transfiguration or the Institution of the Lord's Supper. The climax of the gospel is the crucifixion. Once crucified, Jesus knows that his hour has now come. The last prayer of Jesus is the call to God to glorify the Son by his death. His lifting up on the cross is his lifting up in glory. It is from that point that the Spirit, the comforter, is poured out upon the world as water pours from his side.

In John, Jesus is the revealer. By themselves, human beings are unable to come to God; they need new birth. The revelation of God in Jesus Christ shows a radical contrast between the world and the Kingdom of God, the earthly and the heavenly, the glory of mortals and the glory of God, above and below. Jesus reveals that the world is under the judgement of God and that the Word dwells among us, but only faith can see it clearly.

The teaching of Jesus is framed and summarized not by the institution of the Lord's Supper but by the washing of the disciples' feet and the delivery of a New Commandment – to love one another as Jesus had loved them. John's ethical approach seems to be the insistence on brotherly love within the believing community. This is so that the unbelieving world may know the greatness of the power of God. The text gives no indication of how this might work out in practice, and it lays down no further guidelines for social responsibility within the community.

In the epistles named after John, the emphasis is on the general ruling to walk in the light, to practise brotherly love and to fight heresy. This may of course have been very practical in a context which was threatened by the Gnostic heresy, a tendency which promoted knowledge at the expense of love. Even faithful believers may be tempted to neglect the practical workings of love and feel, in their pride, that their religious knowledge places them above the requirements of sacrificial self-offering.

## Appraisal

Each author writes about Jesus out of a slightly different context and for a slightly different audience. Each has a somewhat different way of looking at Jesus and of expressing, indeed assessing, the importance of what he achieved.

Mark gives us no birth narratives; Matthew and Luke do. Does this mean that for the later writers Jesus has assumed a greater cosmic significance which had not dawned on Mark?

John teaches the pre-existence of Jesus as the Divine Word quite explicitly. Luke does not. But what are we to make of the three songs accompanying the birth narratives? The Gospel Canticles (as they are called) appear to be human responses to a human event yet their grouping together suggests they are being used as markers to express something which goes beyond what is plainly stated.

If one is not involved in the problems of the world, there is a temptation to cultivate the internal, spiritual life, to the detriment of the practical. Could the Johannine tradition (the tradition of the gospel of John) sometimes give comfort to those who are tempted to reject the link between the spiritual and the material, the body and the soul, time and eternity, seeking to undervalue the material at the expense of the spiritual, rather than hold the two in tension?

The gospel texts all express their teaching as they describe the life of Jesus. Yet each has its own setting and concerns.

# 3 St Augustine of Hippo: a Father of the Church

St Paul, on one occasion at Ephesus, was presented as just one more philosophy teacher among so many others. Christianity would come to have much in common with philosophical thinking in the early years of the Christian era. Christianity grew out of the Jewish world and beyond the squabbling of Jewish sects. It was of course more than philosophy, for it presented more than ideas; it presented the Lord of the universe as the redeemer of the human race. God's commitment to human beings was such that they were given a saviour.

The young Church declared to the world a saviour who was the Lord of the world, the *Logos*, rational principle of the Universe. They saw this deliverance as linked to an event: Jesus Christ had 'suffered under Pontius Pilate', been 'crucified, died and was buried'; 'on the third day he rose again from the dead'. Those who believed in him grew together into a close society and companionship which called for a life of purity, self-sacrifice and solidarity with others.

Christianity seems to have first taken hold among the poorer classes of cities; it was only later that it moved out into the countryside. The word 'pagan' originally meant a rural dweller. Christians soon got the reputation of being naïve, ignorant and superstitious. Christians also called into question the values of Roman thought and civilization; they refused to participate in state or civic cults (worship of the Emperor or honour given to a city's protecting god). What is more they ate a community meal in which they appeared to be eating the flesh of their great teacher. Such rumours about them caused them to be outcast, despised and eventually persecuted.

Meanwhile the work of the Church continued and grew a little at a time. Gradually Christian worship moved from private houses to specially built buildings. Slowly Christian ministries also developed, particularly those of bishop, priest and deacon. Little by little public liturgies became established; creeds, rules and regulations were drawn up.

Christian doctrine became standardized. In particular, the doctrine of the two natures of Christ (fully human and fully God) was developed, as was the doctrine of the Trinity. These were given their standard

definitions by the pronouncements of councils of the Church. Much of this work of definition arose because of heresy. Heresy is a teaching concerning Christianity which the church authorities judged to be wrong.

**Liturgy** The words, rites, texts of Christian services.
**Creed** A statement of what one believes. In particular, the Apostles', Nicene and Athanasian Creeds which have high status among almost all Christian churches.

In time Christianity came to confront the pagan philosophical world and eventually, by a variety of means, including the use of state power, to overcome it.

The earliest Christian thinkers had no philosophical system of thought, or means of expressing their concepts of knowledge, other than the prevailing forms of their day. These tended to be mostly platonic with a little influence from Stoicism. Pagan thinkers often attacked Christian thought using the thought categories of their day. Many Christian thinkers borrowed the weapons of their opponents and fought back.

Plotinus (204 –270 CE) taught a development of Plato's thought sometimes referred to as Neoplatonism. He lived at a time when the Roman Empire was breaking up. The world of practical affairs seemed to offer no hope to men and women; only the Other World, a world of abstraction, thought and ideas, appeared promising. For the Platonist that was the real world, the material world was illusion. By and large, the philosophy of Plotinus encourages us to look within rather than without; it encourages us to promote introspection rather than engagement with the world. There is a whiff of otherworldliness in Plotinus; salvation comes by intellectual improvement, ascent to the higher form and absorption into knowledge of God.

It was while reading Plotinus that St Augustine came to accept the notion of immaterial reality and, by thinking of evil as a deficiency, freed himself from a dualistic system of thought according to which the world is the place where good and evil struggle.

## The Fathers of the Church

'Fathers of the Church' is a name commonly given to a number of ancient Christian writers. They were nearer to the sources of faith, to the times of

Jesus, than we are. When we turn to them, there is a sense of returning to sources.

They tried to read all scripture in a Christ-centred way under the guidance of the Holy Spirit. They were people who confronted and held in dialogue a newly evolving religious faith and a rapidly developing secular culture. They stood with one foot in Greek and Latin learning and the other in the Christian message. They are revered for the power of their teaching, the correctness of their thought and the holiness of their lives.

The Fathers of the Church were usually converted to Christianity when adults, they were usually highly educated and well-read. They often were monks or had been monks. That is to say they had lived for a period in monasteries, as hermits or as celibates to heighten their spiritual awareness and sharpen their spiritual discipline. They often came, eventually, to hold pastoral office, as parish priests, bishops or as leaders of religious communities. They came to be our guide to what has been taught as the Christian faith from the earliest times.

In the West, St Benedict wrote a rule for monasteries; it is still in use today. St Augustine is one of the most influential of those early systematic thinkers and is considered, with St Jerome, St Ambrose and St Gregory the Great, to be one of the four great Fathers of the Latin Church.

Augustine engaged in a number of theological controversies and made a major contribution to solving them all. What is more he left behind him a body of theological writing which, for the first time, was beginning to be *systematic*. After Augustine, as the so-called Dark Ages descended on Western Christianity, there would be a body of work which had already laid out the fundamentals of Christian faith in orderly and logical form. His three major areas of contribution were the doctrine of the Church, the doctrine of grace and the doctrine of the Trinity.

**Metaphysics** is the study of being as being, speculation about the meaning of what is, the study of first principles and first causes, the rational knowledge of those realities that go beyond us or the rational study of things in themselves.
**Celibate** Living chastely in an unmarried state: one of the three vows, together with poverty and obedience, taken by those entering monastic orders.

## Life (354 – 430)

Augustine lived from 354 to 430 CE. He was born in Africa, in modern Algeria, though of a Romanized family. His father was an estate owner and a pagan; his mother was a Christian. He pursued what we would now call university studies in a variety of places in Africa, ending up in Carthage. He returned home to support his family, which he did by teaching. He confesses that in his early adulthood he had difficulty in controlling his sex drives. After a number of posts in Africa, he taught Rhetoric in Rome and then in Milan. It was here that he decided to become a Christian. He had fallen under the influence of the great preacher, St Ambrose of Milan.

The story is that when seated in the garden of his house he heard, over the garden wall, the voice of a child saying, 'Take it and read it! Take it and read it!' He happened to open his New Testament and read the words of St Paul, 'Let us behave decently, as in the daytime, not in orgies and drunkenness, not in sexual immorality and debauchery, not in dissension and jealousy. Rather clothe yourselves with the Lord Jesus Christ, and do not think about how to gratify the desires of the sinful nature' (Rom. 13.13–14). His conversion to Christianity was now complete.

He himself witnessed the sack of Rome in 410 by the barbarian invaders from the north, led by Alaric the Visigoth. Rome, the conqueror and ruler of the Mediterranean basin, the city that had lasted for a thousand years, had fallen; all social and cultural certainties had now been shaken to their very foundations.

Following the death of his mother, Augustine returned to Africa with his son and some other friends. He lived a monastic life for a while, apparently waiting for God to reveal what he should do. At Hippo, he was chosen to be a priest of the Christian community and, in 395, became the city's bishop. He remained here until his death, which happened as the city was under siege by the Vandals in 430.

Augustine dedicated his ministry in Hippo to the welfare of his community; he gave much thought to the detail of living a Christian life in the hurly-burly of the everyday world. He was well known and revered as a preacher. These and many other activities occupied his time.

In addition, he thought long and hard about Christian education, in particular educating his flock in Scripture.

We must remember that in those days a bishop performed many of the functions which are now performed by priests. A bishop baptized, heard confession, preached, gave private and public penances, pronounced curses, lifted excommunication, visited the sick, attended the dying, buried the dead, ransomed captives and fed the poor. Bishops founded hospices and hospitals, administered the property of the clergy, heard cases in the church courts, wrote books and letters, sat on councils and engaged in controversy within and outside the church. They had what we would now call philosophical, religious, political and administrative duties.

For Augustine, faith came first, faith was fundamental, but faith still wants reasons. He himself was under the discipline of faith yet aware of the demands of reason. He was conscious that they had to come to co-operative agreement within himself. He constantly struggled to clarify the relationship between the teaching of the man, Augustine, and the eternal truths of the word of God. The mind and what it knows both stand in a supernatural light; this is the only means by which knowledge is possible. The mind is allowed to see truth through the illumination given by God.

Augustine was a prolific writer; his main work was the *Confessions*, a work of autobiography which ended at his conversion. *On the Trinity* is a vast work in 15 volumes. There was also the *City of God* in which he developed his theory of the proper spheres of action of both Church and State. He also wrote on the Psalms and on the Gospel of John.

Augustine is particularly noted for the never-ending war he waged against heresy, even to the extent of being an early advocate of the use of force to compel conformity.

He was a notable controversialist, combating in particular three heresies: Manichaeism, Donatism and Pelagianism. Nevertheless the fight against heresy was not the be-all and end-all of his life and work. He was one of the determining influences on the Western Church, sometimes referred to as the 'Glory of the West' at other times as the 'Doctor of Grace'. The word 'doctor' here retains its old Latin meaning of 'teacher'.

## Timeline

303 Persecution of Christians
312 Constantine becomes Emperor and Christianity becomes the state religion
325 Council of Nicea
354 Birth of Augustine
360 Julian 'the Apostate' declared Roman Emperor
374 St Ambrose becomes Bishop of Milan
384 St Jerome starts to translate the *Vulgate*, the Bible in Latin
386 Conversion of Augustine to Christianity
395 Augustine becomes Bishop of Hippo
396 Augustine starts writing *On the Trinity*
397 Augustine starts writing the *Confessions*
410 Sack of Rome by the barbarian Alaric
414 Augustine starts writing the *City of God*
429 Invasion of Roman Africa by the Vandals
430 Death of Augustine
437 Attila becomes king of the Huns

## Thought

We shall first of all look at the three controversies that St Augustine confronted. We shall then turn to the constructive features of his thought.

### *Manichaeism*

Augustine was at one time a follower of the Manichaean heresy. It was a form of Gnosticism. Reality is a contrast between two opposing principles: between the good principle of light and the bad principle of darkness. This explained the existence of evil. Good and evil were perpetually at war one with each other; all matter was evil; only the spiritual was good.

Within every individual an evil principle is at war with the good, but all humans contain within themselves sparks of the original light and goodness imprisoned within matter. Salvation comes when these sparks of light are delivered from the power of evil. This is a slow disciplined process, helped by many messengers sent from heaven.

In simple terms, the soul had to struggle to escape from the prison of the body. Manichaeism taught an ascetic and ordered morality: people should keep away from meat, wine and sexual activity. But not everybody is able to bear the weight of such a restraint. Consequently there are the elect, who can cope with the high standards required. There are also the hearers; a less difficult standard is established for them.

Augustine was drawn away from this viewpoint by his study of Neoplatonism and with the help of his friend St Ambrose of Milan.

**Gnostic** Gnosticism was a loose set of tendencies, seeing the world in terms of a conflict between two great powers of good and evil and seeking to develop a special relationship with God by means of one's favoured insight, study and knowledge.

Augustine was unhappy with the Manichaean notion that an all-good, all-powerful God could be in danger from, and at war with, Evil. Until the twentieth century it was axiomatic Christian teaching that God is not subject to change. If God is infinite, there cannot be an opposite principle which is also infinite. If God is infinite, only God is infinite and the evil principle must be finite. If God is finite, then God is not what we normally mean by the word 'God'.

Neoplatonism freed Augustine from the materialist metaphysics of Manichaeism. He now saw evil as the absence of Good; it was a deficiency. The very notion of Evil depends on the prior notion of Good. Evil could not be conceived unless one first had the concept of Good.

Mainstream catholic Christianity gave Augustine the notion of the freedom of the human will as a gift from God. Individuals may co-operate with God and use God-given gifts to fulfil the divine purpose or they can do evil when they turn the gifts of God away from God. We do not sin because we have a material component but because we exercise God's gift in a particular way.

### *Donatism*

Donatism was a split in the Christian church which was particularly widespread in Africa. At one time it was in a majority there. It arose because a newly elected bishop was accused of having betrayed fellow Christians, during the persecutions by the Roman Emperor Diocletian. It is also suggested that he had handed over to the authorities sacred texts and vessels used during Christian worship. Books were rare, hand-copied and expensive, so this was a cause of scandal at the time. The Donatists became very numerous; they rebaptized already baptized Christians who converted to them. This was a scandal in the eyes of members of the mainstream (catholic) church.

However Donatism was based on the assumption that only those who led totally blameless lives could hold office in the church. They also taught that, if ministers were sinners, the sacraments they celebrated could not be valid: the effectiveness of the sacrament depended upon the moral perfection of the celebrating minister.

Christian orthodoxy teaches that no person is morally pure. The sacraments do not become ineffective because the minister has faults, be they big or small. Baptism and the Lord's Supper are gifts of God and the grace of God is not constrained or limited by the weaknesses of God's creature.

Augustine fought the Donatists because they shattered the unity of the church. For him, the church was a worldwide fellowship and not a purely local one. The part was not greater than the whole, and a purely local decision could not be promoted in the face of the wider order.

The other question had to do with the purity of the church. Augustine would, of course, have wished that all members of the church were as free from sin as possible, but he did recognize that nobody is perfect and that it can be a dreadful form of oppression to demand impossibly high standards of others. For him the church was holy, because the grace of God was at work within it, particularly through the sacraments.

This was more important than judging the perfection of any particular individual at any particular moment. If it were not so, how could any person know that they were being comforted by a valid sacrament, how might any one know whether the celebrating minister is, at that moment, in a state of sinlessness?

He thus approved the idea that the sacraments had validity, whether celebrated by a Donatist minister or not. Nevertheless he decided somewhat casuistically that, during this crisis, the benefits of the sacraments were delayed until either the minister or the recipient had returned to the catholic fold. He tried to use persuasion on the Donatists, but eventually called on the State to use force against them.

### *Pelagianism*

Pelagianism was the teaching of an Irish monk Pelagius. He was an ascetic man who was disgusted by the lax lifestyle of many Christians, even in Rome. At this time, the bishop of Rome was beginning to claim a major voice in the affairs of the Christian Church, particularly the Latin-speaking churches of Western Europe and Northwestern Africa. Pelagius gave strong emphasis to human freedom and the efforts of the will in leading a Christian life. This trend placed more emphasis on doing good work and earning salvation. It set less store on grace, on salvation as the gift of God and on the commitment of God to the human family.

Pelagius put forward his thinking in Africa and in Palestine. His basic feeling was that Augustine was too negative when he claimed that, because of corrupt human nature, individuals are not able to rebuff evil and look for God, and that they must rely on grace alone. He denied original sin, saying children are born innocent of the sin of Adam. Adam's sin was an example (a bad example) to all humanity and he rejected the Augustinian doctrine of predestination. The value of Christ's redemptive work was, he said, limited to instruction and example.

He taught a doctrine of free will and the innate goodness of human nature. Sin modified human nature, but he denied that the sin of Adam was in some way inherited, causing human nature to be evil in itself. Christ saves by example and the sacraments function as teaching not as power.

He and his followers drew up a list of six doctrines, all of which have been condemned:

Adam would have died anyway even if he had not sinned.
Adam's sin injured Adam alone not the whole of later humanity.

Newly born children are in the same state as Adam was before the Fall.

Humanity as a whole does not die because Adam sinned and died; neither will humanity as a whole rise again as a result of the resurrection of Christ.

The Old Law, as well as the New Gospel, brings humanity to heaven.

There were individuals utterly without sin, even before Christ.

**Sin** is a deliberate missing of the mark; the intentional disobedience to God's known desire; the state of humanity which, in its weakness, cannot attain divine perfection.

**Grace** Supernatural gift freely bestowed by God.

**Predestination** The decision of God by which certain individuals will, no matter what happens, be saved.

**Salvation** In negative terms, the saving of human beings from the influence of sin and from damnation. In positive terms, the destiny of human beings to be in the presence of God eternally.

## Augustine's theory of salvation

When he faced the problem of Pelagianism, Augustine came to express one of the classical statements of the Western Church concerning original sin and redemption. He saw sin as inescapable. Adam, before the Fall, had free will. However, when he and Eve sinned, corruption became part of their nature and was passed on to their descendents. Because all receive their descent from Adam, all have inherited that inclination to sin. It is as though it were part of their genetic programming, as we might say today. Consequently all deserve damnation.

If we are not baptized we are lost. We cannot, by our own efforts, remain free from sin. All humanity is now subject to sin, our resolve is now caged and limited and we are weighed down by shame. We can only be rescued from this condition by God's command.

We can only be virtuous through the grace of God and it is by God's grace that certain people are chosen to go to heaven: they are known as the elect. They are not saved because they are good but by the free gift of God. No reason can be given why some are saved and some not.

But Augustine went further. This divine intervention must be overpowering; we cannot supply anything from our side. But it is clear that all people do not receive saving grace. The obvious conclusion, therefore, is that God must choose who will be saved and who will not. All are equally unworthy; therefore the only standard of choice is the absolute decision of God.

This may seem unjust to us but that is of no account; we must believe it is so, even though we cannot hope to understand why it might be so. Punishment was seen as a necessary statement of God's justice. Augustine appears to have had a harsh sense of universal guilt and the offer of salvation.

Pelagius wanted to preserve the notions of both freedom and responsibility in our moral choice; Augustine wished to emphasize the claims and privileges of grace.

However the Church finally came to a position which seems to be a combination of both outlooks. It tried to express the notion of salvation as co-operation between human freedom and the grace of God. It is a common experience that we would wish to do good, but end up doing something bad. The solution to the puzzle is probably that grace does not take way our nature but perfects it. We frequently seek the best of both worlds; it is only when we have submitted to grace that Good can take over and we are finally free to choose for God unconditionally. We get to the stage where we do not want to sin.

If we look at this in terms of lived experience, then Augustine's experience ran against that of Pelagius. The ascetic Pelagius might have been able to control his impulses by the exercise of self-regulating moral restraint. But Augustine's own personal struggle, particularly against his sex drives, led him to think otherwise. No matter how he struggled, he failed. He only succeeded when he surrendered all to the grace of God which changed his whole outlook, radically and lastingly. The personal experience of most people would probably agree on this point with Augustine.

Nevertheless personal experience would also suggest that moral effort has a role to play. We are not smug enough to assume that future blessedness is inevitable. Nor do we despair that future damnation is unavoidable. We are rarely so indifferent that we feel that, no matter what we do, the future is already decided anyway.

There is no doubt that the struggle against the Pelagians was the most important of all the tussles that Augustine was engaged in. It was another one in which his solution became catholic orthodoxy.

## 'Compel them to come in'

All branches of the Christian Church have, at some stage in their history, exercised force on unmanageable elements in an effort to make them toe the party line. They argue that true charity lies in defending the flock against error. It is the duty of the powers that be to protect ordinary mortals against crime and, in the eyes of many, there was no greater crime than heresy. Regrettably the blame must be laid at Augustine's door.

Augustine said that we should be 'more afraid of the butchery of their (heretics' and schismatics') minds by the sword of spiritual evil, than of their bodies by the sword of steel'. It was against the Donatists that he made casuistic use of the text in St Luke's gospel, 'compel them to come in' in which the guests are forced to attend the wedding feast (Lk. 14.23). This text would come to be used as a justification for the coercion and burning of heretics.

**Heresy** Teachings which cast doubt on or deny the official doctrines of the Church.
**Schism** Division into factions, a breaking of communion, within the Christian family.
**Casuistry** The use of clever, misleading arguments in moral questions.

## Augustine's great writings

Human beings share existence, life and intelligence with other animals. But in terms of reason, humans go beyond the animals. Sense experience allows both humans and animals to cope with the world at any one time and in a given instance. But human beings can do more; they can grasp the universal features built into the many dissimilar instances of experience.

While there are many philosophies, all grasp at truth and there they perceive something greater than all the individual teachings which claim universal allegiance. This notion of a spiritual realm which transcends us is quite independent of us. We must acknowledge this spiritual realm. But we have a duty to do more, we must give it reasoned and systematic expression. This is what Augustine was seeking to do in his great writings.

## *The* Confessions

Augustine started writing his *Confessions* shortly after becoming a bishop and while already engaged in other work, *On the Trinity* for example. In this autobiographical work, he lays out the important stages of his life up to his conversion to Christianity. There are those who consider the quest for God to be the most passionate adventure that any individual could ever embark on; Augustine agreed and he told his experiences in that light.

The *Confessions* is a book filled with God, but it is more. Augustine may have been a saint, but he was above all a human being and that deep psychological understanding gives his work its passion. He experienced all the weaknesses that typical mortals feel. We are left in no doubt about his erotic feelings, and how he considered them to be the last barriers to grace. His erotic impulses never left him; he continued to feel their drag.

He knew all the joys of friendship; sorrow at the loss of friends brought him close to despair. He knew what it was to weep. He loved poetry and knowledge.

The *Confessions* is the book of a Christian who is trying to state his faults with a penitent heart. He must humble himself before his brothers so that he may sing the goodness of God. Those two movements echo throughout the work: telling the uncomfortable truth and praising God.

**Penitence** Regret for wrong done and a wish to reform.
**Redemption** This is the act of freeing humanity from the power of sin and restoring the world and its inhabitants to communion with God. In Christianity, redemption became effective with the dwelling of Jesus on earth and his death on behalf of others.
**Speculation** Resulting from meditation and reflection. Often referring to conclusions based on conjecture rather than hard evidence.

## On the Trinity

Augustine accepted and worshipped the Trinitarian God of orthodox Christian teaching. In the West this was coming to be known as the 'catholic faith'. The term 'catholic' was often used to distinguish Western orthodoxy from heretical and schismatic forms of thought. This Trinitarian teaching was known by faith; reason might seek to give it rational, coherent and organized expression, but reason did not invent it. It is the most complex and bewildering of all Christian teachings; some might even say impenetrable.

It may be expressed as story: God, experienced as Father, is the creator and ruler of all. Concerned about the waywardness of the human family, this father sent his son, Jesus, as a special messenger, the Christ, to rebellious humans in order to persuade them of the error of their ways. This son was sustained by the messenger from heaven, the Spirit.

This God is not three gods, but one experienced in different manners and working in different ways to sustain creation and redeem it. The Father is shown through the activity and being of Christ, through the witness and inspiration of the Spirit working on us. Furthermore this threefold-single God always works in agreement, singleness of mind and harmony of spirit. The work of one is at the same time the work of the other two.

That was not of course good enough for the intellectual climate of late classical antiquity. So the early theologians struggled to show that God was Trinity: 'three persons and one substance'. We owe the specialized vocabulary we use about the Trinity to the Christian philosopher, Tertullian (160–225). 'Trinity' comes from the Latin *Trinitas* and is designed to suggest three in a unity (*unitas*).

'Person' comes from the Latin *persona*, which was a mask worn by an actor. When the actor appeared on stage you knew by the mask if he was the villain, the hero, the assistant or other. When we think in terms of 'person' we think in terms of the role God is playing at that time: creator, redeemer or inspirer. But behind each mask there is always the same God.

'Substance' comes from the Latin *substantia*. This is what the three persons have in common. The notion already existed in Greek philosophy to designate something fundamental, something capable of having attributes. A substance is what we would now call a proper name, not a class name. All three persons of the Trinity share the substance of Godhead; it gives them their foundational unity. When we contemplate their work we contemplate them under their 'personal' identity, but they only appear to have outer variety.

The early church was asking the question, 'Who was Jesus?' The whole idea of the Trinity has to be seen relative to the way people were trying to answer that question. The answers are part of the Christological teaching of the Church. Christology is the area of theological speculation and reasoning about the person of Christ.

The traditional theory is that Jesus was both fully God and fully man. Jesus is 'of one substance with the Father'. This made Jesus much more important than a mere human being for Christians. But it also meant that all thinking about God had to become much more subtle. Traditional Jewish thinking about God, for instance, no longer worked.

Various attempts have been made to express the idea of the Trinity in simple words or images: '1+1+1=1' is one effort; St Patrick famously used the three leaves of a shamrock on a single stem. Augustine used the language of psychology and personal relations to express the idea.

Augustine was aware of the developing thought concerning the Trinity and made a contribution to it. His first contribution was to reject any notion that the Son and the Spirit were in any way inferior to the Father within the Godhead. The position of the Son and the Spirit does not mean they were created after, or were subordinate to the Father. It merely means their role in the story of salvation came into play after that of the Father.

In the early Greek Church, the Son was thought of as 'begotten of the Father'; the Spirit as 'proceeding from the Father'. This is the way the Nicene Creed talks about Son and Spirit. The Father is the only origin of Godhead (the quality of being God). Augustine noted that when Jesus breathed on his disciples, telling them to receive the Holy Spirit (Jn 20.22), the Spirit proceeded not only from the Father, but also from the Son.

This led theologians in the West to disagree with theologians in the East and eventually, much later than Augustine's time, an extra word, *filioque*, was added to the Western, Latin-language version of the Nicene Creed. In the West, the Holy Spirit was now described as 'proceeding from the Father and the Son'.

Augustine identified the Son as 'wisdom' and further identified the Spirit as 'love', the love uniting ordinary mortals with God. The community of Christians is therefore the work of the Spirit. This gift of tying us in to God reflects the nature of the Trinity itself. God is a community of 'persons' bound together by the Spirit, forming a single entity.

When God created the world, traces of Godhead were, according to Augustine, left in that creation. He felt that those traces are to be found at the very height of God's creation, the human mind. Augustine reserved an important part for the human mind in all his theological speculation. He thought he detected various triple sets of function in the mind. The names and functions vary: 'mind', 'ideas/concepts' and 'love' is one such triple set. On other occasions he put forward 'memory', 'intelligence' and 'will'. Such sets of three reflect, in his mind, the structure of the Trinitarian God.

## City of God

Augustine's great work, the *City of God* , was written to defend the Christian Church from the subtle propaganda being whispered against it. Christianity had been, it was suggested, responsible for the fall of Rome to the barbarian leader Alaric in 410. So Augustine set out to make a statement about the rights and duties of the Christian in the State, on the role of the Christian State and on the responsibilities of the Church in civil affairs. Augustine's ideas had great influence during the Middle Ages and he has been an influential thinker on the role, duties and rights of civil government right up to modern times.

Augustine based his idea of a Christian State on his understanding of human psychology and in particular on a Christian psychology. Human beings have a twofold nature: body and spirit, they are citizens both of this world and of a heavenly city. This means that they are constantly involved in two spheres of interest and activity. There is conflict between the two urges in all human beings and in all institutions.

The city of God is the goal of human development. In human history, the heavenly and the earthly city struggle against each other. The earthly city is the province of Satan; the heavenly city is the realm of God. God will inevitably have final mastery; only when the heavenly city is permanent will peace and salvation be secure. Christians, of course, do not set their hopes on this world or on this life.

Augustine spends some time pondering the correct meaning of 'love'. He notes that all human beings desire happiness and that our stretching out to God is part of that desire for the highest good. Augustine sees love in two ways: as enjoyment and as use. We can love some object as an end in itself, and we can love it as a means to something else. When love is directed towards God, only love as an end in itself is appropriate. Created things are only used correctly when they are used for God's sake. This is the meaning of his saying, 'love and do as you please'. When we love in a way that is directed towards God, then we are bound to be engaged in doing what is good.

In the heavenly city the supreme good is God; in the earthly city the good is peace. Peace is of course more than the absence of strife; it is the earnest striving of all the parts of the population, the correct ordering of civil society and the actuality of justice. We can now see that humans living in a civil state experience both a will to power and the untiring quest for peace, but the civil state is only Christian if that power is co-ordinated, directed and dedicated to the achieving of peace.

At times it appears that the term 'city of God' is the Church and the 'earthly city' is paganism. On other occasions the 'city of God' is the juridical church, the church as a corporate body with its officers, hierarchy, rules and property, while the 'earthly city' is all society outside the confines of the church.

Eventually Augustine comes to see the 'city of God' as the whole of the people of God, known only to God and intermingled with the whole of society, including those not belonging to God. Such citizens of the 'heavenly city' are 'partly known and partly unknown'. They will only be distinguished on the Last Day. This distinction was obscured throughout the long period of Church supremacy in the Middle Ages and was revived at the Reformation.

Augustine proposes that, from now on, in the Christian era, the only valid state possible is the Christian State, serving a community that is a unit because of its Christian faith. Pre-Christian states are not in truth proper states at all; the application of Christianity to civil power is what gives validity to a State.

The role of the civil power, particularly the coercive civil power, is confusing here. Augustine was willing that the Roman Emperor of the day should play a role in stamping out heresy but did not allow the same Emperor a say in the running of the Church.

The problem of sexual desire occasionally raises its head here also. People asked if Christian virgins had lost their virtue when raped at the sack of Rome. Augustine answered that another's yearnings cannot soil one. Chastity is a virtue of the mind and cannot be lost through suffering rape. He agreed that sexual appetite was not wrong in marriage, provided one intended to have children. The desire for privacy in love-making shows that people are ashamed of sexual activity, it is shameful because it is not ruled by will. The element of lust in intercourse is the consequence of Adam's sin. Virtue is achieved when the will has control over the body.

## Appraisal

Augustine had had a vigorous and dynamic life; he had lived sinfully, and been a member of more philosophical schools of thought than most. He did not come to Christianity through philosophical speculation, but through an encounter with Christ occasioned by his reading of Paul's *Letter to the Romans*.

In writing his *Confessions* he invented a new literary form; many would follow, Pascal and Newman among them. From this work would also flow the great autobiographies of Western literature.

He had debated the problem of evil with the Manichaeans: he had argued that God was the sole creator and sustainer of all things, while evil was an absence of good, arising out of the human being's misuse of freedom.

Do people commit dreadful, brutal and evil acts out of the simple absence of good; or do they make a positive choice to do these actions?

He had debated the freedom of the will with the Pelagians: human beings cannot help themselves, only God can put right what is wrong in people's lives and free them from the results of their own sin.

He had argued with the Donatists over what made sacraments valid, maintaining a high view of the church and of the sacraments. The weaknesses of the minister cannot invalidate the sacraments which are an expression of the grace of God freely given.

From Augustine, the Christian Church got its teachings about the sovereignty of God, the lost condition of human beings when left to their own devices and the necessity for grace.

You will see that by the time of Augustine, the Christian Church was wedded to the notions of correct and incorrect teaching; furthermore, because what was at stake was eternal life or eternal damnation, the Church had now abandoned the exclusive use of gentle persuasion and had sometimes adopted the means of compulsion, force and penalties.

It has been said that inside the head of St Augustine took place one of the great operations of the human spirit: the synthesis of ancient and Christian thought, and that from this point, the course of Western civilisation had started out on its long adventure. Through him the culture of ancient Greece and Rome joined hands with the Bible; platonic wisdom came to terms with the 'scandal of the cross'.

# 4 St Thomas Aquinas: Revelation and Reason

Up to the twelfth century, philosophy was strongly influenced by Plato (427–347 BCE). Plato believed that the world of spiritual Ideas or Forms was the real world; the chief Form was the Form of the Good. The world we experience was but a pale reflection of this world of the Forms. If a ball is hard, green and round, there is (in another mode of being to which we have no direct access) a 'hardness' of which our ball is an instance; the same might be stated of 'greenness' and 'roundness'. Aristotle (384–322 BCE) thought that ideas existed only in so far as they were realized in actual objects and was more interested in the physical world. He was also interested in change, in how we can describe it, in how something changes yet retains its identity and in causes. Aristotle's work was not widely available in Europe until the twelfth century.

By and large, the Middle Ages were not very interested in the physical world and was more interested in metaphysics, the reality that lay behind the physical world and how we might get to grips with it – how the natural and the supernatural are related. Scholastic philosophy and theology tried to puzzle out, by deep and persistent thought, the relationship between God and the world. Theirs was a mixture of Christian dogma and pagan philosophy. Many minds were trying to bring about a marriage of the two. Thomas Aquinas worked to achieve a union of Christian teaching and the newly rediscovered Aristotelian philosophy.

**Metaphysics** is the study of being as being; speculation about the meaning of what is; the study of first principles and first causes; the rational knowledge of those realities that go beyond us; the rational study of things in themselves.

Aquinas was a man of great intellectual capacity and competence; he lived at a time when many new things were being discovered. In Thomas' century, the new preaching orders of the Franciscans and the Dominicans were founded to engage with the world. They saw themselves as having a special mission to address what we would now call poverty, marginalization and social exclusion. Their main aim, however, was to bring spiritual comfort, rather than effect economic and social reform. Thomas was to be a teacher at several of the new universities now being founded all over Western Europe.

What makes Aquinas so much a child of his times, and so unlike a person of the twenty-first century, is his unshakeable belief that his two loyalties (to the gospel and to the rational exploration of the natural world) were not in contradiction; they could advance hand in hand. In his rational theology he affirmed that God's providence and intelligence resulted in order and beauty in the created world. There was only one valid *truth*, guaranteed by God, and nothing reason might uncover could conflict with that truth of God.

His key achievements are his discussion of the role of reason in faith and his rational clarification of elements of Christian teaching (the divinity of Christ is an example). He also developed his principle of analogy and his five arguments for the existence of God. Both of these help us to reflect on the nature of God and on how we use human language to illustrate it.

## Life (1225–1274)

Thomas Aquinas was born in a castle near Naples in 1225; his father was Count of Aquino. He was educated at the famous Benedictine Abbey of Monte Cassino. He decided to enter the Dominican Order at the age of twenty and upset his family so seriously that he was kidnapped by his brothers and held prisoner in the family castle for about a year. Legend recounts that his family introduced a young and beautiful girl into his room in the hope that he might discover the delights of the flesh and turn away from his priestly calling, but the future saint drove her angrily from the room quoting psalms.

Thomas was determined to pursue his vocation and eventually managed to resume his studies. This time he went to the University of Paris. Here he was greatly influenced by St Albert the Great (1200–1280), an erudite teacher of great intellectual curiosity. Albert was particularly interested in the works of Aristotle. This was to have a profound effect on the development of the thought of Aquinas.

Aquinas possessed an exceptional capacity for systematization. Thomas was to express Christian thought in terms of Aristotelian philosophy. Until the twentieth century his approach and Aristotle's thought were to be the vehicle by which Roman Catholic teaching was expressed and handed on. The process was not without risks of abuse.

Thomas stayed in Paris until 1248, he then travelled to Cologne, where a new Dominican house of studies (*studium generale*: an old term for university) was being established. He returned to Paris in 1252 and continued his biblical studies. He subsequently completed his commentary on the *Sentences* of Peter Lombard. This was a necessary step in acquiring his Licentiate, the degree that allowed him to teach Theology. He took his Master's degree in the same year, 1256.

In 1259 Thomas went to teach Theology at a *studium generale* attached to the papal court. He was back in Paris from 1268 until 1272. He was in Naples between 1272 and 1274. He was then summoned to Lyon by the Pope to take part in a Council, but died on the way, at the age of 49.

He devoted his life to study, to the defence of Roman Catholic orthodoxy, to the meticulous systematization of Catholic truth and to writing. It is said that it was his custom to dictate to three or four different secretaries simultaneously! He had been nicknamed 'the dumb ox' in early life. It is claimed he was large and fat, very tall with blond hair, though slightly bald; he had a dark complexion. However he was robust enough to have covered, on foot, the 15,000 kilometres that took him from Naples to Paris, to Cologne and back to Paris again, to Rome and back and from there once more to Naples.

He was a man of piety and spirituality, with great devotion to the Eucharist and the humanity of Christ. Those who pleaded the cause of his canonization described him as being of smiling countenance, gentle and affable, with rare humility and patience, never upsetting anyone with harsh words. His feast has been observed in the Western Latin Church since 1264.

His two great works are, first, *Summa contra Gentiles* (1258–1260), which sets out to establish the truth of the Christian religion by argument and is addressed to a non-Christian thinker (probably a Muslim Arab), and then *Summa Theologica* (1265–1274). He thought and wrote at a time when Christianity was challenged by a vigorous Islam, from which it had also much to learn, and Thomas' own achievements confirm this. 'Summa' means a compendium and, depending on format, each work can run to about fifty volumes.

He is buried in Toulouse in France, within the astounding architecture of the Eglise des Jacobins. After his death, the universities of both Oxford and Paris condemned his writings. However this suspicion did not last long and he was canonized (declared to be a saint in heaven) by Pope John XXII in 1323.

## The influence of Aristotle

Aquinas' starting point was the existence of individual material objects; they were the first source of knowledge. From them he inferred the existence of a spiritual reality; note how this process operates in the Five Ways. Those Five Ways owe much to Aristotle, particularly the argument of the Unmoved Mover and the argument from causality. Thomas also follows Aristotle in seeing all beings (apart from God) as coming to be, through the co-operation of the two elements of matter and form. He rejected any notions that would combat the Christian teaching of personal immortality. Many thinkers have fought against his teaching of the materialistic account of the human soul; others have been suspicious of his high regard for human reason.

**Matter and Form** What something is made of is matter: wood, stone, play dough. The form is the shape one gives it. Form gives matter its substance. Matter without form is only potentiality.

Aquinas, together with all the scholastic philosophers, was fascinated by logic and determined to apply it wherever they could. Aristotle's logical works were the first ones to reach the West and in the early Middle Ages they were only known in incomplete form. We had to wait until the nineteenth century for their influence to be seriously criticized by scholars.

Aquinas' contribution to the method of the medieval Christian theologian–philosophers (the Schoolmen) was to use Aristotle's teaching as a framework on which to hang religious faith. This gave Theology the status of systematic enquiry.

### Timeline

1160–1170 Averroes' *Commentaries* on Aristotle
1214 Genghis Khan conquers northern China
1215 Signing of *Magna Carta*
1225 Birth of Thomas Aquinas
1230 Education of Thomas at Monte Cassino
1239 Thomas at the University of Naples
1241 Building of the Sainte-Chapelle in Paris
1245 Thomas enters the Dominican Order and is 'kidnapped' by his family
1246 Thomas a pupil of Albert the Great in Paris
1248 Thomas in Cologne
1256 Thomas takes his degrees
1257 Founding of the Sorbonne
1258–1260 Thomas writing the *Summa contra Gentiles*
1260 Birth of the German mystic Meister Eckhart
1265–1274 Thomas writing the *Summa Theologica*
1271 Marco Polo begins his travels in China
1274 Thomas summoned to a Council in Lyon, dies en route

## Thought

Thomas' work is so vast that we could not deal with it in detail here. We shall take a very short look at each of his big works and then we shall briefly look at four aspects of his thought. These are the created order, God, theological language and, finally, the mysteries of faith.

Thomas' work is divided into questions; each of these is divided into articles. Every article has a statement of objections to the point Aquinas is promoting. Aquinas next states the authority on which he bases his case and then states the case proper. He usually ends with a number of minor points designed to clear away any remaining objections. It is overall theological systematization and a fusion of all previous thinking on each point. It works from the unshakeable conviction that all questions can be authoritatively answered and that all such answers inevitably fit together into a solid, coherent system of thought. So we can sum up his aims as comprehensive vision and intellectual synthesis.

**Synthesis** The process of putting together individual parts to form a coherent whole.

## Summa contra Gentiles

This is Thomas' first great work and its aim was to convert Jews and Muslims to the truth of Christianity. It provides material for preachers working among non-believers. All particular goals are subordinate to the overriding goal of the universe which is the good of the intellect, that is to say, truth. The pursuit of wisdom is the most perfect, sublime, profitable of all pursuits. All this is proved by appeal to Aristotle.

When Aquinas sets out to declare the truth which the Catholic Church possesses he must have recourse to natural reason, since the Gentiles, (non-Christians) do not accept scripture. Nothing in faith is contrary to reason. Nevertheless it is important to separate what can be proved by reason from what cannot. Natural reason lacks understanding in the things of God. It is possible to use reason to prove the existence of God and of the soul, but one cannot prove the existence of the Trinity, the Incarnation or the Last Judgement in this manner.

We understand temporally, but God understands eternally. God knows individuals as well as universals.

**Trinity** The Christian understanding of God: the unity of Father, Son and Holy Spirit in a single Godhead.
**Incarnation** The Christian teaching that the Son of God became a human being as the historical Jesus, both fully God and fully man, permanently, without the integrity of the manhood or of the godhead being compromised.
**Last Judgement** The end of time when, according to Christian tradition, all who have lived will be expected to give an account of themselves before God.
**Essence** What an item or event is by its nature. An essence can be an idea or plan without realization.
**Existence** When an idea or essence has come into being, is realized in the world, it has existence.

**Sacrament** Any one of seven ritual actions seen as being special channels to God and that guarantees of God's grace.
**Resurrection** is the theological teaching that God would raise up each individual after death to stand in the divine presence and be judged fit for the company of heaven (or not). The early Christians believed that the experiences they had of the presence of Jesus after his death were proof of resurrection teaching and a promise of such a hope and destiny for all committed to Jesus.

If one wants to understand first and last things, first cause and final end, one must first of all consider the divine nature. The only cause of God's will is the divine wisdom, so God's will is free having no cause outside itself. God of necessity loves himself, but does not love other things of necessity. Some think the existence of God is self-evident; this would be true if we knew the essence of God, but we only know it imperfectly.

God's essence and existence are one; no creature knows God's essence sufficiently to be able to deduce God's existence from God's essence. God has no potentiality: God is active power. God is essentially infinite; God's knowledge and understanding are infinite. The existence of God is proved by the argument of the unmoved mover.

The second part is mainly concerned with the soul in human beings. All intellectual substances are immaterial and incorruptible; in humans the soul is united to the body, the intellect is part of the human soul and created afresh with every individual.

Ethical problems are discussed in the third part. Evil is unintentional and is not an essence. All things tend to be like God who is the end of all things. Our ultimate happiness consists in neither the pleasures of the senses nor in moral virtues; they are means to the contemplation of God.

The Divine Law orders us to love God and our neighbour. Fornication and divorce are forbidden as children need the presence of a father. The possession of many husbands or wives together with the practice of incest are all forbidden on grounds of complications in family life and the arguments are rational; Aquinas later introduces texts of Scripture to support reason.

The fourth part deals with the Trinity, the Incarnation, the authority of the popes, the sacraments and the resurrection of the body. The identity of the post-resurrection body is not dependent upon the persistence of the matter that composed it during life.

Religious truths which can be proved can also be known by faith; faith is necessary for the ignorant, for the young and for those without time to study philosophy. Since human beings are rational creatures, their final happiness lies in the contemplation of God – an end which cannot be achieved in this life.

## Summa Theologica

The *Summa Theologica* is Aquinas' second great compendium of Christian thought. Here much of the material appears, on the face of it, to be similar, but the method is slightly different. In the first work, Thomas was inclined to set out arguments without first of all assuming the truth of Christianity. Here his thoughts are more likely to start from a convinced Christian standpoint, and he lays out arguments in a systematic and rational manner.

Human persons, he affirms, require more that philosophy in their search for truth. Some truths are beyond human understanding and only available to us because God has revealed them. Theology depends on revealed knowledge and supplements natural knowledge.

**Revelation** Truths revealed to humans by supernatural means.
**Genus** a class of objects divided into several subordinate kinds: for example quadrupeds can be dogs, cats, pigs and so on.

The five proofs of God's existence (The Five Ways) are set out. By using them we can prove the existence of God from the facts of motion, efficient causes, possibility and necessity, gradations of perfection in the world, the order and harmony of the world. God alone can account for the facts of motion, efficient cause, necessity, perfection and order.

We describe God as being simple (non-corporeal and without genus), actual, perfect, good, infinite, unchanging, one and present in the world. It is by God's grace alone that human persons, as created beings, can know God. We can only grasp God; we cannot understand God (through apprehension, not through comprehension).

## *The Created Order*

Aquinas viewed everything that was created as having its own autonomy. It could, insofar as it possessed reason, decide for itself what it should do and how it should go about it. Nevertheless there is a delicate distinction. Created beings, and in particular humans, are not independent of God, but totally dependent on the divine being. God does not set a limit to our activity; rather it is because of God's activity that we are capable of acting. Free acts are permitted by God, unfree acts are when others interfere and force patterns of behaviour on us.

We might pause here to note that we should not think of freedom and lack of freedom in terms of the political freedoms which have since been won in the West: freedom of thought, speech, action, political association or religious practice. These have all been gradually accumulated as controlling political and religious powers have been eroded. That is a very bad way of looking at our freedom with regard to God.

Aquinas' view of our relationship to God and to grace is totally different. We stand in a relationship to divine omnipotence, which cannot be at all resisted, manipulated or avoided as can political and social pressures. God is the creator and sustainer of the universe, of everything in the universe. God is not part of the universe. To put it in logical language, God is not a member of any class of creatures in the universe.

Aquinas believed that the more we acknowledge nature's order, the more we come to understand God's creativity and God's creative plan. God's plan is seen in the continuing creation we observe around us. This fulfils itself in an ordered pattern over which God remains in control. God has decided that within this ordered scheme of things, each creature moves according to its own nature and, within that pattern, human beings have a higher degree of independence because they are endowed with intelligence.

### THE MATERIALITY OF THE CONTINGENT ORDER

When we come, after hard struggle, to recognize the transcendence of God, we get some notion of the limits and restrictions of what it is to be human. God is more than Necessary Being as opposed to contingent beings; yet it is by such a distinction that we come to appreciate the being of God and to know our contingent and finite status. Contingent beings are perishable. The creation consists of both necessary and contingent beings. Aquinas saw the angels, for instance, as both necessary and created. The fact that we are composed of matter means that we are liable to be destroyed: our materiality changes as its form is replaced by another form.

**Transcendence** Above, independent of, surpassing the material universe.
**Necessary** What has to be. Without which some other thing cannot be or some other event cannot take place.
**Contingent** What does not have to be, usually caused by, or dependent upon, something else.

Nature is valuable to human beings because God gave it existence. When one is a creature of the Creator, one is not separated from God; rather one has a relationship with God. Divine grace perfects nature. Human reason and freedom are valuable in themselves; when they come into a state of actualization they glorify God. Human freedom of will and mind are not limited by God's omnipotence; they are reflections of God's own nature, for we are made in the image of God.

Aristotle's idea of cause saw the highest form of causation as teleological; that is so say, we understand change best when we see it as directed towards a goal. Human nature is created by God in such a way that we have the potential to move towards perfect communion with God. All movement in the direction of perfection tends towards that goal.

When we actively promote human goals, striving to realize human values, we promote the will of God. We have to realize our humanity fully in order to be as God intended us. We are an autonomous part of God's universe and only when we are really free can we freely turn to God in worship and love, and only then accomplish our destiny.

But if the soul is the form of the body, to use Aristotelian terms, the body is matter and totally necessary for our existence. In fact, it is only when we come to learn through our physical sensations that we succeed in understanding. We observe the visual and the particular; we come to understand the universal. Aquinas asserted the essential value and substantiality of this world's being. The forms are embedded in matter.

For Aquinas form was an active principle. It is not just the structure, how something *is*; it had a dynamism, it is actually in the process of being realized, it is changing, is being realized in relation to the ultimate goal which is God.

### THE VULNERABILITY OF THE HUMAN

Thomas held that that the substantial form of any material object, including human beings, is the principle which makes it what it is, which makes it act as it does, which gives it identity. Matter is the principle of vulnerability, the possibility of not being and also the possibility of not being what it is now. If something is alive, its life is its form; its living is its being. In all living creatures, its vital acts are acts of the soul.

In the human being, however, some of these acts of thinking and deciding are acts of the soul but not processes of the body, whereas in other animals such acts are bodily acts of the soul. No doubt Thomas wished to emphasize that for humans there are acts which transcend the body. So humans have a unique relationship with God and are destined to be in the divine presence.

Irrational beings press on towards their goals because of the natural causes controlling them; rational beings (humans) act in terms of the natural causes controlling them but also may have in mind the good towards which they aim as political, social and rational beings; aims which promote their well-being and help them towards fulfilment, happiness and moral virtue.

Humans therefore have to acquire an intellectual sense of practical virtue; Aquinas called it *prudentia* (practical knowledge and discretion). It is nevertheless entering into one's share of the human calling towards grace and glory.

## *God*

Let us now try to get an impression of how Aquinas reasoned about God. We shall take a brief look at the five arguments he used to illustrate the idea of God.

THE FIVE WAYS OF THOMAS AQUINAS

*Way 1: The Unmoved Mover* Everything is in movement, something must have started that movement; to find this initial point we cannot keep taking one step back for ever, a chain of moved movers must have had a beginning in a mover who was not moved. We call this Unmoved Mover God.

*Way 2: The First Cause* Everything has a cause. Cause does not just come before, but actively produces its effect. But there must be a starting point (terminus) that actively willed and produced all that exists. We call this First Cause God.

*Way 3: The Argument from Contingency* Many things exist, although nothing in their nature demands that they should exist. They come into being and pass away: they are expendable. If that is so, there must have been a time when nothing existed unless there was some necessary being to account for them. We call this being, which must necessarily exist to account for all contingent beings, God.

*Way 4: The Argument from Degrees of Being* Things either exist or they do not. When we say metaphorically that some things are more real than others, we mean they are richer in content and significance. This ascending scale of being, truth and goodness must have a limit, a Being who has these qualities to the highest degree. We call this Being God.

*Way 5: The Argument from Design* When we look at the world we observe signs of design and purpose. We call this overarching design and purpose, which indicates a Designer, God.

In modern times these arguments have been sternly criticized by Christian theologians and philosophers of Religion. In the first four arguments – from movement, from efficient causality, from contingency and from degrees of being – God is treated as one being among others that exist. However each of the descriptions is essentially qualified. God is *unmoved* mover, *first* cause, *necessary* being: the superlative which is the *source* of qualities in all things. Thus God is each time removed from the series of items or events from which deity is deduced. The arguments show the divine being to be of a different order from the series of entities from which the argument appears to arise.

The fifth (teleological) argument is of a different type: all things are directed to a goal by an intelligent being. The final outcome is that God is the efficient cause of the universe and its intelligent ruler. Even if these arguments cannot logically establish the existence of God, they all stress what we mean by the word 'God', rather than demonstrate that God actually exists.

We might pause here to note a distinction between Natural Theology and Theology of Revelation. There are certain truths which we can grasp by the use of our own reasoning powers. They might include the existence of God and the immortality of the soul. When we reason in such a way we are engaging in Natural Theology. There are other truths, the Incarnation and the Trinity to mention but two, which we could not have discovered by the use of unaided reason; they had to have been revealed. We remember that Aquinas was an Aristotelian and set out from the starting point of sense-perception (what we can know through our senses).

### THE NOTION OF 'EXISTENCE' APPLIED TO 'GOD'

God is not bound by any of the categories which we usually use to make sense of experience. Aristotle for instance drew up a list of categories where the most important were 'substance', 'quality', 'quantity' and 'relation'. God is outside all such distinctions of understanding which belong completely to the created world.

God cannot exist in any place or at any time. God's existence is essentially outside of time and place. Nevertheless God is present as creator and sustainer to any and every object that does exist in space and time. The sentence 'God exists' is true whenever and wherever it is pronounced. This is God's attribute of eternity, and God alone possesses it. This does not mean that the actions of God can be arranged in order, they are essentially outside any pattern or arrangement of priorities, nor can they be timed or limited by duration.

### THE OMNIPOTENCE OF GOD

The notion of God's omnipotence means that God can bring about any thing or situation that anybody might like to mention. Does this mean that God can square the circle or change the past? The usual answer given to such a question is that it is a contradiction in terms, a nonsense. It just does not make sense and so we do not ask it; it has nothing to do with the omnipotence of God. In the same way God cannot do, perform or promote evil, for evil is not something that is; it is something that is a deficiency or failure, the non-presence of what we might reasonably expect.

#### THE TRANSCENDENCE AND UNINTELLIGIBILITY OF GOD

God is totally beyond our understanding. We cannot know what God is or what God is like. However when we question the experience we have of creation we come to ask questions about what is beyond or behind it. Aquinas' arguments for the existence of God try to lead us from thought about the familiar world we know to thought about a form of existence we cannot experience.

We can know that God is and that God is the cause of all that is. After that we can only know what God cannot be. We are led to forms of negative theology. God is not contingent. God is not a member of a class of things. God is not created. God cannot cease to be.

God is, for Aquinas, the ultimate Form causing nature to be, but God is also the ground and foundation of being. God is an active principle, a dynamism towards realization. God's essence is existence. God communicates existence to creatures, is more than a distant and unresponsive unmoved mover. Creatures achieve reality through nature's constant process of becoming, its untiring dynamic from potentiality to actuality. To be is to participate in existence, and existence is the gift of God's own being.

### *Theological Language*

Since God is totally transcendent (but also immanent) how can the language that we normally use apply to the Divine Being?

How can we say anything about God? If we say God is our Father this suggests that God has a head, two arms and two feet, that God is male. But God is held to be Spirit, not body. Therefore God has no sex, is personal, but is neither male nor female. So people tend to say, 'When you say God is our Father, you don't really mean that, so why do you say it?' The person who makes that objection is using language *univocally* as if each word only had one fixed meaning. On the other hand, people begin to think, 'Oh, he says one thing but really means something different!' This is using language *equivocally*, using double meanings. To get over such problems, Thomas Aquinas set out his theory of Analogy.

### THE LANGUAGE OF ANALOGY

A tourist brochure will often say that a holiday destination is a lively resort. What does that mean? It is easy to understand what is meant when we say that a person is a lively person. When we say the resort is lively, we do not mean that it is vivacious, likes telling jokes, laughs a lot, likes to go dancing and so on. We mean that in this resort all the facilities exist for lively people to enjoy themselves and that they do enjoy themselves when they go there. The description of the resort is analogical. When we say that a town is a lively resort or that a certain group is a lively group the meanings come from a core meaning (*prime analogate*), in this case a lively person. But we cannot use prime analogates with regard to God; for nothing comes before God to which God may be compared.

Analogical language sets out to be ambiguous. If I say I love my wife, my car and my job, the meanings may all be similar, but they are certainly not identical. When we say God loves us or that God is good, we may not say precisely what these sentences mean, but by consulting how we use the important words in everyday life, we come to have a sense of how they operate when applied to God.

Analogy for Aquinas is a technical use of language which warns us not to use certain words in the same way as in other contexts.

All valid statements about God are analogical. When we say that God is our Father, God is neither wholly like a human father nor wholly unlike a human father.

We use the *Analogy of Proportionality* which states that properties of created beings are related to their existence in the manner appropriate to the existence of a created being. On the other hand properties of uncreated being are related to its existence in the manner appropriate to uncreated being.

We may use the *Analogy of Attribution* which describes a relation which obtains between God and God's creatures by using terms drawn from the relationships that hold between creatures. When we say, 'God is Father', we are not speaking as if God was a human. We are not speaking symbolically. What we are really saying is that this manner of speaking points up the relation of dependence between creature and Creator by using the analogy of child and father.

There are two ways we can speak of God. One is to use positive expressions and ideas. We say that God in some way possesses all perfections. We can also use a negative way: we say that God cannot possess any imperfection; so our talk about God is in terms of what God is not. Theologians often like to hold these two ways of speaking in tension.

## *The Mysteries of Faith*

### THE TRINITY

The Christian doctrine of the Trinity is a difficult idea. It is that there is one and only one God, who has three identities, each of which is equal to the others and all of which together form a unique and single being.

Thomas saw the conception of the earthly body of Jesus as the work of the Trinity together. Sending the Son is the work of the Father, bringing the Incarnation about is the work of the Spirit, accepting the mission is the work of the Son. The Incarnation is the supreme demonstration of godly love, in which the Father, Son and Spirit are equally involved.

### THE MYSTERY OF CHRIST

The deep consciousness of every human person is how we experience separation from God. However the eventual success of the work of creation is the return of the human person to God. This ultimate success is led by the person of Christ and is realized through the work of Christ.

Thomas starts his thinking about Christ with the Incarnation and goes on to consider the work of Christ. He analyses the hypostatic union (the union of two natures, divine and human, in Jesus), the perfection of Christ and his grace. He next thinks of the consequences of this union, the unity of Christ's being, his will and his actions.

**Redemption** This is the act of freeing humanity from the power of sin and restoring the world and its inhabitants to communion with God. In Christianity, redemption became effective with the dwelling of Jesus on earth and his death on behalf of others.
**Word (The)** is a translation of the Greek word *Logos*, meaning word or reason. It was seen in the Old Testament and in Greek thought as referring to the universal reason which ordered everything in the cosmos. In Christianity it refers to the second person of the Trinity. Jesus was identified as The Word.
**Atonement** The reconciliation of God and the human race brought about by Jesus Christ.

Here Aquinas deals with the theology of redemption, the satisfaction made by Christ, the merits of Christ and the redemption offered by Christ. He gives due importance to the introduction of the incarnate Word into historical reality.

Aquinas' view takes account of all stages of Jesus' ministry. His thoughts are not limited to the suffering and death, but give importance to all these phases of Jesus' ministry. It is a theology of all the mysteries of Christ, revealing God's plan of salvation and how it was brought about by Jesus. The life of Christ thus reveals the mystery of God which is revealed in history and has effect in history.

### SALVATION

For Aquinas, the human race is more than a random collection of individuals; it has an organic unity of being. Adam was born with an original sense of justice which was to have been the inheritance of all. In this situation Adam acted not just as a private person but as representative of all and lost what he held in trust for us. We are now without the power to control the senses by reason. As time goes by each generation passes on to the next this legacy of unjust desire and randomness. This is known as original sin and declares that the whole human race is guilty in this manner.

Salvation cannot come from any imperfect human; salvation must come from God and did so in the person of Jesus Christ. Aquinas attaches special importance to the Atonement.

God's perfection and justice are so great that nothing sinful or impure can approach it. The Atonement is the reconciliation brought about between the human and the Divine as a result of the sacrificial death of Jesus Christ.

Aquinas sees Christ as making satisfaction to God for all sin by offering to God his perfect obedience. What is more, the Cross is the absolute call of God's love to human hearts, thus urging us to repentance. Aquinas further sees the sacrifice as bearing the punishment due for sin.

### *Christian Lving*

#### THE GRACE OF GOD

Grace belongs to human beings as part of their nature. This is part of the political, social and moral nature we are given and this is how we participate in the divine nature. We acquire (by education) certain virtues which enable us to live with other human beings and develop our social and political potential. Similarly, because the grace of God develops our natures, we are given certain virtues – faith, hope and charity – to allow us to respond to God and fulfil our destiny. These include a willing acceptance of God's Word and a willingness to allow ourselves to be moulded by the Holy Spirit into hope and practical love. Sin is always present as a corruptor and we need the grace of God to take us beyond it into a sharing in the divine life.

#### THE CHURCH AND THE SACRAMENTS

All of Aquinas' thinking was governed by a very specific context: the fact of the medieval Catholic Church. The church was a society, set on earth to be the visible sign of the life and being of Christ and to continue his work in time on earth. The church had important characteristics or marks: it was one, holy, catholic and apostolic.

The church was a unity; it was a communion under the headship of the Pope. This unity was a sign of perfection, as opposed to the broken and fragmented quality of heresy. The church was more than a civil society; it was devoted to the work of God and received its mission from God and the power and grace to perform that mission; it was holy. It was for the entire world; it was catholic. In Aquinas' time its organization did not stretch all over the world as it does today; so catholic meant for all. The salvation of God was for all people; its teaching was what had always been proclaimed by all. It was apostolic; it taught what the apostles taught. Its doctrine was in an unbroken line with their witness to the resurrection and their teaching about salvation.

What was important for Aquinas was that the church was the mystical body of Christ performing the work of Christ on earth through the varying actions of its many members. Aquinas saw this as an analogy with the physical body: each member performing different functions on behalf of the total body. In the church, the seven sacraments nourish the spiritual life of every individual throughout life and in different circumstances and callings. They contribute to our ability to be open to grace.

### THE MYSTERY OF THE EUCHARIST

Aquinas' crucial teaching about the Eucharist was transubstantiation. He got from Aristotle the distinction between *substance* and *accident*. The substance is what makes something what it is. A chair is for sitting on; a spoon is for transferring food from plate to mouth. Accidents are how one might describe them. A chair might be made of wood or stone; it might be comfortable, adjusted to the height of the table or awkward to get out of. A spoon might be big or small, metal or wooden. When we think about it we can see there is a difference between the description of a given chair and its core meaning.

In the Eucharist we start with bread and wine; by the power of God working through the church, the substance of the bread and wine was changed so that they became the substance of the body and blood of Christ. The outward appearance of the elements remained unchanged.

Aquinas did not treat the Eucharist in one precise place in his Summa. His treatment is scattered throughout it. He thought about it in the context of spiritual sacrifice. If our attitude is one of love and surrender, then the action we engage in must in some sense be sacrificial. Because a sacrament brings into effect what it signifies, the Eucharist is the sacramental sign of the sacrifice of the cross. It contains the sacrifice and brings its effect into our reality when we celebrate it.

Aquinas talked of the Eucharist being the 'immolation of Christ'. This came to be seen as in some way repeating the sacrifice of Calvary every time Mass was celebrated. Some even thought that the Mass in some way added something on to the sacrifice of the Cross, thus giving the celebrating priest power in the communication of salvation to the faithful. This was not the intention of Thomas and the theory of transubstantiation became one of the most bitter of battlefields at the time of the sixteenth century Reformation.

Calvary is not repeated in the Eucharist; the Eucharist is not the suffering of Christ but the presence of the Christ who suffered. His death is not present as historical fact but in its effects. In his account of the Eucharist, Thomas was looking for a degree of reality that avoided total literalness and utter materiality, and a degree of objectivity that made it more than a woolly symbol. His treatment of the Eucharist has been described as trying to move us out of imaginative categories and into intellectual ones.

### NATURAL LAW

Aquinas' ethical thought has a two-tier structure. The cardinal virtues of prudence, justice, fortitude and temperance are at the lower level. At the upper level were the theological virtues of faith, hope and charity. A basic principle running through all of Aquinas' work is that grace does not take way our nature, but perfects it. The cardinal virtues in a Christian are not just human achievements; they result from the submission of the human will to God and are prompted and supported by grace.

Aquinas said moral action is based on reason. The fundamental rule of reason is that good should be done and evil avoided. When we come to appreciate our various inclinations to goodness in ordinary human and social life, we understand how this basic principle functions. Our first preference is to protect our own existence; we also want to reproduce and to live together in community. He saw all these tendencies as being expressions of one central and fundamental natural law – to do good and avoid evil.

Let's look a little more closely at his analysis. All creatures are inclined towards good in a way that is natural to their capacities and being. Humans incline towards good in a way that is specific to their being as rational creatures; their tendency towards good has a rational factor. We must not fulfil our inclinations willy-nilly but in a way that suits our capacity to discern human good in a rational manner.

A practical working out of this principle is to be found in the Ten Commandments. They are a working out of our basic principle – do good and avoid evil. This therefore is, for Aquinas, a natural rule or law. By acting in the approved manner our existence as individuals and in community is enhanced.

Human reason comes about because we are capable of intelligent thought, but it goes out beyond this capacity in speculation, while at the same time respecting its essential structure. Nature may be a pre-rational ground for human action, but nature does have significance for that action, since our reason presupposes what is ordained by nature. The order of right reason is within the human being, but it is consistent with the order of nature which is from God. Reason opens out towards the world and also opens upwards towards God.

## The influence and weight of Aquinas

The Schoolmen were the teachers of Philosophy and Theology in the Middle Ages. They based their approach on the writings of many thinkers but particularly on those of Thomas and gradually elaborated a way of dealing with intellectual questions. It was quite formal. During a disputation (an academic exercise) the student would be asked to state a thesis (an argument, a truth). The student would next supply a proof of that thesis, using Scripture and Tradition, faith and *magisterium* (the authoritative teaching of the Roman Catholic Church). St Thomas himself became a favourite source of supporting quotations. Then the student would be required to state a contrary argument but go on to reject it, basing his arguments on Scripture, the Church Fathers and other authoritative sources. Finally, the student would have to give a speculative elaboration. It was accepted that if one could find a rational, coherent answer the problem was solved; all was well.

## Appraisal

Aquinas had an extraordinary impact on Western thought. He made judicious use of the human capacity for empirical and rational intelligence to serve the Christian cause. The human intellect can cognitively penetrate the many created things and appreciate their order, their dynamism, their finiteness and their dependence; intellect thus comes to apprehend the infinite highest being, which is God, and play its part in the spiritual quest. Faith may go beyond reason, but it does not contradict it; rather it is enriched by it.

Aquinas did not believe that the mind's unaided reason could come to the deepest understanding of nature and the supernatural. Faith, but above all Christian revelation, was necessary for that. If we want to move towards the highest spiritual realities, we require the light of the incarnate Word, and that is only approached through love.

Aquinas' expression of the five arguments for the existence of God have been freely criticized in contemporary theology. Aquinas appears to be building an argument on what may be talked about, our experience of the world and moving in logical order to God, but God is shown to be outside the range of what may be talked about. Therefore God cannot be reasoned about in this manner. Aquinas appears to be building up a picture view of a transcendent, monarchical God. The only human reaction possible to such a God is on our knees. This is now frequently found to be an unsatisfactory response; it does not address the sort of question people ask in the twenty-first century, which is, after all, the task of contemporary theology. It fails to address the anguish of people asking questions such as 'where was God in the 2004 tsunami?'

The modern technological world assumes that by being precise and technical in the way we use language we can 'squeeze and freeze' language into set meanings and thus obtain mastery over language, and thereby achieve technical control over nature. Does Aquinas' use of analogy deliver a degree of precision and control in technical theological language? Or does it anticipate a twentieth century rediscovery that there is a basic undecidability about language. We can never get to final bedrock meaning; language always operates within that quality of undecidability.

Forms of discourse are acceptable ways of discussing certain subjects. Aquinas' way of discussing Theology became, in time, acceptable; the preferred way of doing Theology. Such acceptable forms of discourse became, in time, methods of wielding power. Should Theology be a means of wielding power, the preserve of a highly trained elite or should it be a subversive activity? What might it be subversive of?

Thomas saw Evil, not as something that actually exists but as the absence of God. Is this a credible response in the face of the Holocaust, Russian Gulags, Cambodian Killing Fields or the Rwandan massacres?

Do you find revelation and reason to be in agreement, or is there tension between them?

# 5 Martin Luther and the Protestant Reformation

With Martin Luther we are brutally thrown out of the familiar and comforting set-up of the Western, all-European, medieval, Latin Church and propelled into the modern world. It is both more nationalist and individualist in feeling and outlook. Luther was not a systematic theologian. His writings were often produced in response to particular circumstances, his *Shorter and Longer Catechisms*, possibly the nearest things he wrote to systematic theology, were produced to meet a pastoral need. His basic theological protest was that the church was no longer the servant of the gospel, but sought to use its important role in society as master, ruler and judge. Much of Luther's protest was a protest against the power of the popes.

## Why the struggle?

Following the collapse of the Roman Empire in Western Europe the only functioning institution capable of exercising control, and influencing people and events, was the Church. Because the Church was developing, particularly in the West, into a centralised institution, with the bishops of Rome seeking a role of oversight and direction, the papacy came to fill the power vacuum there.

By the sixteenth century, it regulated many matters now considered purely secular and civic. It imposed treaties, admonished kings and regulated their marital and dynastic disputes. There were parallel systems of church and royal courts, often hearing cases with no religious overtones or interest. Much of the history of the Middle Ages was the story of how rulers sought to establish their own authority in the face of papal power.

## The state of the Papacy

By the late Middle Ages, the absolute power of the papacy over the Western Church was well established in practice, though not dogmatically defined. This concerned much more than the moral weight and teaching authority of the papal office; it concerned oversight and involvement in every aspect of tight central government: appointments to a wide range of positions, the payment of large sums of money into the papal coffers and the inevitable venality of clientelism and hangers-on. The luxurious lifestyle of all living at the papal court had become notorious and the Great Schism (late fourteenth and early fifteenth centuries) with two and, on occasion, three popes caused great scandal. Reform of doctrine was occasionally raised but was not the burning issue; reform of administrative and financial matters was widely debated.

> **Pastoral** Aspects of the clergy's work in offering help, care, advice and guidance.
> **Dogma** A system of religious teaching authoritatively considered to be absolute truth.

## Earlier reform movements

The reform of the Church was debated from one end of Europe to the other and had started in the early fourteenth century. The figures of John Wycliffe (*c.*1330–1384) and Jan Hus (*c.*1372–1415) will briefly serve as examples.

Wycliffe, an early English reformer, started his academic career as a philosopher. He was opposed to the radical separation of natural and supernatural knowledge which was fashionable in the Oxford of his day. He hoped for a Church which would be 'holy' in the pursuit of spiritual gifts, abandoning its external and worldly trappings. He opposed the notion that human beings have a right to private property and rejected any hierarchical organization of society. He taught that the Bible was the only standard of doctrine and he is credited with the first translation of parts of the Bible into English.

John Hus is still a national hero in the Czech Republic. He too was a well-known preacher in Prague, where he attacked the notion of pilgrimages and the lax morals of the clergy. He was a firm supporter of the ideas of John Wycliffe, many of whose writings have been preserved because they survived in Czech translations. Hus was eventually condemned, tried and executed in circumstances that now appear highly dishonourable.

Despite their differing settings and circumstances, both thinkers had common concerns: the way the Church held and accumulated property and the high levels of papal taxation. They opposed ritualistic religion, seeking an inner religion of the heart; they both rejected claims of spiritual authority made by hierarchical organization and the temporal power of the Pope.

They both identified the church with the whole body of believers, not with the clergy; believers had a spiritual bond with God which was more important than their obedience to clerical control. But how, in order to reform the Church, does one wrest power away from the clergy and the Pope? They had absolutely no interest in giving it up.

The only natural ally that a church reformer was likely to have was princely power! The gradual progress of political nationalism was developing alongside calls for Church reform.

One other movement for church reform came from what is known as the conciliar movement. This was a movement of intellectuals; it did not arise from a popular base. Its fundamental idea was that government of the Church should be based upon consent rather than a notion of absolute authority and that the organism for expressing that consent was a general council of the Church. The whole body of the Church, the totality of the faithful, is the source of the Church's authority, and Pope and clergy are its servants.

## Life (1483–1546)

Martin Luther was born in Saxony in 1483. He was first a student at the University of Erfurt where he enrolled in the Faculty of Arts and studied Philosophy. He then joined the Augustinian order and took up Biblical studies. He was ordained priest in 1507. He made a business trip to Rome on behalf of his order in 1510–1511. In 1512 he was appointed Professor of Biblical Studies at the University of Wittenberg. He gave a series of lectures on the *Psalms* and on *Romans, Galatians* and *Hebrews.*

He became uneasy about traditional teaching on salvation and gradually developed his doctrine of justification. The fact that he came to question traditional teaching is sometimes blamed on his zealous but somewhat glum nature; he was over anxious about his own salvation. It appears that the routine carrying out of his religious duties, daily recitation of the Divine Office and daily celebration of Mass, failed to reassure him.

The central event of his life, which is usually referred to as his 'tower experience', is variously dated between 1512 and 1515. He appears to have had a sudden and revealing insight that the core teaching of the Christian Gospel is that faith is the only thing which justifies a sinner before God. This means that in order to have a right relationship with God, to be in good standing before God, all one need do is trust that God will put away one's sin. One does not have to perform any duty or act. Salvation cannot be earned; it is given as a free gift out of the unimaginably generous love of God. Faith brings with it the certitude of salvation because it is guaranteed by God and not earned by our efforts.

This led him to abandon all belief in the mediation of the Church and its priests in the pursuit of salvation. When John Tetzel arrived in Wittenberg preaching indulgences (the forgiving of sins in return for financial contributions to, on this occasion, the rebuilding of St Peter's Cathedral in Rome) Luther reacted.

This was when Luther first came to public attention and it happened during 1517 when he published *Ninety-five Theses on Indulgences* and invited scholars to debate publicly with him. His reputation as a vigorous critic of traditional teachings grew quite quickly and he moved into the camp of those calling openly for reform of the Church. His main idea was that the medieval institution had drifted away from the early New Testament ideas of what the Church should be like. He wrote in German; this was a startling novelty as learned debate was, at that time, normally conducted in Latin. His use of language was vigorous and engaging.

Rome hoped at first that the matter could be dealt with within the Augustinian order, but Luther's energetic disputations won him supporters within his own order and indeed in other religious orders also. He was tried in Rome for spreading heresy. He was summoned to appear before Cardinal Cajetan at Augsburg, where he refused to abandon his new doctrines. He then fled to Wittenberg, where he was protected by the Elector Frederick III of Saxony. We must remember that people were still burned at the stake for heresy well into the seventeenth century and that both Catholics and Protestants alike practised this brutality.

**Salvation** In negative terms, the saving of human beings from the influence of sin and from damnation. In positive terms, the destiny of human beings to be in the presence of God eternally.
**Mediator** One who seeks to bring about a peaceful settlement between opposing parties. In Christian theology it refers to the work of Christ reconciling God and the human race.
**Heresy** Teachings which cast doubt on or deny the official doctrines of the Church.

By 1520 Luther had quite definitely broken with the medieval church. He was condemned in that year by the Papal Bull *Exsurge Domine*: 41 of his theses were branded heretical. Luther responded by publicly burning the Bull. He was summoned before the Diet of Worms in 1521. He again refused to withdraw his teaching and was denied safe conduct for travel within the Holy Roman Empire.

However his prince, the Elector of Saxony, continued to support him, arranged for him to be 'kidnapped' and brought to a place of safety. During his eight months in isolation he wrote many pamphlets, but his finest achievement was to begin work on his translation of the Bible into German from the original tongues. It is an enduring monument to his genius and was prized for the energy and warmth of its language.

While Luther was living quietly and safely, his ideas spread rapidly, large areas of Germany abandoned traditional practices and popular enthusiastic religious practices became common. Many monks left their orders, priests married and popular religious demonstrations got out of hand; there were also disturbances over economic issues. Luther returned to Wittenberg to restore order, in this he was helped by the civil authorities. He now abandoned his religious dress and married a former nun, Catherine de Bora, in 1524.

At this time there was a popular Peasants' revolt, which Luther denounced severely, urging the German princes to go to war against those who had rebelled. This cost him some popular support, but his ideas continued to spread. He wrote many hymns which were a popular way of spreading his ideas and which are still among the treasures of the German language.

The Reform movement had by now spread to a number of other countries, but serious disagreements quickly appeared among the reformers themselves. In a confrontation held at Marburg in 1529, Luther and Ulrich Zwingli (1484–1531) disagreed strongly over the nature of the Eucharistic Presence. He was still unable to move freely around the Empire, because of the sanctions imposed on him, but Luther agreed the *Augsburg Confession*, a document drawn up by Philip Melanchthon (1497–1560), a disciple who acted as leader of the reform movement while Luther's movements were restricted. The purpose of this document was to try to make peace within the reform movement; but Luther refused any moves in the direction of reconciliation with the Catholic Church.

Towards the end of his life, Luther was saddened by the frequent disagreements that broke out between Protestants of various types. Eventually the task of making peace would fall to the civil authorities.

He was a deeply pessimistic man, but also one of strong feeling. He had considerable powers of oratory which he did not always place under reasonable control. We see the positive side to his mastery of language in his lively translation of the Bible and in his confident, compelling hymns. We see the negative side of this eloquence in his hatred of the Papacy. His attacks on those who opposed him were often violent, abusive and obscene. Martin Luther died in 1546.

## Timeline

1483 Birth of Martin Luther near Mansfeld in Saxony
1492 Columbus discovers the New World
1501–1505 Luther studies Philosophy at the University of Erfurt
1503 Julius II elected Pope
1507 Luther ordained priest
1510–1511 Luther visits Rome
1512 Professor of Biblical Studies at the University of Wittenberg
1512–1515 Luther's 'tower experience'

1514 Albert Dürer's *Melancolia*
1517 Tetzel's Indulgences campaign
Luther publishes his *Ninety-five Theses on Indulgences*
1520 Luther condemned by the Papal Bull *Exsurge Domine*
Suleiman the Magnificent becomes Ottoman Emperor
1521 Luther summoned before the Diet of Worms; refuses to withdraw
1523 Zwingli successfully upholds 67 Reformation Theses in Zürich
1524 Luther marries Catherine de Bora
1524–1525 The Peasants' War
1525 The Reformation spreads to the Netherlands, Denmark and Norway
1529 Luther's debate with Zwingli over the Real Presence of Christ in the Eucharist
1530 Luther agrees the *Augsburg Confession*
1531 Henry VIII declares himself head of the Church of England
1536 Calvin publishes his *Institutes of the Christian Religion*
1546 Death of Martin Luther
Michelangelo takes charge of the building of St Peter's in Rome
1555 Division of Germany into Catholic and Protestant principalities

## Thought

### *Luther's writings*

While Luther was returning from the Diet of Worms (1521) he was 'kidnapped' and taken to the Castle of Wartburg. This was really a device to ensure his safety, as he no longer enjoyed the protection normally granted a citizen of the Holy Roman Empire. From now on he must rely on the goodwill of the Elector of Saxony. He stayed at Wartburg castle as a guest and was afforded every facility there. It was a period of intense depression but also of much literary activity. He wrote several famous pamphlets there and it was during this period that he started his famous translation of the Bible into German.

In his *Appeal to the Christian Nobility of the German Nation* Luther argued for the reform of the church, hoping that the nobility would use their social and political position to favour this aim. He proposed that taxes no longer be paid to Rome, wanted to do away with the celibacy of the clergy and close down religious orders. He also wished to discontinue practices like pilgrimages and masses for the dead.

The *Babylonian Captivity of the Christian Church* was next issued; in it Luther engaged in a powerful polemic against the Western, institutional Church. He argued that Christ's message was no longer permitted to impact with all its force upon the world. The gospel had been kidnapped by the institutional Church which had perverted its meaning, because it used it as a means of holding power over people and populations. The sacramental system of the Church, he argued, had become the property of the clergy, which now controlled the gospel rather that acted as its servants.

The third pamphlet of this set was *The Liberty of a Christian*. Luther now thought about how the doctrine of justification by faith affected Christian living, trying to work out its implications for the practical activities of daily life. Can one just believe and do as one pleases?

These three works became known as fundamental Reformation texts. They are not systematic works of theology; they are polemical works written to persuade, and they arose from the immediate promptings of circumstance.

He also wrote more devotional works including a commentary on the *Psalms* and a meditation on the *Magnificat*, the Song of The Blessed Virgin Mary in Lk. 1. Here he asks for the intercession of the mother of Jesus; this is not often considered a 'Protestant' practice.

The great work of his creative genius must be his translation of the Bible into German. He started the New Testament in December 1521; it was on sale by September 1522. This timetable alone is staggering: he could only write by hand, print setting was in its crudest infancy. He used Erasmus' Greek text. What is more there was no well-established German language into which to translate the work. There was a form of official, administrative German, spoken and understood by very few. There were many local dialects. By the time Luther had finished, the German language, as we understand the term today, had come into being.

It was mentioned earlier that the Reformation was a time of developing nationalism. This trend was given further encouragement by the insistence that the Bible be available to ordinary people in their own language. The English translator and reformer William Tyndale (*c.*1494–1536) once told a scholarly clergyman, 'I shall cause a boy that driveth the plough to know more of the scripture than thou dost'. The translation of the Bible into the common language of the people often promoted the use of that language. Luther's translation was but the first of many. But it also provided a people with a well-constructed, vigorous language, well adapted to everyday life, and it became the focus of national awareness. Many Bible translations incidentally served in this way to 'establish' the nation's language.

### THE *NINETY-FIVE THESES ON INDULGENCES*

When on 31 October 1517 Martin Luther nailed *Ninety-Five Theses on Indulgences* to the door of the Wittenberg Church, he was acting, as he was entitled to do, as a teacher of Theology. It was his right to put forward new ideas and invite other scholars to debate publicly with him, so that those ideas could be tested. Luther was not inciting the people to revolt; he was requesting scholars to discuss with him. He had at this stage no notion of breaking with Rome, or of founding a new church, but he did want to reform abuses and the sale of indulgences was a glaring one: one which, in fact, diminished the office of the Pope.

His constant theme in the *Ninety-five Theses* was that indulgences have no effect, only the cross of Christ guarantees salvation. Penitence is not a passing, momentary thing; it is a permanent attitude of the heart, mind and soul.

### THE *CATECHISMS*

Luther wrote two catechisms, which are the nearest things he wrote to systematic theology. During the Diet of Worms (1521), held under the patronage of the Holy Roman Emperor Charles V, Martin Luther defended his religious doctrines and refused to deny them. The various princes of the many states making up the Holy Roman Empire were divided in religious opinion and each applied the outcome of the discussions at Worms in his own way.

The Elector of Saxony asked Luther to organize the evangelical church in his territories and Luther set to work energetically. He found that the educational level of the clergy, including their theological education, was poor. So he wrote the *Longer Catechism* to instruct the clergy, and provide them with a handy reference book. He also wrote the *Shorter Catechism* for the instruction of the faithful. This is still very much the standard reference book in the Lutheran communion in many lands.

This shorter work takes the form of a father instructing his children in the Christian faith. It includes the Ten Commandments with a very short explanation of the meaning of each. The explanation is always a single sentence, never more than about six lines. This is followed by an explanation of the Apostles' Creed in three articles headed Creation, Redemption and Sanctification. There follows an explanation of the Lord's Prayer in eight short sections, including a commentary on the word *Amen*: it signifies that these requests are certainly pleasing to God and that God hears them, for they were taught by Jesus Christ. Next come two short sections on the sacrament of baptism and the sacrament of the altar. It finishes with a short passage on how a father should every morning teach the members of his family to ask for God's blessing for the day ahead.

### *Justification*

Luther often meditated on how we come to salvation and on the problem of Predestination. Are we predestined to be damned or to be saved? One of his superiors is said to have remarked to him that he should not meditate on the position of the sinful human before a holy God. He would be far better off meditating on the wounds of Christ, placing Jesus at the centre of his thought rather than himself. If we do this our fears concerning predestination will disappear, for God has predestined Jesus to suffer for sinners. Thus God has taken the steps required for salvation; salvation is in God's hands, not ours.

Thus Luther's meditations, particularly his meditations on Scripture, came to see the Bible as the great witness to a saving Christ and as the only rule for faith.

God may be a merciful Lord, but God is also a just Lord. Luther could not take God's grace seriously if it in any way watered down the total justice of God. The despair one experiences when confronted with God is not a logical stalemate, but grace, for one is already placing one's life before God. The way one judges oneself in the sight of God can only come from encounter with God; it is to admit that God is right! The just person, in contrast to the sinner, is the one who accuses self and admits God is right.

Luther said that he expected from God the exercise of 'formal' or 'active' justice: the justice of God compels God to punish sin and sinners. As Luther meditated on Rom. 1.17, 'the righteous will live by faith', he came to see the whole weight of the gospel in terms of the 'passive' justice of God. Divine mercy judges sinners to be in fellowship with God because that sinner believes. The negative impact of the sinful condition is abolished because of faith. Salvation is the work which God accomplishes in us, the power of God working in us.

Consequently the justice of God is not what God demands of human beings, but what God gives to the sinner who comes seeking mercy in humble repentance and in the obedience of faith. Someone other than us has submitted humbly and willingly to the demands of justice and suffered instead of us on the Cross. Jesus has undergone the judgement of God. We need not climb to heaven, God comes down to earth. The remaining question is to see if our lives can now show the love which God has shown us.

Luther, in his *Commentary on the Epistle to the Romans* summed up the human situation like this: *simul peccator, et justus ac semper paenitens.* The Christian is 'always a sinner and always just and always repentant'.

So Christians must look at themselves in three ways:

- experience themselves as sinners when they confront the holiness of the God who is Love;
- experience themselves as just when they accept through faith the benefits that God has provided for them in the work of Jesus the Son;
- experience repentance, as they stand before God, knowing they have nothing to offer the God they tirelessly offend and also thankful to the one who gives all and repeatedly gives all.

If one wishes to misunderstand all this, one may do so. But Luther never lapsed into a too easy, even cynical, attitude that everything necessary had been done and one didn't have to bother oneself. This attitude would later come to be labelled 'cheap grace'. It is the thoughtless acceptance of a happy mediocrity in the face of an indulgent God. He remained haunted by the idea of holiness, the desire to accept and obey the will of a God whose justice saves but whose grace draws us into service.

**Catechism** A booklet of questions and answers about the Christian faith used for teaching.
**Predestination** The decision of God by which certain individuals will, no matter what happens, be saved.
**Repentance** To regret the bad things one has done in the past and to resolve to change one's behaviour.

## Sola fide, sola gratia, sola scriptura

This Latin phrase which means 'by faith alone, by grace alone, by scripture alone' sums up the Reformation teaching of Justification by Faith.

'By faith alone' is the answer given by Luther to the question, 'how can one become just, or innocent, before God?' This emphasizes the heart of the answer Luther took from St Paul. We are not made innocent before God because we have obeyed the religious law, but because we have accepted Christ and accepted Christ's just, honest and innocent standing before God which brings about our salvation. This faith is more than a casual assent to a proposition; it involves a vibrant involvement in a living reality, working itself out at every moment of life.

'By grace alone' is how we experience salvation, how it is realized, how it becomes effective within us. It involves two views. God's love gives us strength to live as God wants, but in addition, and more importantly for Luther, God turns towards us and accepts us as we are, even when still estranged from God. The Christian is always dependent upon grace and the sinner is always dependent upon the innocence of Christ. Faith perceives the mercy of God and grows because nurtured by the gifts of God, which we receive even though we do not deserve them.

'By scripture alone' is Luther's understanding of the authority by which we come to knowledge. Luther increasingly distrusted the authority of the papal office and the sacramental system of the Church. He did not abandon sacraments. He protested against their use as a lever of clerical control. It means that no revelation is given to the Church outside scripture. Scripture has weight because, in it, Christ is made known.

Obviously with three principles standing 'alone', it means that each has power in its own area. We are dealing with the means of salvation, the dawning awareness of salvation and the authority by which we accept it.

### *The Freedom of the Christian*

We are saved from damnation and despair by the grace of God which is received by faith and taught in scripture. This is the certainty announced by the gospel. Luther contrasted this basic idea with all the duties and securities offered by the traditional church of his day.

Luther did not denounce works, nor say we were free to ignore them. On the contrary, the Christian is not relieved of the performance of duties. Luther just did not believe that works brought about or guaranteed salvation. Salvation is the gift of God. But once we come to an understanding of that gift, then works spring from the joy of a believer's heart; we do not perform them in order to gain some advantage from them. We perform them because, when we realize our new state, we cannot avoid expressing our love for God through them.

Christian liberty is therefore a wonderful gift which, by faith, we receive from God. From now on the only concern of that new insight is how best to give thanks for the grace received. All the Christian can now do is live a life of thanksgiving and that is expressed by seeking to please God.

### *Luther's 'Theology of the Cross'*

This is a strand in Luther's thought which he contrasted with the 'Theology of Glory' where God is revealed in the wonders of creation and in good works. Through this particularly Lutheran insight, the revelation of God comes in a veiled inner way through the experience of suffering. Only faith can really understand this concealed communication which reveals the hidden God (*deus absconditus*). Believers see the reality of a God who loves us in the mystery of the Cross, in the sacrifice of

Christ crucified. This not only reveals the extent of human guilt but also reveals how it can be taken away.

In the Old Testament, God has chosen a small, rather than a powerful, people. In the Cross God is revealed and God's saving work is successful through an act of suffering. It is not achieved through a work of power. The mystery of the kingdom of God is shown in good news to the poor, the blind, the lame and the marginalized. All these things are hidden from the wise. Christ crucified is, in the words of St Paul, 'a stumbling-block to Jews and foolishness to Gentiles' (1 Cor. 1. 23).

There is a stress on humiliation here. There is a paradox because apparent failure achieves success.

So Luther sees the Theology of the Cross as central to all understanding of the Biblical message. Individual Christians may often have to take the Theology of the Cross on board at a personal level. When they do this, they rediscover the meaning of the pain of God in the world. By the Theology of the Cross, many Christians come to a deeper understanding of the divinity of Christ (they reflect on his humiliation) and to a finer appreciation of the humanity of Christ (they meditate on his exaltation).

### *Luther on sacraments*

Luther was powerfully disappointed and frustrated by the organization of the Church of his day. He considered it to be a mockery of gospel teaching. He was particularly angry with the supremacy and control of the popes. He constantly taught that where bishops and pastors, including popes, were not obedient to the word of God, then the ordinary believer was not obliged to obey them.

In those days this was a revolutionary way of understanding Church. Most people believed that the Church, like any other power structure, had to rule and impose authority. To believe that the authority of the Church was something to be accepted by individuals, because they were impressed and attracted by the goodness they saw there, was startling.

These thoughts turned the received understanding of the doctrine of the Church upside down. The Church was no longer a power structure, it was not even a visible organization; it is, rather, the free association of true believers.

In the traditional understanding, the agreed and accepted power structure was the cast-iron guarantee of the authenticity of the Church and, because of that, of the validity of her sacraments; everything flowed in a seamless line of authority from the Pope, whose own authority flowed in a seamless line from St Peter and the Apostles. In the new understanding, the Church was an association of genuine belief and holiness, partly visible, partly unseen. The authenticating spirit was faithfulness to Christ.

This also had profound implications for the understanding of Christian sacraments. They were no longer visible signs of authenticity and supremacy; they were an expression of faithfulness before God.

Luther gave some importance to the traditional sacrament of penance. But it was no longer the act of making reparation before God by good works; it was now to be the renewal of the believer's life of faith in a spirit of repentance. For Luther however only the two New Testament ordinances of Baptism and the Lord's Supper had compelling sacramental power.

In Baptism, water makes remission of sins effective and grants eternal life to all who believe in the promises of God. This happens because it is laid down by commandment of God and because the community is operating under the authority of God's word.

Regarding the Lord's Supper, Luther rejected the notion of transubstantiation where the substance of the bread and wine changes to become the substance of the body and blood of Christ. He also rejected Zwingli's teaching that the Eucharist was no more than a memorial feast. He emphasized bodily presence, but it does not come about because of the actions of an authorized, ordained priest; it happens because God's word is made real and apparent as the believer participates in the sacramental action.

### *Luther's political thought*

Luther was by no means a revolutionary in either a theological or a political sense. He was not particularly interested in change. He was more concerned to recapture a lost, fundamental and original spirit. He believed he had no competence in political matters but believed that the world in which the gospel was preached could not be ignored.

He constantly warned all Christians against revolt, sedition and even minor occasions of public disorder. All Christians had a duty to obey the authorities, which were instituted by God and had the duty of overseeing the public good. The role of the people was to urge the authorities to do what was right. In this matter Luther believed that the duty of the government was to oppose both Catholics and those who wished to abolish all government.

He nevertheless was quite clear in his mind that there was a difference between religious life and public life; there is a quite definite separation of spiritual and political power. Each of us is a blend of worldly and spiritual components. The worldly side of us is subject to authority, government, princes and laws; the spiritual side is freed from authority, government, princes and laws.

But he would never have wished to see himself as the father of modernity, clearing the way by sweeping aside a collapsed medieval mindset or rocking medieval institutions. His overriding passion was to convince all that God is love and that they should hold that truth with unshakeable certainty.

## *The* Confession of Augsburg

Although Luther had been condemned at the Diet of Worms (1521), the Holy Roman Emperor had many other problems on his hands than religious commotion in Germany. By and large, the decisions of the Diet of Worms were not followed through and the Lutheran Reformation was allowed breathing space to consolidate and develop. However, things did not always resolve themselves in a satisfactory manner and other councils were held to arrange matters. Eventually, in 1530, another assembly was held in Augsburg so that each side might be heard. John Eck (1486–1543) was to speak for the Catholic side; Philip Melanchthon, for the Protestant one.

Melanchthon drew up a statement of belief that was agreed by all the Protestant delegates: the *Confession of Augsburg*. It contains articles on God, Original Sin, the Son of God, Justification, the preaching Ministry, Obedience in faith, the Church and many others. This document nowadays has the status of a foundational document among the churches of the Lutheran tradition.

The Emperor asked his theologians to draw up a refutation of this text, which they did. He considered it now refuted, but there was no agreement. A final decision was put off to a general council. So, at last, the demands for a council were to be met. But that council was the Council of Trent; it opened in 1545, and no Protestants were present.

In 1555 there was a gentleman's agreement called the Religious Peace of Augsburg. According to this, the prince of each state of the Empire was free to settle whether the official religion in his lands was to be Catholic or Protestant. It was the principle of *cuius regio, eius religio* and that roughly means 'if your prince is Protestant (or Catholic), so are you'.

### *Christian orthodoxy*

Protestant Christian teaching continued to develop and refine its teaching and awareness. Reformation teaching did not rely on new sources of inspiration and authority. We have seen how Luther insisted that his teaching be in agreement with the word of God as found in the Bible. He was not a believer in the literal inspiration and infallible truth of the Holy Scripture. His teaching often took its authority from simple traditional texts. We have noted his use of the Ten Commandments and The Lord's Prayer. But he also was alive to the tradition of the Church outside scripture and we have also seen how he used the Apostles' Creed.

## Appraisal

Luther had a pessimistic outlook. This may have led him to exaggerate the sinfulness of the human person and to be suspicious of the role of reason in coming to knowledge of God. On the other hand he was deeply conscious of the need for salvation and came to see that only the merits of Christ could guarantee this. His doctrine of Justification by Faith understood that the merits of Jesus were accredited to sinners, without their deserving them.

Human persons are totally under the sway of sin and cannot escape from that situation. So God regards us as sinless because of the sacrificial work of Christ, though in fact we remain as we were before.

Luther retained a most negative view of all human religious effort. So he left all external religious behaviour in the control of the civic authorities, his thought concentrated on the interior life.

Faith was absolutely central for Luther. This was not assent to certain teachings, for the sake of appearance. It had to be an inner, vibrant, core reality, out of which one comes to an understanding of life.

Luther increasingly distrusted the power structures of his day. He particularly distrusted the remote functioning of the institutional Church in Rome. His vibrancy and passion made him seek something more immediate than that. Following the Reformation, Protestant power structures would tend to be more national. It was a time of increasing national awareness; the power of the medieval Papacy was, in some areas, being whittled away. Power was now increasingly passing to the civil authorities.

None of the three, the Reformation, Luther's teaching or the slow and thoughtful meditation on theological truths, can be expressed by slogans. Theology's insights are matters of careful, sober and calm reflection.

Luther's work is less the calm reflection on a given body of theological data; it is more the excited meditation on a real, profound and personal experience.

What are Luther's contradictions?

# 6 St Ignatius Loyola and John Calvin: the two sides dig in

This chapter considers two of the most unlikely bedfellows. They are Ignatius Loyola and John Calvin. They were rough contemporaries. They were both highly influential figures in the religious turmoil of sixteenth-century Europe. They both studied at the University of Paris. They both had an experience of profound religious conversion. They were both personally austere men. They both set up lasting religious organizations. Loyola founded the Society of Jesus, and Calvin, the religious government of Geneva and the Reformed/Presbyterian tradition of Western Christianity. They both wrote an influential work: Loyola is the author of the *Spiritual Exercises*, and Calvin wrote the *Institutes of the Christian Religion*. They both have reputations for rigour in thought, action and organization.

None of this should blind us to the enormous differences between the two men. As the sixteenth-century Reformation took its course, these two men are examples of how it went in two opposite directions.

At the end of the last chapter we left our survey of Western Theology with a consideration of Martin Luther and the Protestant Reformation. We noted that the constant demand for a general council had at last been answered with the calling of the Council of Trent. However Western Christianity had now been splintered. There were no Protestants present. The work of the council would be to bring about a Catholic Reformation.

This movement is often called the Counter Reformation. One of its purposes was to reform longstanding abuses and to reaffirm Catholic traditions following the severe criticisms levelled against the late medieval church. However it appeared to be doing so in the light of the Protestant movement earlier in the sixteenth century and indeed in resistance to it. There is no doubt that the Roman Catholic Church confronted the Protestant reformation by reforming itself from within. It is difficult to give due balance to the various movements of reform, reaffirmation and resistance following the calamity that had occurred.

Three other points might briefly be mentioned. First this period of history was a time of frequent criticism of the Church, but it was a humanist rational criticism, chiefly aimed at widespread church abuses. The unique contribution of the Protestant reformers was to mould that criticism into a rediscovery of the fundamental function of Scripture as the foundational authority of the Church. Secondly this was a time of adventure, searching, exploration and discoveries of new lands. The adventurous spirit was also active in the world of ideas. The third point is that the Reformation came just after the inventing of printing. Books were becoming cheaper. The word had acquired a new potency and fascination; the new emphasis on Scripture was not a total accident! The Reformation took place at a particular moment in European civilization when new things were avidly grasped after and new tools were available to channel new ideas in a particular way.

## Ignatius Loyola

### *The Council of Trent*

This council met, with disruptions and gaps, from 1545 to 1563. The Roman Catholic tradition holds it to be the 19th General or Ecumenical Council in the history of Christianity. However it was not attended by Orthodox bishops (there had been few formal links between Orthodox bishops and Rome since 1054) nor by Protestant Christians. Its deliberations are considered to be the classical statement of the ideals of the Catholic Reformation and it took place against the background of the spread of Protestant ideas and the urgent necessity for moral and administrative reform, not to mention the need for discipline in many lax and wildly varying local practices. There was widespread resistance to setting it up, not least from the Pope, but there were other internal squabbles.

The council did not meet under ideal conditions; it was suspended from 1547 to 1551 because of an epidemic and later because of a revolt against the Holy Roman Emperor, Charles V. This led to a ten-year suspension.

The Tridentine documents covered a wide range of subjects, both doctrinal and administrative. It considered, among other subjects, the equal validity of Scripture and tradition as a basis for doctrine, the sole right of the Church to interpret Scripture, the authority of the Latin *Vulgate* text, Original Sin, Justification, the Seven Sacraments, Transubstantiation (together with a repudiation of Lutheran, Calvinist and Zwinglian Eucharistic teachings), Holy Orders and the reform of the *Index*.

**Tridentine** Concerning the Council of Trent (1545–1563).
**Doctrine** A set of principles presented for belief by a religious group: the teachings of a church.
**Scripture** The sacred writings of a religion. Here, the Bible.
***Vulgate*** The Latin text of the Bible translated from Greek by St Jerome in the fourth century. Later revised.
**Transubstantiation** The official Roman Catholic doctrine of Eucharistic change. The substance of the bread and wine changes to become the substance of the body and blood of Christ, even though there is no change in outward appearance.
***Index*** Here, an official list of books which Roman Catholics were forbidden to read. Now abolished.

There were hopes in the early days that the council would, to some extent, move to meet Protestant criticisms, but as the sessions dragged on, were suspended, new popes elected and the balance of power and persuasion shifted within the composition of the council, these anticipations failed. Protestant hopes were dashed; many Catholic wishes for more radical reform were unsuccessful. The Roman Catholic Church came out of the council, more authoritative, sure, clear-sighted and disciplined.

## Life (1491–1556)

Ignatius Loyola was born in 1491 to a noble family in one of the Basque provinces of northern Spain. He was sent at an early age to court, where he developed a taste for high society life, including courting young ladies, gambling and sword play; all this led to the neglect of formal academic education. He saw military service, particularly against the French.

He was wounded in 1521 when his leg was struck by a cannon ball. He walked with a limp for the rest of his life.

During his convalescence he asked for frivolous novels to relieve his boredom, but none was available and he was supplied with a life of Christ and lives of the saints. In desperation he read them, discovering that he might like to imitate the saints. At the same time he entertained romantic thoughts concerning an unknown lady, but noticed that when he thought of her he was restless, whereas when he contemplated Christ and the saints he was at peace. This is held to be the beginning of the long discipline, later known in the *Spiritual Exercises* as 'the discernment of spirits', and to be a stage on the way to his religious conversion.

Having decided to go on pilgrimage to Jerusalem he went to the monastery of Montserrat near Barcelona where he spent the night in vigil, left his sword at the altar, gave his clothes away and set out on his journey. Before leaving Spain he had an experience near the town of Manresa, then lived in a cave for ten months engaging in prayer, fasting and good works. The *Spiritual Exercises* had started to take shape here, and he also had a vision about which he never talked but which appears to have involved a profound conversion experience. A core conviction of this time was the experience of grace as the ability to see God in all things; consequently all times and experiences were times of prayer.

He eventually arrived in Rome, received the pope's permission to go to the Holy Land but on arrival was told it was too dangerous and that he must leave again.

He now decided to be a priest, returned to school to learn Latin and, though he was 33, studied in the same class as young boys. He later went to the University of Alcalá. Here his keenness to expound the Scripture and to teach people to pray attracted the unwelcome attention of the Inquisition and he was imprisoned. He had a similar experience in Salamanca and decided to study at Paris. He enrolled at Montaigu College in February 1528; four years after Calvin came to that same college.

In the French capital he met Francis Xavier and Peter Faber, gathered followers around him and taught them to pray using the method of the *Spiritual Exercises.* He and his friends decided to form a group who would go to the Holy Land but if that was not possible, to go to Rome and offer to serve the pope; the pope received them favourably.

It was in Rome in the Church of St Mary Major that Ignatius said his first Mass.

Ignatius summoned his companions to Rome where they discussed their future and they decided to take the three traditional vows of poverty, chastity and obedience; an additional vow placed them especially at the disposal of the pope for whatever duties he might decide. The new company, the Society of Jesus, was approved in 1540. Ignatius was unanimously elected Superior.

Loyola would spend the next 15 years directing the members of his order, writing thousands of letters and overseeing their activities all over the world. The Jesuits would found houses in every part of the planet. They acquired a strong reputation for rigour and thoroughness and three members of this very new order were influential theologians at the Council of Trent.

The Society of Jesus was involved in education, a subject dear to Ignatius himself. Schools, colleges and universities were soon founded and the Jesuits became a major force in the educational world, a role which continues to this day. Throughout the Middle Ages there had been frequent movements of retreat from the 'world' in order to promote one's salvation. Loyola's vision involved a reconciliation of the spirit and the 'world' and a definite ministry to it and in it. The Jesuits often became the educators of a new Catholic elite in Europe and elsewhere.

Loyola was quietly loyal to the established church of his day, the Roman Catholic Church. He had a special degree of loyalty to the pope and his order was dedicated to furthering the pope's wishes. He wished it to defend the established institutions of his day from attack.

Ignatius Loyola's health had never been robust, he often suffered from stomach ailments, and his physical condition gradually deteriorated in Rome. He died in July 1557. He was beatified in 1609 and canonized in 1622.

## Thought

Loyola wrote few works. He wrote the *Spiritual Exercises*, he wrote many letters and he wrote the *Constitutions* of the Society of Jesus. It is generally agreed that he wrote the *Spiritual Exercises* by himself, but it is pointed out that he only became a prolific letter writer after Juan Alfonso de Polanco became his secretary. The same may be said of the *Constitutions*; so it is difficult to rule out the influence of Polanco from these later texts.

The *Spiritual Exercises* are a method of spiritual retreat. The *Constitutions* are a recipe for living in community. Other works include The *Pilgrim's Story*, which is a set of confidences which he hoped would be helpful to others. The remaining fragments of his *Diary* tell of his thoughts, deliberations and experiences as he struggled to deal with the concrete problems he met day by day. His works are not an ordered treatise, but all have the quality of encouraging the reader to action. A considerable quantity of correspondence also remains.

Loyola's academic studies were in the faculty of Arts at Paris: he graduated both Bachelor and Master it is known that he attended Theology lectures there, but he never took a degree in that subject.

He is known to have disliked the Protestant Reformers and their thought; he certainly encouraged some of his followers to combat their ideas and influence. There is, however, no evidence that he ever read them.

Even though the Jesuits were to achieve the reputation of being the spearhead of the Catholic Reformation, Loyola was not himself a controversialist and did not confront Protestant Reformation ideas head on; his main interest was in how he could 'help souls', and he seems to have decided that this could best be done through educational, pastoral work and missionary work. Nevertheless he could not avoid being deeply touched by the sixteenth century doctrinal turmoil.

The Jesuits were particularly active in the Far East and in South America. Indeed Loyola is credited with inventing the word 'mission' in the sense of the spread of Christianity to non-Christian lands. Yet he never wrote a treatise on such subjects. He was a doer rather than a thinker but a doer who wished to share his particular experience of spiritual insight with others. 'The world is our house', one of his closest assistants used to repeat. In this, there is an implicit, though rarely explicit, element of pastoral theology to Loyola's work.

Loyola's concern was less with doctrine and more with a way of praying. This way had two chief components: the gospels, particularly the gospels of Matthew, Mark and Luke; and an attitude of interior meditation which is particularly attentive to gospel narratives. Thus the *Spiritual Exercises* played a role in the development of the spiritual retreat.

Loyola, of course, was convinced that by spiritual meditation Christians have direct access to God and that God is actively at work within them. This inner conviction and spiritual richness were the sources out of which believers can best minister to the world.

In this, as in many other aspects of life, Loyola's practical common sense shows through. He did not insist on the daily observance of the Divine Office in community; this would tie people to one place and get in the way of efficient and effective ministry, but he also laid down specific instructions for care of the body and concern for self so that health and strength might be maintained for active mission.

Loyola had a strong and positive sense of the world. He did not try to flee from it but appears to have been reconciled to it. He was strongly aware that Divine Love was constantly operative within it: grace perfects nature.

Humans have been created to praise, worship and serve God. Other things on earth were created for human use. We should use these things in so far as they help us to attaint the goal for which we were made and distance ourselves from them in so far as they impede our progress to that end. This rule of 'in so far as', known to Jesuits as the rule of *tantum quantum* has two components: the correct use of this world's gifts and a rule of detachment or indifference. This was to help Jesuits to be more open to the promptings of divine inspiration.

**Inquisition** A tribunal of the Roman Catholic Church operating between the thirteenth and nineteenth centuries, with special responsibilities for rooting out error, heresy and unbelief. Responsible for regrettable excesses.

**Spiritual retreat** A long or short period of quiet and mediation during which people concentrate on their relationship with God.

**Ascetics** are individuals who seek spiritual enlightenment by severely disciplining the body. They tend to shun comfort, luxury, fine clothes, good food and live very simply, even imposing harsh conditions upon themselves.

**Spiritual director** An individual, usually a priest, who offers advice, help, counsel and confession to other individuals concerning their relationship with God.

## *The* Spiritual Exercises

Following his conversion Loyola entered upon a phase of extreme asceticism: giving away his clothes, living in a cave on alms, eating a minimum of food, tortured as to whether he had confessed all his sins, even contemplating suicide. It was doubtless at this time that he first started making the notes that would, in time, become the *Spiritual Exercises.* The earliest text we still possess dates from 1541.

The text is a difficult work for the outsider. It is more a series of notes which guides a priest helping those in his pastoral care towards 'discernment'. Discernment is a word used by Christians when they have a feeling that God has a plan for them, a mission for them to accomplish, and they are trying to discover (discern) what that plan and mission might be.

Obviously in business, industry, administration and so on one consults a document or gets in touch with a superior when learning what one is supposed to do. Getting in touch with God is more problematic; our main models are the Scriptures, particularly the gospels, and the example of Christ. So discernment is an activity of prayer.

The *Spiritual Exercises* were written as a sort of course in prayer; the person following the course is known as an *exercitant.* The aim of the *Exercises* is to help exercitants (both men and women) work out the will of God for their lives, to provide them with the strength and open them to the grace which will equip them to follow that path. The *Exercises* are by no means restricted to members of the Society of Jesus, though they are usually followed under the guidance of a Jesuit director.

Normally the exercises are completed in a four-week cycle. Loyola did not intend the exercises to be some sort of substitute for a daily office; it is probable that he only intended them to be completed in their entirety once or twice in a lifetime. Shorter retreats of three or four days using the exercises are now more usual but unlikely to be undertaken more than once a year.

The first week usually concentrates on sin and its cost, the second week deals with Christ's life on earth, the third week deals with the passion and the fourth week with the risen life of Christ.

This is a broad outline; there are additional features designed to help the exercitant to pray, to avoid being over-conscientious and on how to avoid self-consideration when choosing a vocation in life.

We shall just consider one element of Ignatian meditation: the *composition of place*, which is an integral part of the first week. It is a method of praying the gospel narratives. Loyola talked of 'seeing the place'. This means that he wanted to get a mental image of the place where the story took place, to see the landscape, feel the heat and smell the smells; he wanted to get a vivid impression of the setting so that he could experience the events more clearly. Thus he would ask himself questions about the road from Bethany to Jerusalem, for instance; he would wonder if it is wide or narrow, flat or hilly.

Other more abstract efforts at composition of place involve trying to see his soul imprisoned in a perishing body, exiled among wild beasts. This element then became an introduction to more intense meditation.

The *Exercises* contain a rich store of spiritual insight; some people even claim them to be inspired. The work has a lyrical quality where deep religious feeling is often illustrated by military images, recalling Loyola's background and training.

The central idea in the *Exercises* is obedience. It was not a theoretical virtue; rather it was one which promotes a practical truth and inspires action. It flows from the respect and adoration which are due to the majesty of the Creator and Saviour and promotes total submission to the will of God. Loyola took the phrase, 'thy will be done on earth as it is in heaven', quite literally.

The central principle of the *Exercises* is directed towards the possibility of acting in accordance with the divine will. Thus he (and all Christian people) must know what that will is and conform his own will to it. The first step on the road is to acquire inspiration and counsel from on high. This means meditation, searching, prayer and discernment.

The aim of the Society of Jesus has been stated as 'contemplation in action'. This is less a question of arriving at a mystical state of contemplation through, or while involved in, action; rather it is a formula aimed at contemplation but never separated from action.

This is an optimistic outlook. It does not renounce the world but accepts it and acts within it. It seeks the contemplation of the divine but never forgets that there is work on earth to be done. It balances love of God and duty towards God with love of neighbour and duty towards the same.

At the same time it has a negative side. The emphasis on obedience suggests a nagging pessimism concerning the resources human beings possess in order to accomplish the will of God. Nevertheless that is overcome by discipline and obedience – military virtues!

The *Exercises* have been widely studied and commented by theologians and mystical writers. They have their critics as well as their admirers; St Teresa of Ávila, for instance, said she was incapable of using such a system. Others have seen in them an overweening confidence in the human ability to raise oneself to God. However, prayer is always a work and gift of grace.

For those who eventually decide they wish to enter the Jesuit order, Ignatius Loyola has prepared another document, the *Constitutions*, to help them live in a community. The desire here is to help individuals together to discern the will of God.

### *The* Constitutions

In the early days, there was great discussion among the companions as to what their mode of life should be. They fell into the habit of meeting, usually in the evenings, to discuss the drawing up of a rule.

The first draft was probably made by Loyola's secretary, Polanco, and the text then revised by Loyola himself in 1552. Papal approval was sought and granted, and the rule put into effect throughout the society. Loyola made some revisions up to the time he died. They were not printed until after his death and remain largely untouched today, though Loyola foresaw that modifications would be necessary.

According to the *Constitutions* Jesuits are not to accept ecclesiastical dignities, they have no special religious habit, they are forbidden to keep a choir and they were the first order whose constitutions directed them to undertake active work in foreign missions, schools, hospitals, prisons and so on.

Loyola's diary, containing the record of his devotions at the time he was working on the *Constitutions*, still exists and he appears to have experienced visions and special insights at this time.

The *Constitutions* begin with a general outline of what is proposed to all who seek membership of the Society of Jesus. There follows an account of the rules of the order, starting at the point of entry into the society: admission of candidates, sending away unsuitable entrants, training new members. The *Constitutions* then outline how the order is organized. The final sections deal with the relations a member should have with his fellows and how he should get on with his superior. They detail the qualities required in a superior, how the superior should run the order and how to keep the society in good working order.

Jesuits claim that the *Constitutions* follow logically from the *Spiritual Exercises* and that they are the temporal rules of those who, having finished their second week of the *Spiritual Exercises*, have decided to join the order. Here obedience to God, the basic principle at the heart of Loyola's own mystical life, has been transposed into a rule for community living. But to do this Jesuits must sacrifice their own freedom and place it in the hands of the society's superior known as the General.

The *Constitutions* also contain regulations for the running of colleges and the election of the General. However every element is inspired by the spirit of obedience. All members are to see their formal obedience in all things as eventually directed towards God. In this exercise of obedience members should not be guided by either fear or anxiety but only by love. However if a subordinate member of the order disapproves of a command or considers it unjust, inappropriate or wrong, then that subordinate has the duty to make respectful representations to his superior.

## Appraisal

It is often stated that Loyola was not much interested in entering into controversy with the Reformers; his interests lay elsewhere. Nevertheless it is interesting to note that his work lays out rules for spiritual discipline which consciously or unconsciously contrast with the issues that the Protestant Reformers had raised.

At the beginning of the *Spiritual Exercises* rules are laid out for the spiritual life. They include the necessity of obeying the 'Church Hierarchical'; frequent recourse to confession and attendance at Mass, the use of the Divine Office. Ignatius values religious orders and the practice of continence and chastity; these are to be preferred to marriage.

In addition Loyola praises the 'perfections of supererogation' (the merits gained by working over and above the call of duty), the adoration of relics and the practice of indulgences, pilgrimages and penance.

Loyola sees value in the belief that people cannot be saved without being predestined and without saving faith and grace; nevertheless he advises caution in speaking of such things. He is also cautious about speaking of saving faith as opposed to work, in case lazy people use it as an excuse for doing no good work at all.

Loyola may not have engaged in controversy, but his outlook was firmly in continuity with the Medieval Latin Church.

### Timeline

1488 Bartholomew Diaz is the first European to round the Cape of Good Hope
1491 Birth of Ignatius Loyola
1492 Christopher Columbus lands in the New World
1505 The Portuguese arrive in Ceylon
1508 Michelangelo starts painting the ceiling of the Sistine Chapel
1509 Birth of John Calvin
1517 Martin Luther publishes his *Ninety-five Theses on Indulgences*
1519 Charles V becomes Holy Roman Emperor
1520 Suleiman the Magnificent becomes Ottoman Emperor
1522 Conversion of Ignatius Loyola
1523–1528 Calvin at Montaigu College in Paris
1528 Loyola at Montaigu College
1525 The Reformation spreads to the Netherlands, Denmark and Norway
1533 Calvin's conversion experience
1534 Henry VIII declares himself supreme head of the Church of England
1536 John Calvin publishes the *Institutes of the Christian Religion* in Latin and makes his first visit to Geneva
1540 Founding of the Society of Jesus
The final shape of Loyola's *Spiritual Exercises*
Calvin marries
1541 Calvin's definitive return to Geneva
1545 Council of Trent called
1547–1551 Council of Trent fails to meet
1549 Francis Xavier begins his mission to Japan
1552 Suspension of the Council of Trent
1556 Death of Ignatius Loyola

1558 Elizabeth I becomes Queen of England
1560 Protestant Conspiracy of Amboise in France and its suppression
1562 Council of Trent back in session
1563 Council of Trent closes
1564 Death of John Calvin
1572 St Bartholomew's Day Massacre

## John Calvin

### *Life (1509–1564)*

John Calvin was born to a solid middle-class family in Noyon in northern France. His family had always intended him for a career in the church and he was tonsured (the first step in the process of ordination) when only 12.

He studied Theology in Paris from 1523 to 1528. He was for a number of years a member of Montaigu College, the college Ignatius Loyola would join in 1528. While there, Calvin may have questioned his vocation and indeed his faith. He left the very scholastic University of Paris, enrolling in the more humanist University of Orleans, later studying law at Bourges where he first came under the influence of Protestants. Some of his teachers in Paris had been active in arguing against the thinking of Wycliffe (*c.*1330–1384) and Hus (*c.*1372–1415).

In 1533 he underwent an experience of religious conversion and believed he had received a command from God to restore the church to its primitive purity.

It was probably in 1533 that Calvin first read Luther; he developed a high regard for him at first, though he would later be critical of him. He also appears to have broken with the Roman Catholic Church about this time and resigned the church benefices he had already obtained; he may also have suffered persecution and imprisonment. He settled in Basle for a period, intending to devote his life to study. Here he worked on the first version of his *Institutes*, published in 1536. This was in Latin; a French translation was published in 1541. It was the first work of Theology ever to be published in the French language.

At this time there was turmoil in the city of Geneva which had recently become an independent entity and which had expelled its bishop. Here the reformation movement had two sources; one was experimentation with a republican form of government, the second was humanist reform in matters of morals and worship.

Calvin was invited to the city to stabilize the church and give it a sound basis of reformed teaching. He drew up rigorous regulations concerning who should be admitted to Holy Communion and the sort of profession of faith that should be demanded of all citizens on pain of exile. He started to work on regulations for the exercise of excommunication. His attempts were deeply resisted and he was eventually expelled from the city.

He took refuge in Strasbourg where he settled down to a period of intense theological work, also ministering to the French-speaking congregation of that city. It was at about this time that he married Idelette de Bure and their marriage appears to have been tranquil and successful.

By 1541 his supporters had gained the upper hand in Geneva and Calvin returned there, and, for the remainder of his life, devoted himself to establishing and maintaining a Puritan theocratic regime which was quite severe. Government of the reformed church was placed in the hands of pastors, doctors (teachers), elders and deacons. There was a consistory, or church council, which had far-reaching powers over the private lives of citizens and functioned as a sort of moral police. Pleasures such as dancing and games were forbidden, and tough penalties for religious offences were in force.

**Theocratic** Government by God or by ministers representing God.

Calvin's opponents were ruthlessly combated and on occasion tortured and executed; the most shameful case is probably that of Michael Servetus (1511–1553) who had been in correspondence with Calvin. He had written a book in which he had abandoned the doctrine of the Trinity and denied the divinity of Christ. He was denounced to the Roman Catholic Inquisition, probably by somebody close to Calvin and arrested. He escaped and fled to Geneva, where he was arrested and burnt as a heretic.

By 1555 Calvin had overcome all opposition and he devoted the remainder of his life to Bible study (he wrote a number of commentaries on various books of the Bible), giving advice to religious reformers in other parts of Europe and founding the Academy of Geneva to place the training of ministers on a sound academic basis. He was, in effect, a dictator in Geneva, being known as 'the Pope of Geneva'. However he made that city the intellectual centre of the Reformation.

He was a man of great learning;, he was well grounded in Latin, Greek, Hebrew, Theology and Law, and he was a formidable organizer. His written work is precise and clear. The ideas are well expressed in logical sequence, the style is firm and clear and there are passages demonstrating all the eloquence of persuasive power, highlighted by well-known and pleasing images.

Calvin himself was an austere and distant man; he had little interest in personal gain, but his character is marred by cruelty and overbearing claims to be the ultimate arbiter of matters of faith and biblical interpretation. He died of overwork in 1564.

## Thought

With John Calvin we are able to see more clearly the principles on which the Protestant Reformation grew and flourished. They are as follows:

- the desire to reform the established religious tradition rather than to found a new one;
- if a doctrine cannot be demonstrated by Scripture, it is to be discarded. From now on Scripture was to have the dominant status in the church;
- Bible-based sermons, biblical commentaries and biblical Theology were all given a leading role in worship and theological thought.

Calvin's major work of Theology was the *Institutes of the Christian Religion*. Its first edition was in 1536 and had eight short chapters. The final edition published by Calvin (1559) had 80. It has four major sections: the sovereignty of the creator God; the human need for salvation satisfied in Jesus Christ; how human beings make this salvation their own and, finally, the church and society.

His thought declares the following:

- In order to hold the true faith, human beings must take direct inspiration from Scripture, rather than rely on the tradition of the Church.
- The human being is a fallen creature, corrupted by original sin and destined to Hell without the saving aid of God.
- The elect are predestined to be saved; this salvation does not depend on good works, but on the choice of God who has already decided who will receive faith and the assistance of grace.

### *The reading of Scripture*

The reading of Scripture by all was Calvin's central aim. He felt that the Medieval Latin Church had let the importance of Scripture slip out of sight and that the centrality of the Bible must be restored, and restored for all. He was not afraid of the unlearned reading it for themselves; this clashed with a central principle of the post-Tridentine church, which held that the teaching authority of the church alone had the ability to interpret Scripture and was nervous of letting the Bible be read by all without supervision.

### *Calvin's method*

Calvin liked the way other Reformers expounded Scripture. Melanchthon in particular impressed him. He dealt with topics in a clear, orderly and simple manner. His method was to interpret Scripture but to do so in a way that examined everything in context; he wanted the clear intention of the biblical author to be brought out by this method. When one had come to some sense of the authentic meaning of Scripture, then one could use it to draw out general doctrine.

Ministers were encouraged to teach the doctrines found in Scripture and only those doctrines. This basic general doctrine was to be drawn up into catechisms and taught to all. Having established basic Christian doctrine, the next step was to preach from Scripture and apply both Scripture and doctrine to the lives of those who listened to them. When they were well grounded in this method, the ordinary people in the pews were to be encouraged to read the Bible for themselves.

### *Calvin's doctrine of God*

Calvin was watchful against trying to capture the essence of God through human reasoning. God's essence is as incomprehensible as the divine majesty is hidden. Our task is to come to knowledge of God as we learn to fear God, to reverence God, to love and praise God. To do this we must school ourselves in the Holy Scriptures.

But in every page of the Bible we see the divine face of Jesus and it is in that face that we see the reflection of God.

This operation is both clear and obscure and it requires the help of the Holy Spirit, who must shine a light into human hearts. This contact from the Holy Spirit gives us a supernatural feeling for the being of God which inborn human sinfulness would otherwise prevent.

Calvin did not believe that, left to their own devices, human beings were capable, by reason alone, to come to knowledge of God or to construct a natural Theology. The original human condition is miserable. Even though he personally found such a reality painful, Calvin's severity was unbending on this point.

Even though sinful humans are offensive in the sight of a just God, Calvin realizes they are divinely created and that God has lavished much care and attention on them. So the mystery of God's love stretches out to the created order and that love, which has always existed from the very beginning, has already made provision for the human race to be reconciled to God.

### *Justification*

Human beings have fallen into sin and therefore cannot rightly see how God is present in the universe. This inability is sometimes referred to as 'depravity'. That means that every part of our being is faulty, and we are consequently unable to come to God unaided. So we are subject to the anger of God.

Because of our flawed nature, God has made special provision to allow us to be attentive to the divine being and to be brought into a relationship with that being. Our attention is turned, not merely to the fact that God offers us gifts and benefits but to a source that removes the fault and stain of sin. It is the duty of Christian preaching to set this vision of God before us and it does so by announcing Christ crucified.

When we reflect on the cross of Christ we see how God has placed all our guilt on Jesus. The curse of God, which should be ours, and the eternal damnation, which is rightly ours, are the burden taken up by Christ and taken away from us. In the resurrection we see that God has accepted this atonement made for us. In the ascension we see Jesus display all the qualities missing in us and are encouraged to turn to Jesus alone for our comfort, support and salvation. Instead of death, God now offers us eternal life.

By means of faith we are now invited to become one with Christ; through union with Jesus we are freed from our separation from God. Calvin refers to this as the 'double grace of Christ' and involves repentance and justification.

**Damnation** Endless punishment in Hell: endless existence shut off from the presence of God.
**Atonement** The reconciliation of God and the human race brought about by Jesus Christ.
**Repentance** To regret the bad thinks one has done in the past and to resolve to change one's behaviour.
**Justification** Because of the sacrifice of Christ, God does not consider human beings guilty of sin, but grants the sinlessness of Jesus to them as a gift.

### *Predestination*

The Doctrine of Predestination, which is plainly taught by a number of Christian teachers, is suggested in Mt. 20 and clear in Rom. 8. It was developed by St Augustine and also taught by Luther. It received very clear emphasis in Calvin and is considered a typical mark of Calvinism.

Calvin did not necessarily see it as the foundation on which his theological work rested but considered it an important component nevertheless. He held it to be a wonderful secret of the judgement of God. The true Christian will maintain a degree of intellectual sobriety in approaching it, will not seek to understand it deeply but will meditate on it without fear.

Calvin held that it was God's will that salvation should be offered to some yet withheld from others. He admitted this posed difficult problems for many. He noted that salvation flows not from human judgement but from God's free mercy. The grace of God is illustrated by the fact that God does not adopt everybody 'promiscuously' to the hope of salvation but gives to some and refuses to others.

If we do not accept this principle then we lack humility. But if we do not accept that all whom God wants to save are in fact saved, we suggest that Christ's sacrifice was in some way ineffectual. We then detract from divine glory.

God saves those who have no claim to salvation and anyone who tries to prevent people from experiencing this teaching does an injury to both fellow human beings and to God. Predestination is, according to Calvin, the only basis for solid confidence to deliver us all from fear and through this teaching Christ promises to preserve in safety all those the Father has committed to his care.

He warns that when we inquire into predestination, we try to penetrate the deepest recesses of God's mind. We must trust in Scripture as the only way of discovering what ought to be believed concerning God. It is foolish to seek any other source of knowledge of predestination and we should avoid it.

On the other hand it should not be considered a banned subject. Holy Scripture is the 'school of the Holy Spirit' and nothing necessary and useful to know is left out of it, while nothing is taught there which it is not beneficial to know. We should not examine what God has concealed and we should not ignore what God has revealed.

God's foreknowledge extends to the whole world and all in it. Predestination is an eternal decree and by it God has determined what is to happen to every individual: eternal life is foreordained for some; damnation, for others.

Sanctification is still required from the chosen, and love is the source of their protection. We are to be content with the good pleasure of God. Throughout sacred history, in particular Old Testament history, Calvin sees the varying fortunes of the people of God as demonstrating their election. Election remains unchallengeable; its tokens are not always visible. When we come to consider the members of Christ we see conspicuous evidence of the superior effectiveness of grace; those individuals are united to their head and can never fail of salvation.

The trouble is that, out of the great multitude of those who hear the call, the many fall away; only a small portion remains. Even if God covenants with a people, God does not give everybody the spirit of renewal which allows them to persevere to the end in the covenant. He issues an eternal call without the internal efficacy of grace.

**Sanctification** The continuing work of the Holy Spirit renewing and purifying sinners and enabling them to perform good works.
**Election** is the idea that God in every age chooses a people, or an individual, in preference to others to carry out some task. It often refers to those who do God's will and remain steadfast in times of trial.
**Covenant** originally an agreement between two parties; it came to be seen as the faithfulness of God towards Israel in return for the inner righteousness of the people before God. Jesus restated it as humanity receiving a gracious gift from God by which their desire to serve God was made perfect. It requires a response. It has its highest expression in the example of the life and death of Jesus.

God's gathering together of a church was because of his covenant but the covenant was dishonoured by the majority. So God has restricted this covenant offer to a few, in order to prevent total failure.

So Calvin asserts that God has determined, 'by eternal and immutable counsel', who would be admitted to salvation and who would be excluded. God's choice of the elect is founded on 'gratuitous mercy', irrespective of human merit. When God condemns people to damnation it is by a 'just, irreprehensible, but incomprehensible, judgement'. It also implied that once one was saved, salvation could not be lost. This was to be a major cause of controversy, particularly involving the eighteenth century preacher John Wesley.

Calvin's theology makes a clear distinction between the 'order of nature' and the 'order of grace'. The dominant idea behind predestination is the sovereign power, awe and majesty of God. If God offered salvation and people refused the invitation, then the sacrifice of Christ would be in vain. Since God has already decided whom to save and whom to damn, the sacrifice will without doubt achieve what it set out to do.

This short summary is an attempt to state things simply without distorting them:

- In the eternal covenant, the Father gave a number of people to the Son and the Son came to redeem them.
- Human beings are sinful; they do not become sinful by wrongful actions. They commit wrongful actions because their condition is sinful.
- Because of that 'depravity', humans cannot understand God or come to God.
- A sinful (apparently free) human being cannot in fact choose freely but can only do so in a sinful manner.
- Therefore God must predestine.
- God alone is capable of all-powerful and sovereign rule.
- Predestination is the only way the loving mercy of God can be effective and evident.

### *The right worship of God*

All the Protestant Reformers were dismayed by the use of rituals and images in worship; they felt that the current practices of the sixteenth century did not raise the worshipper to the contemplation of heavenly realities but kept worshippers' attention anchored on earth. Calvin's goal was to encourage and enable ordinary people to read the Bible for themselves; only when they were capable of doing this would they be capable of offering proper worship.

Calvin saw the popular use of images, processions and the adoration of the Eucharistic bread as encouraging defective forms of worship, rather than offering authentic worship to God. People's attention was being distracted towards the worship of representations of the mystery, persuading themselves that what was in fact invisible could, and had, become visible.

Imposing ceremonies were condemned as fraudulent and counterfeit. So Calvin set out to restore a true worship of God, rescuing it from the objects of false devotion promoted by the medieval church.

The creation is able to give us an impression of the power, majesty and awe of God. But because they are sinful, human beings are unable to appreciate this. Therefore God has provided for us, in the Bible, a means by which we can come to contemplate the truth of God. Calvin did not want people to be distracted by illusions; so he simplified the order of worship and stripped churches and ministers of their traditional ornaments.

Calvin accomplished this by reducing services to bare necessities. There was no impressive music; hymn singing was to be done by all. Church buildings had no ornaments; crosses and images were removed, even stained glass was replaced. The ministers wore a plain black gown and there was little liturgical movement. The high pulpit, rather than the altar, became the focal point of the church building. The church was the faithful people; the building was only its meeting place.

### *Sacraments*

Together with all Protestant Reformers, Calvin insisted on two sacramental ordinances only. He was not inclined, as Luther was, to see confession as sacramental.

Since the thirteenth century the Latin Church had tried to separate the validity of sacraments from the personal attitude of either the ministering priest or the recipient. Sacraments were valid *ex opere operato*, that is 'by virtue of being performed'. The purpose of this attitude was to underline that sacraments are instruments of grace and as long as they are done within the rules laid down, God acts through them.

Calvin felt that the doctrine of *ex opere operato*, tied the value of the sacraments too tightly into the ministry of the church, particularly stressing a valid ministry. It did not allow enough scope for the free grace of God operating through the sacraments and without human constraint. He rejected the medieval understanding which placed the stress on a human programme and on the legal structure of the church, rather than on the initiative of God.

In Calvin's view baptism showed how Christians have been grafted into God's people; in particular it demonstrated the 'double grace of Christ' of repentance and justification. The Holy Supper demonstrates how we are united with the flesh of Christ and how we draw sustenance from him in order to be united with God in eternal life. We can see here the comparison with bodily food leading us to appreciate the heavenly and spiritual feeding which is the gift of God to us.

Calvin believed that the outwards signs of bread and wine really bring to us, and set before us, the body and blood of Christ. But we feed on Christ in our souls, not by means of our mouths. Calvin abandoned Roman Catholic practice, but he equally rejected Zwingli's argument that the Lord's Supper is no more than a memorial feast. He did not consider the Eucharistic elements to be empty signs; they were essentially linked to Christ's self-giving.

Calvin reaffirmed energetically that the Body of Christ is really present in the sacrament of the Lord's Supper but made a fine distinction between reality and materiality. The bread and wine are visible signs which represent the body and blood of Christ to us. We give the title body and blood to them because they are the instruments by means of which the Lord Jesus gives them to us.

The body and blood of Christ are a spiritual mystery which the eye cannot see and human understanding cannot comprehend. By this means, it is figured for us in visible signs in a way our human weakness can grapple with.

### *Christian living*

Christian life arises out of the experience of repentance and justification. Calvin sees that God has prepared a plan for us, which we find through the study of Scripture and meditation on the life of Jesus. The Law of God for all had already been revealed in the Law of Moses. Jesus has given us the correct interpretation of it.

This Law of God, or Christian pattern of living, is something which has its source in the gospel, the same source out of which justifying faith and repentance arise. It is something which must swell up in the heart and become concrete in the actions of our daily lives.

But Calvin went further; he was concerned that the whole of the city of Geneva should be a model of virtuous living, according to the freshly presented divine law. The whole city was to be transformed into a vast uniform and religious community.

The city was to be improved, but without ostentation or luxury. Its citizens were to live without any form of self-indulgence. There was to be no dancing, no outrageous behaviour, no swearing or blasphemy and no frivolous badinage. All works of superstition, witchcraft or heresy were to be removed from libraries, as were anything suspected of doubtful, obscene or erotic inspiration. They would go frequently to church so that they might always remain, wherever they were, in a state of continual silent prayer.

Calvin also had to face up to those who disagreed with him. As well as fighting the Roman heresy (as he now considered it to be) he had to confront extreme forms of religious sedition, including those who felt a special personal illumination. During the sixteenth century there was no shortage of small and secretive groups given to excessive scepticism and libertinism, as well as, on the other hand, to unbalanced religious enthusiasm.

## *Calvinism*

During the period 1618–1619 the Council of Dort adopted an expression of Calvin's teaching that has received widespread and popular attention. It is sometimes called 'Five-Point Calvinism' and (in English) the word TULIP is used to help remember the five points taught. It is important to remember that both this way of expressing the teaching, and the mnemonic itself, date from after Calvin's death:

T Total Depravity of sinful human nature: 'Depravity' here means imperfect, flawed. 'Total' means every part of the human personality is affected by the flaw.

U Unconditional Election: Individuals are not predetermined for salvation because of some personal good point or accomplishment, which God already knows they will possess. Election is granted without conditions.

L Limited Atonement: Christ did not die for the whole human race but only for the elect.
I Irresistible Grace: The elect are inevitably saved; they have no choice or decision in the matter.
P Perseverance of the Saints: Those who are predestined cannot fall away or opt out of that condition.

## Appraisal

Was predestination Calvin's major concern? Some see this teaching as totally necessary. If we say that human beings are free to accept or reject the gracious offer of God, we suggest that the sacrifice of Christ was in vain. Only those whom God wants to save, will in fact be saved, in this way we know that God has total power and is in full control. Others see this as a minor concern of Calvin's; his chief anxiety was to be faithful to Scripture and to be utterly clear in his teaching.

His final arrangement of the *Institutes* had four parts:

God the Creator
God the Redeemer
The Holy Spirit
The means of grace and the church.

This arrangement has been influential and is still widely used.

Calvin's teaching was powerful and respected. His followers prefer to talk of the 'Reformed Tradition' rather than of Calvinism. This strand is widespread in continental Europe and from there spread to America. In Britain it played a decisive role in the development of Puritanism.

### *Christianity in the West since the Reformation*

There was no great debate at the Reformation about a whole range of theological subjects, such as the Doctrine of Creation, of Jesus Christ, or of the Trinity. Everybody agreed about them. Controversy centred on how Scripture related to tradition, who had authority to interpret the Bible, the nature of justification and the role of the sacraments. There was also controversy about non-theological issues such as church corruption and abuse of power.

Both the Protestant and Catholic Reformations were followed by periods in which theologians 'bedded down' and consolidated their positions, defined new forms of orthodoxy, usually in the form of apologetics for their own side and in opposition to the other.

Within Protestantism, both Lutheran and Calvinist (and both frequently disagreed), there was a renewed concern for methodical exposition of doctrine. Aristotle's metaphysics was used as a central organizing tool for the expression of teaching. Human reason played an important role in drawing up 'systems' of Christian teaching. All sides thought that Christian teaching was capable of being expressed in a clear, logical and methodical way. Calvin and Luther had not been very interested in method but, once they had passed away, Natural Theology became fashionable again.

The Council of Trent ended much of the corruption people had been complaining about for centuries. There was now clear and authoritative teaching about matters of contemporary theological controversy and the Roman Catholic Church was now in a position to critique the new theologies which had issued from the Reformation.

In England the Reformation was political rather than theoretical. The difference between before and after the 'Reformation' was defined by the form of public worship rather than by the struggles between schools of theological teaching. There was theological debate but members of differing theological outlooks and schools could all belong to one church. Sharp and bitter controversy did indeed break out and the struggle between theological schools was to continue well into the seventeenth century.

Puritanism was a variety of reformed theology in sharp distinction to the Church of England. It was usually Calvinist and laid great importance on a personal experience of salvation and developed intense pastoral supervision of adherents. It often had connections with political radicalism and, following a significant instance of emigration to the New World, would have a profound influence there.

Continental Protestantism was, in time, seen by many as dry, dull and theoretical, capable of expressing formal belief statements but unable to promote vibrant, life-changing faith. The Pietist movement wanted to relate Christian thought to issues of day-to-day living and to revitalize the church. Personal conversion, conviction and Bible study were its methods. We shall meet such concerns in the person of John Wesley.

# 7 John Wesley and Evangelical Revival

John Wesley was one of the major figures of the great eighteenth century Evangelical Revival. Many revivals gripped America, Britain and Ireland during the late eighteenth and nineteenth centuries; there were even one or two examples in the very early years of the twentieth century. Indeed, the Revival spirit lives on, the Pentecostal movement is a case in point.

## Setting the scene

Before discussing Wesley, it may be useful to get a feeling for a number of terms, ideas and situations and keep them at the back of our minds.

### Evangelical

Evangelical is a general word which means anything to do with the gospel. It comes from the Greek word 'euangelion' which means 'good news'. It is widely used with reference to the good news about Jesus Christ, to the four New Testament texts and the way they tell the story of his earthly life, and moreover, it refers to the message preached by the Christian Church about Jesus.

It also has a special, restricted and particular meaning, being used to refer to 'Scriptural Christianity'. Here Christian faith and witness is fed by almost exclusive reference to the Bible, without the prop of time-honoured Church structures, tradition or sacramental worship. Evangelical faith is firmly Protestant and at least some of its drive has been found in strong feelings against 'Popery and Puseyism' (disparaging terms denoting Roman Catholic practice and Anglican ritualism).

Evangelicals tend to be orthodox in faith. What is quite distinctive about evangelical thinking is that, first, it insists on personal conversion, a 'new birth', that each individual should undergo a life-changing religious experience. Secondly, it emphasizes the Bible as the decisive religious authority, often insisting on a literal interpretation of the text. Thirdly, all Evangelicals are activists, energetically sharing the faith. Fourthly, they focus powerfully on the redeeming work of the Cross.

### Revival

Revival and 'revivalism' are aspects of the Evangelical outlook where emphasis is placed on the building up of religious fervour and energy in order to renew the life of the church community. Revival tends to be promoted at mass rallies, by forceful preaching, in sustained (often emotional) prayer and in the lively singing of hymns frequently set to invigorating tunes. Revival seeks to convince individuals of their sinfulness, to encourage them to seek the forgiveness of God in conversion and to stimulate them to engage in Christian witness and service in the world.

### The Great Awakening

Finally we should take a look at the eighteenth century Great Awakening in the American colonies. This too was a revivalist movement. It was a mass movement and its origins were varied, though mostly native to America. It brought many thousands of people to a vital, active commitment to Christianity. It was not the transfer of masses of the population from one faith system to another; rather it was a radical infusion of energies into a nominally Christian population. The Great Awakening influences Christian life in America to this day and strongly influenced John Wesley in his time.

The results of the Great Awakening were sometimes explosive and controversies were bitter. It caused disruption within settled denominational life: for, while fresh converts were fired with activist zeal, they aroused suspicion among traditional and conservative members and led to the growth of sects. On the positive side it led to a huge expansion in active church membership, particularly among Americans of European origin but less so among African and Native Americans.

The Great Awakening was thoroughly Protestant in both tone and theology. It was not, however, confined to any one expression of Protestantism. It involved Congregationalists, Dutch Reformed and Presbyterians. George Whitefield, a well-known revivalist preacher in America, was a priest of the Church of England. It gave great impetus to the spread of Baptists. It touched all age groups.

Rallies of the Great Awakening often featured extreme varieties of behaviour, suggesting forms of possession: people roaring, trembling and falling down. Wesley's rallies were no exception, although it is not certain that he encouraged such symptoms.

The Great Awakening laid emphasis on Bible teaching; it bred strongly independent individuals and promoted non-hierarchical church structures; these were by and large democratically governed by the membership. The movement promoted puritan values and an austere life style. Education was highly valued. The Great Awakening disapproved strongly of sexual wrongdoing, profanity, the breaking of one's word, drunkenness, quarrelling and gambling. This outlook became the accepted norm of respectable social behaviour, although it never stamped out the condemned practices. Occasionally, this tendency expected the Kingdom of God to be realized on earth and, at the other extreme, saw it as the perfection of the American way of life.

Keeping these elements of religious culture in mind, we might now turn to John Wesley.

## Life (1703–1791)

John Wesley was the fifteenth child of a north of England clergyman and his wife Susannah. His father, Rev. Samuel Wesley, was rector of Epworth in Humberside. When John was 6 years old the rectory barn caught fire and, since no one noticed, spread to the house. It was only with great difficulty that little John escaped from the flames.

Wesley was educated at Charterhouse in London and later at Christ Church, Oxford. He was ordained deacon in the Church of England in 1725. He had read *The Imitation of Christ* by Thomas à Kempis (1380–1471) in his early twenties and was attracted by the notion of a religion of the heart. His early spiritual growth seems to have to have had three pillars: reading the Bible, reading *Holy Living and Holy Dying* by Jeremy Taylor (1613–1667) and the search for a true spiritual friend who would convince him that he was truly a Christian.

He was due to help his father with parish work but did not immediately return to the north. Rather he visited the parishes of friends; apparently he was already feeling the urge to preach in many places. He was known to have an earnest manner and pious habits. He was silly about women for most of his life, and it is doubtful if he ever matured emotionally in this regard. He had several infatuations but did not yet marry.

In the early spring of 1726 he was elected to a fellowship at Lincoln College, Oxford, and took up his duties. However his salary would not be paid for a year so he had to scrimp and save. He returned to Epworth for the summer, again to help his father. In order to save money, he walked the entire journey; it took him a month. At that time it was normal for college fellows to be in holy orders, and Wesley was ordained priest in September 1727.

He plunged into college life and his college duties but felt they were 'worldly'. He was tireless in his own study and reading, drawing up lists and timetables of subjects to be covered. He gradually became associated with a group of serious young men and they drew up plans for systematic fasting, Bible study and prayer. This band of solemn youths were laughingly referred to in the university as 'Methodists'; we shall meet the word again!

At this time he came under the influence of William Law (1686–1761) and other writers with a mystical tinge. One of the great formative experiences of his life came when he set out with his brother Charles on a missionary journey to Georgia, one of the English colonies in America. During the sea voyage, his ship met a frighteningly violent storm and Wesley feared for his life. He was impressed by the calm and fortitude of fellow passengers who belonged to the Moravian Brotherhood and ashamed of his own fear. Their trust in God was so complete, and so contrasted with his own, that Wesley feared he was not a Christian.

When he arrived in Georgia the American colonies were experienceing the Great Awakening and the conversions he witnessed there also left a lasting impression. His own preaching was not successful as he tended to be over-fussy in his interpretation of church law. He also preached strongly against slavery and gin, which did not make him popular with the colonists. The Georgian experience could be described as a chapter of misfortunes, growing mostly from Wesley's inexperience. But he did learn.

He arrived back home in 1737 and struck up a friendship with Peter Böhler of the Moravian Brotherhood. Böhler persuaded him to open himself to 'saving faith'; consequently Wesley experienced religious conversion on 24 May 1738, having just read Luther's *Preface to the Epistle to the Romans*. From then on, he decided that his mission would be to promote vital, practical and saving religion. By and large he was not welcome in churches of the Church of England, so he took to preaching in the open air. This was to be his mission for the rest of his life.

His preaching was soon successful and he made many converts. In order to minister to these converts he set up a body of lay preachers to be pastors to the newly converted. He also opened preaching houses to accommodate his missions in the big centres of population. The most famous was the Foundry at Moorfields in London. Wesley's chapel still stands there and contains his eighteenth-century pulpit. He was most successful in London, Bristol and in the north of England.

Clergymen of the Church of England (and Wesley considered himself one all his life) exercise their ministry by 'incumbency'; they are responsible for an area and live within it. Wesley exercised his ministry by 'itinerancy': he travelled. He would continue to travel and preach for the rest of his life. He travelled on horseback, frequently 8,000 miles a year. This is a stupendous achievement, for the roads were dreadful. He had a special desk made to fit in front of him on the horse, so that he could read and write while travelling. He was often greeted with enthusiasm; some complained of the noisy hymn singing; there were occasional riots.

The Church of England was particularly suspicious of Wesley's preaching. Sober churchmen condemned his 'enthusiasm'. Others feared they were seeing another outbreak of the Puritanism that had so troubled England during Cromwell's time, less than a hundred years previously.

In 1749 or 1750 Wesley met Mary Vazeille, the widow of a London merchant. She had been a recent convert and had come seeking spiritual advice from him. Wesley never had much luck in his dealings with women and this relationship was no exception. The association became more personal and they married in February 1751.

He refused to lighten the load of his itinerancy and Mary did not like travel, although she appears to have accompanied him for the first three or four years of their marriage. However Wesley's habit was to set out at about four in the morning, ride till noon, change horses and continue riding until midnight. The only reason he stopped was to preach sermons on the way. His wife came to resent his frequent absences and the relationship deteriorated.

In 1744 Wesley organized the first conference for Methodist lay preachers. In time this became an annual event. These lay preachers were beginning to form a 'parallel' ministry with the clergy of the Church of

England, but they did not work in co-operation. Wesley drew up a constitution for the conference in 1784. There were continuous pressures on Wesley from now on to ordain his own clergy, but he doggedly resisted them. He never wished to enter into schism with the Church of England.

His field of missionary work gradually extended to Ireland, where he was moderately successful, and to Scotland, where he was less so. The American mission field was also productive and it was there that the break from the established church was most keenly felt. Wesley liked the *Book of Common Prayer*, and he preferred it to the extempore prayer of the Dissenters; he would have preferred it to be the service book for all, but did allow some changes to be made in it for American Methodists.

America was now independent, and American Methodists were not inclined to accept direction from England. Finally, in 1784, he appointed two men, Thomas Coke and Francis Asbury, to act as superintendents in America. This was practically the same as ordaining them bishops, and the break with the Church of England was now a reality.

Wesley worked at a time when England was undergoing rapid change. The new spirit of scientific enquiry had caused a new 'industrial' revolution; the same spirit was revolutionizing agriculture and the methods of land holding were changing. As the village commons were gradually fenced in, landless country folk could no longer grow their own food, and machinery was reducing labour on farms. Canal and railroad building was creating a wandering population of labourers; the factories were demanding a steady supply of workers.

These trends were creating vast upheavals in the population, and the traditional parish system of the Church of England could not minister to the vastly different way the population was now structured. What is more, it did not want to adjust to meet changed needs. Many of the people to whom Wesley preached had no church background and felt no loyalty to the established Church. This, coupled with the fact that Wesley was usually excluded from Church of England pulpits, and the fact that a new organization was necessary if Wesley's work was to continue, made the break with the Church of England inevitable.

Wesley himself sat strangely between two extremes. He was, after all, a traditionally trained, logical scholar and fellow of his college. Nevertheless he came to accept that religious conviction must be accompanied by emotional involvement. His management of his organization was quite autocratic, yet he appears to have tempered conviction with discipline, individualism with community responsibility and personal inspiration with sound organization and leadership. He was able both to take initiatives and to rein in the exuberance of followers who wanted to go too quickly.

Wesley was a brave, stubborn and persistent man. He appears to have had a magnetic personality and much of what he earned from his writings was put aside for charitable work. He founded a new religious movement, which, by its promotion of hard work and the values of sobriety, austerity and honesty, profoundly influenced the tone of Victorian England. Wesley is considered by some to be one of the architects of modern Britain. That, however, is to display a very parochial view of the situation; the area of his influence extended far beyond Britain. He died in 1791.

### Timeline

1703 Birth of John Wesley
1707 Halley studies the movement of comets
1709 The Wesley family narrowly escapes death when the rectory caught fire
1712 St Petersburg becomes capital of Russia
1715 John Wesley enters Charterhouse
1719 Daniel Defoe's *Robinson Crusoe*
1720 John Wesley elected exhibitioner and enters Christ Church, Oxford
1725 John Wesley ordained deacon
1726 John Wesley elected Fellow of Lincoln College
Jonathan Swift's *Gulliver's Travels*
1727 John Wesley ordained priest
1729 Wesley joins the Holy Club or 'Methodists'
1735 Wesley sails for Georgia to act as chaplain in the colony
1736 John Harrison's marine clock
1738 Wesley returns to England
John Wesley's conversion
1739 John Wesley takes up field preaching; his itinerancy has begun
1740 David Hume's *Treatise of Human Nature*
1744 Wesley organizes his first conference for Methodist Lay Preachers

1751–1772 Publication of the *Encyclopaedia* in France
1751 Wesley's marriage to Mary Vazeille
1762 Rousseau's *Emile* and *Social Contract*
1781 Kant's *Critique of Pure Reason*
1784 Wesley appoints two 'Superintendents' in America; break with the Church of England
1789 Beginning of the French Revolution
1791 Death of John Wesley

## Thought

Like other breakers of the theological mould, Wesley was not a systematic thinker. His writings were for the instruction and strengthening of the converted. His greatest work, one which is given almost canonical status within Methodism, was his sermons. Editions of his works, including Journals, Diaries, Letters and Sermons run to over thirty volumes. His theology reaches us through sermons, hymns, pamphlets, letters and journals.

Wesley did not invent a new creed which he then peddled to the innocent. He was nothing like twentieth century promoters of new sects. He did not set out to reform some perceived error. He wanted to make the Christian gospel a deeply felt reality in the hearts and minds of every individual, and he wanted to do this with special concern for the ordinary people of the land.

### *Wesleyan foundations*

#### ARMINIANISM

Jakob Arminius (1560–1609) reacted against the teaching that Christ died just for a certain number of pre-chosen individuals. Arminius held that God had decided to elect from fallen humanity all those who believed in Jesus Christ and continued to obey his commandments. Jesus the Saviour of the world died for all, and salvation, pardon and reconciliation are offered to every individual, even though only the faithful will enjoy them. Here the notion of predestination is maintained, but it does not deliberately exclude anybody. God has predetermined that a group will be saved. By believing, individual sinners freely opt in to that predestined group. This view, known as Arminianism, is regularly criticized by Calvinists. Wesley was Arminian in his teaching on salvation.

Efforts have been made to distinguish a 'Wesleyan quadrilateral' for the sources of his doctrine:

- The Scripture guided by the Holy Spirit
- His personal religious experience
- Reasonableness
- Tradition (as he received it through the Church of England).

Later Methodists have summarized the content of Wesley's teaching as the 'four alls'. This outline dates from 1903:

- All need to be saved.
- All can be saved.
- All can know they are saved.
- All can be saved to the uttermost.

Wesley insisted on an active search for holiness. He accepted the Biblical analysis that all people are sinners and fall short of the standards expected by God. His own sense of his sinfulness gave sharpness to his theology. He wanted to be holy and to have a living relationship with God. He tried continually to lead a life of organized piety, but this routine of religious study, meditation and prayer failed to satisfy him. He felt constantly separated from God and insisted that it was the common lot.

Wesley believed that individuals could not guarantee their own salvation; so salvation must be a gift from God. But every gift has to be appreciated and cared for; otherwise it will get broken and become useless. God's gift of salvation must be accepted and responded to. Wesley felt that each individual was free to accept this gift; it was not forced on any person. This 'Arminian' outlook was to place him in prickly disagreement with the Calvinists. For Wesley everybody can be saved because God has made that salvation possible.

If people have been saved by God, then their relationship with God is a close and comfortable one and not one governed by conflict. They now have new life and possess new power. They are certain of this because of the assurance of the Holy Spirit of God working in them. God's Spirit speaks to them directly in their hearts. Wesley referred to this as 'inward consciousness' which leads to Christ-like attitudes and behaviour. These are obvious and observable in the lives of all saved believers.

Wesley believed that individuals can be saved to the uttermost: can experience Christian perfection within their own lives. He stressed this as part of his conviction that there can be no limit to the grace of God. This must inevitably result in a change of lifestyle and that change must involve loving both God and neighbour. Conversion brings about renewal of inner being in the image of God; one is cleansed from all stain of sin, both of body and of soul, and one seeks to live as Christ lived. Converts devote their whole being to God; they submit to whatever design God has for their lives.

### *Works of Piety and Works of Mercy*

Wesley upheld the traditional Christian teaching that Jesus Christ is the means by which God's grace is made available to sinful humans. Nevertheless it was important for individuals to engage in spiritual disciplines backed up with good works. Wesley believed that all Christians should practise the Works of Piety and the Works of Mercy.

The Works of Piety included such things as Bible reading, prayer, regular attendance at Holy Communion, fasting, having a concern for Christian community and living a healthy lifestyle.

For Wesley, prayer was an essential part of Christian living, and Methodists were to pray without ceasing. All their lives were to be times in which they spoke to God or thought about God, suffered for God or acted for God. These continual acts of prayer were to be performed at work, at mealtimes, even when preparing for sleep. This involved a life of Christian simplicity.

Wesley was a passionate reader of the Bible and encouraged it in others. But such reading of the Bible also involved seeking to know for oneself what the message of Scripture was and acting upon it. It was attentiveness to 'word of God'. He was also an advocate of regular fasting, usually on Wednesdays and Fridays. This was in order to advance holiness.

The Works of Mercy included visiting the sick and those in prison, providing food and clothing for the poor, earning one's living, saving as much as one could and giving away everything one did not need for oneself. Medicine was a feature of his missions. Wesley was also a fundamental opponent of slavery and forbade Methodists to own any. Personal holiness could not be promoted without social holiness.

### *Grace*

Wesley taught that God offers to us three kinds of grace. They are prevenient grace, justifying grace and sanctifying grace.

Prevenient grace means 'grace that comes before'. It is grace that prepares us for our encounter with Jesus Christ. This prevenient grace has accompanied us at every moment of our lives. All the gifts and accomplishments we have are the fruits of God's prevenient grace. This means that Wesley did not accept a Calvinist view of total depravity by which the imperfections of human nature prevent us from contact with God.

Justifying grace was the experience of conversion, of being 'born again'. It is through justifying grace that we come to experience a totally new life in Jesus Christ and to know that God has given us salvation. We are however, according to Wesley's teaching about Free Will, capable of accepting or of refusing this gift of justifying grace. The grace of God is 'free in all' it does not depend on any capacity or merit in any individual. The grace of God is given; it is 'free for all'.

But once believers have accepted the free grace of God in conversion, they can then progress in a relationship with God, and God will keep and support them in that relationship. This is sanctifying grace. Wesley believed it was possible to fall from grace. One could not sit still and do nothing. Conversion must issue into holiness of life, which itself is part of the continuing quest for Christian perfection. One has to be pro-active in sustaining the relationship, but God's grace will be there to support and encourage.

These three elements of prevenient grace, assurance of salvation and Christian perfection are very distinctive features of Wesley's theology.

### *Christian perfection*

Wesley believed that individuals play a part in the quest for salvation but not in the sense that they earn their salvation. He did not subscribe to the Pelagian heresy. Individuals are free to accept God's offer of salvation. That offer is part of the grace of God freely given, but it is also freely received, not forced or imposed.

More controversially, Wesley taught a doctrine of Christian perfection. He did not intend to boast that certain people had acquired sinless perfection on earth. Rather he thought that once a person has made perfect surrender to God, wilful sin can be stamped out.

On this point he entered into controversy with the Moravians, who taught a form of quietism or passive illumination. Wesley promoted an active spirituality. Works of charity were a crucial ingredient of holiness. In controversy with the Calvinists he rejected predestination, limited atonement, the perseverance of the elect and the reprobation of sinners. He could not picture a God who had decided everything in advance, leaving no room for human response or responsibility.

Nevertheless in all his teaching Wesley laid great emphasis on grace, equally stressing how dependent human beings are upon it.

**Pelagianism** The heresy that human beings can, by their own efforts, and without divine grace, ensure their salvation.

**Quietism** The suspect notion that human beings must reach a state of total passivity and annihilation of the will; they must abandon themselves to God in order to achieve salvation.

**Predestination** The decision of God by which certain individuals will, no matter what happens, be saved.

**Atonement** The reconciliation of God and the human race brought about by Jesus Christ.

**Perseverance of the elect** The steady continuance in faithful belief and action following conversion. Some versions of the teaching hold that God will not allow the converted Christian to fall away from salvation.

**Reprobation of sinners** God's action of condemning sinners to eternal punishment.

### *The Eucharist*

Wesley saw the Eucharist as a memorial of the sufferings and death of Jesus on the cross. But it was more than just a memorial. It had a vital, life-giving aspect. It was a calling to mind of everything that the sacrifice of Calvary can mean. It recalls all this before the human race but it also recalls it before God. It is therefore a pleading before God of that beneficial sacrifice and a prayer for its effects and benefits to be effective in the lives of those who pray.

The Eucharist is a means of grace; it is a communion with the risen Christ at a particular moment in a believer's life: now! It is also a sign of grace, an assurance that Christ has not left his people comfortless.

The Eucharist is promise and memorial of Christ, response of the believing heart and active co-operation with the continuing work of the Holy Spirit. Christ is present; the Eucharist stirs up faith and arouses response to God.

The Eucharist is a preview of heaven, a promise of what is to come. It anticipates by faith the great rejoicing when Christ and all his disciples are finally one, when all sorrow, toil and difficulty are abolished and happiness is complete.

The Eucharist is not a sacrifice; there is only one effectual sacrifice – that of Christ at Calvary. But Holy Communion suggests sacrifice. It does so by recalling the sacrifice of Jesus; but it also suggests sacrifice in the yielding response we are asked for: the sacrifice believers offer in return to God.

Wesley thought of the sacrament as a 'converting ordinance', a sign of how Christ offers himself for fallen humanity and how believers must turn to God in self-offering.

### *Folk theology: the religion of the heart*

Wesley was not a systematic thinker; nor did he set out to write theology. Professional theologians, indeed, have often scoffed at his theological ability as well as highlighting his tendency to lift ideas from many quarters. One critic decried his work as 'simply condensation'. In so far as a theological system underpinned his thoughts he was Arminian and an opponent of Calvinism. On this point he differed strongly with his contemporary George Whitefield (1714–1770), although their friendship held firm.

In Wesley's day there was strong opposition to forms of religious expression that valued strong feeling. Such an attitude was referred to as 'Enthusiasm', often a term of contempt. Wesley valued religious 'experience' highly. His followers all valued religious experience and evangelical witness. People witnessed, preached, persuaded and pleaded on the basis of their own experience and feelings and not on the basis of religious, metaphysical or theological systems. Self-fulfilment as experienced by individuals for themselves was sought and valued.

But it was not the self-fulfilment of 'anything goes' as the thrill seekers of postmodern disintegration and licence might envisage it. Wesley gave very clear priority to Scripture and had a feeling for tradition as he had received it through the Church of England. He called his followers to disciplined, healthy living and a loving concern for others.

Another element of Wesley's teaching was his notion of perfectibility, being 'saved to the uttermost'. This notion has attracted criticism as it raises fears of spiritual pride and complacency. This danger is particularly strong when faced with those who may not have reached the same stage on the journey.

Wesley was and must always be seen as a folk theologian, seeking to express plain truths for plain people. His theology, such as it was, was forged literally 'on the hoof', as he travelled on horseback from place to place, with his specially designed writing desk fitted in front of him on the saddle. With this he read, thought and wrote his letters and his pamphlets, working out his responses to the controversies which confronted him. 'He was not,' said Ronald Knox, somewhat smugly, 'a good advertisement for reading on horseback.'

Wesley's theology was best taught, indeed caught, in the hymns written by his brother Charles, one of the great hymn writers of the English language. Charles Wesley (1707–1788) is said to have written over 9,000 hymns, although not all are of first rate quality. Among the best known are 'O for a thousand tongues to sing', 'Hark, the Herald-angels sing!' and 'Love divine, all loves excelling'. It is not unusual, to this day, to consult Charles' hymns if one wants to learn aspects of Wesleyan doctrine. The core of that teaching is found in the *Collection of Hymns for the Use of the People called Methodists*, first published in 1780.

### *Wesley's anthropology*

How did Wesley view the human race? Wesley lived at the time of the Enlightenment, though he was not a supporter. Nevertheless he was known to be acquainted with early empiricism (Locke), psychology and experimental methodology. He was a promoter of religious toleration, supported the abolition of slavery and was concerned for public health.

The Enlightenment saw human beings as essentially good; they could be made better by the sustained use of reason and provided they abandoned all superstition, including religion. This was very much the view of the French Enlightenment, although English Enlightenment figures, particularly the Deists, were open to some expressions of religion, provided they were carefully and rationally controlled.

The Calvinists saw the human race as essentially fallen. Calvinist theologians were conscious of evil in the world and in the individual. They believed that, by their own efforts, human beings could not overcome such tendencies. Only God could do this for them. They were also gloomy about human efforts to remain on a path of virtue and they considered that only God could keep them holy, hence God chose some to be predestined to virtue; the rest would be lost.

Wesley was conscious of evil and hopeful about grace. The world was fallen, yet God could heal a human heart. Holiness and the transformation of society were both possible. Human beings were not predestined puppets without choice. Wesley saw the human heart as free and capable of responding to God's offer of love. Nevertheless he did not preach a religion of the unaided effort of the will. God's grace was an ever-present resource.

Wesley's view of the human being might be summed up as follows:

- The human heart is sinful, but can be justified by faith
- A new birth is possible by responding to God's call in Jesus Christ

- The Holy Spirit is a constant witness and protection to help believers on their pilgrimage
- Human beings are dependent on grace but still free: perfect love is a gift from God and can be demonstrated in human lives.

Wesley never abandoned the quest for perfection.

Before his conversion, Wesley had professed 'the faith of a servant', where believers do all in their power for God. Following his conversion he professed the 'faith of a son', where believers thank and praise God for all God has done for them.

## Political and social consequences

Wesley's 'itinerancy', his campaign of revival preaching to large numbers of the unchurched and displaced, had profound social consequence. All over England, but particularly in the north and in the rapidly growing cities, it created a large population of sober, hard working, reliable people. Some historians have even claimed that it saved England from revolution.

Wesleyanism was widely seen as a religion for the poor. It was a very lively religious organization which eventually operated outside the boundaries of the Established Church and outside the corridors of power. It gave emotional outlet in hymn singing, yet tended to organize people in small groups.

When, in the early twentieth century, the working classes began to organize themselves politically, the Methodist Church was undoubtedly an organization which provided a common culture for political allies. The Labour Party, it was said, owed more to Methodism than to Marx. In many ways, Methodism defined the robust, no nonsense, down-to-earth, North of England Non-Conformist.

It is probably dangerously easy to overestimate the numbers of drunkards and feckless individuals converted in Wesleyan rallies. But the movement did contribute to a stable population of 'little people', shopkeepers, artisans, farmers and factory workers who settled for simple comforts and thrift. They were advised to make all the money they could, save all they could and give away as much as they could to good causes.

However, as Methodism established itself, it tended to become socially conservative. On the whole, Wesleyans supported the magistrates against the radicals during the 'Peterloo' massacre of 1819. Some suggest that because of Methodism, England acquired a working class that was in large part compliant with government policy, narrow-minded and repressed. On the other hand, many individuals were taught the workings of democracy through church business meetings and learned the elements of political rhetoric as they sat beneath the pulpit.

Women played a wide role in early Methodism. In Wesley's lifetime there were probably more women than men acting as visitors, evangelists, leaders of classes and prayer groups. By the late eighteenth century there were large numbers of women preachers. However, as respectability grew, the role of women, regrettably, became less conspicuous. This probably came about because of notions about social correctness and feminine reserve, together with strict adherence to the Apostle Paul's injunction that women should remain silent in church.

## Appraisal

Wesley found his authority in the Scriptures, which was the most important record of the continuing redemptive work of God in the world, accomplished through the ministry of Jesus Christ.

Wesley valued the tradition of the Church, particularly as he had found it in the Church of England, which, in fact, he claimed he had never left. However he abandoned the divine right of episcopacy and denied the apostolic succession.

He initiated and supported a ministry of evangelism to every human being of every social status and condition. The Gospel was to be proclaimed to all and had only to be accepted through faith.

He demanded that holiness be a visible result of conversion. The Gospel made an offer to all, but it also made a claim on every individual.

He never toned down his quest for Christian perfection.

He encouraged social concern and social action, being concerned for physical conditions and individual health and wellbeing.

He proclaimed the Lord' Supper as a sacramental sign of the fellowship of believers.

Like all before him in the Reformation tradition he was orthodox with regard to the doctrines of God. He laid Protestant stress on the doctrines of salvation and on how individuals can come to it.

Might any emphasis on conversion as a normative, once-for-all, precise and definable moment be a weakness in a theological system? Why might this be?

# 8 The Contexts of Modern Theology

Christianity makes much of the 'faith once for all entrusted to the saints' (Jude 3) or 'Jesus Christ . . . the same yesterday and today and for ever' (Heb. 13.8). Popular opinion sees it wallowing contentedly in a message and a mindset that has never changed since 33 CE. However, if we look at things a little more closely, we can see that this is an illusion, that the priorities of Christians of different ages have been quite varied and that the understanding of basic concepts like salvation or ministry or sacraments has also subtly altered.

Christianity has never simply stated a bald fact; Christians have always been obliged to offer a message adapted to the world in which they found themselves: Christians in all their incalculable diversity, addressing settings of wonderful variety. Consequently Christian ideas have had to be presented in ways that were marked by the particular flavour of the times and by the particular concerns within those different settings. In this process Christianity has opposed many contemporary ideas but has also taken on a colouring from the world in which it proclaimed its message.

In this chapter we are going to take a look at some of the ideas that have shaped the contemporary world and so try to get a sense of the many settings in which the Christian faith has been called upon to give an account of itself and which have, of course, influenced how that account was expressed.

## The Scientific Revolution

The sixteen centuries before Newton all have an air that is unrecognizable and can just about be understood by modern individuals. The cultural foundation of every one of those centuries was theological. God was an undisputed given, a force that was always present to be reckoned with. It is likely that, in terms of deeply felt theological feeling, the sixteenth century, the century of the Reformation in Western Europe, was the most theological of all. It was certainly so in its negative, and violent, results.

I wish to outline in brief the work of three thinkers and to hint at how they changed the geography of the human imagination. They did not solve all scientific problems. Inventors and thinkers continue to do important work.

After Newton (1642–1727) a theological account of the world was no longer necessary. Such an account did not immediately drop out of sight, but it has gradually faded from human concerns. Newton demonstrated a system by which the universe continued to function, following mathematical principles and laws, and we can understand it without any reference to the idea of God.

The scientific outlook combines two stages of action. The first, the stage of analysis, is when the scientist collects, little by little, observable facts. The second part of the process, the stage of synthesis, is when that same scientist makes a daring guess at what might be the laws governing the way those facts pull together. That hypothesis is then tested against observable fact.

Building on those who had gone before him, Newton's triumph was to state the three laws of motion which explained the motions of the planets, the orbits of heavenly bodies, the tides and all movement. Before Newton it was assumed that a lifeless body would quickly become still if the influence of soul on matter ceased. It was now suggested that lifeless matter would keep moving for ever if an outside material cause did not stop it. God was no longer necessary to keep things working. All could be explained using mathematical principles.

The second thinker is Sir Charles Lyell (1797–1875) who published his *Principles of Geology* between 1830 and 1833. Earlier geologists thought that our planet was only about 6,000 years old, and had suffered catastrophic geological transformations on a scale unknown today. There had been many of them, and they had taken place over a comparatively short period of time. On each occasion the flora and fauna had been destroyed, and the world had then been repopulated by a fresh creative act.

Lyell's work suggested that the Earth was, in fact, thousands of millions of years old. The landscapes which we take for granted, mountain and plain, had not been created as we see them today, but were in fact the result of geological transformations which had gone on for thousands of centuries. The natural forces controlling these changes had remained constant and are still operating today.

Archbishop Ussher (1581–1656) had famously declared that the creation, as described in Genesis, had occurred in 4004 BC. Lyell upset this worldview. The suspicion that science contradicted the Bible, and that science was therefore hostile to religion, was beginning to grow.

This suspicion burst into raging controversy with the publication of Darwin's *On the Origin of Species* in 1859. Human beings had been around for much longer than 6,000 years. Human beings were not created, but had gradually developed, as had all life on earth, from earlier forms. Two laws governed the change: first, all life forms adapt to the situation in which they find themselves and, secondly, only the fittest survive. So when a species adapts itself in order to supply all its needs more efficiently, it then has a greater chance of surviving. All life is the story of that gradual change over millions of years, a slow change that still continues. Here Darwin (1809–1882) offered a view of human history that passionately upset every person of delicate feeling.

These changes shocked, even enraged the sensibilities of the nineteenth century. That probably explains why the ideas were so fiercely resisted rather that calmly evaluated. The world and human history now stretched back so far that it is difficult to get one's head around it. They overturned the assumptions that European history, supremacy and standards were central to the development of human civilization. There was nothing lasting or secure about Western civilization's eminence or values. Could human beings be seen, from now on, as possessing any special relationship with God? Can one say any longer that there is a God-breathed spirit within each human person? The modern outlook was to be more individualistic, more sceptical and increasingly secular.

## The Enlightenment

The term 'Enlightenment' is frequently applied to the intellectual temper of the eighteenth century. This mindset grew out of the Scientific Revolution of the seventeenth century. Thinkers increasingly felt that everything could be explained by reason and were unwilling to entertain old forms of thought or old forms of authority. Kings had claimed to rule by divine right. However by the eighteenth century this was increasingly contested.

In addition there was increasing conflict between thinkers of this outlook and the Christian Church. Dogma was distrusted; clerical authority was mocked. The church was inevitably seen as a selfish power structure. It was not seen as performing any vital or necessary pastoral function.

There were several important intellectual developments here. One was the conviction that a population is capable of developing reasonable laws if it is given the freedom to do so. Note the insistence that laws can be reasonable. When they are reasonable, it was assumed they command respect and assent by that very fact.

Secondly, there was an assumption that what the mass of the people think, feel and desire is more important that what the king thinks, feels and desires. So people's mental outlooks started to move in a democratic direction. Aristocratic, authoritarian mindsets were being left behind.

Thirdly, there was a growing belief that by limiting the power of government, by providing checks and balances on the way power operated, personal freedom, economic growth and religious toleration could all be promoted, with a proportional increase in the happiness of populations. The success of the newly independent United States of America was a forceful argument here.

The Enlightenment did not, of course, promote a definite and agreed philosophical programme. There was widespread debate and fierce disagreement; religious and political intolerance were still found everywhere. Views ranged from constructive criticism of both religious and political power to total atheism and degenerate lifestyles.

## Empiricism

Empiricism is the conviction that all knowledge comes from experience: I know it is raining because I look out the window and see the rain. Here sense experience is the starting point for knowledge. The senses (touch, taste, hearing, smell and sight) give us our basic knowledge about the world. They are the raw material which we process as we gather knowledge. The empirical outlook insists that we test all our conclusions to see if they are correct. But empiricism also insists that we can be mistaken and that new evidence may arise which forces us to correct and re-evaluate what we had believed before. Chief amongst those who thought in this way were John Locke (1632–1704) and David Hume (1711–1776).

However many thinkers have disputed that we are capable of getting all our knowledge from sense experience alone. We do make logical connections between ideas. They are just that: logical connections. Can we observe logical connections or do we reason towards them? If we use both raw facts and logical connections, then we use more than sense experience.

## Immanuel Kant

Immanuel Kant (1724–1804) was interested in what our experience can tell us about what lies beyond physical reality. Hume had really distrusted the mind's abilities, but Kant could not accept that degree of mistrust. Our senses do, in fact, tell us a lot about how reality appears to us. Reality points beyond experience to a unity of how the world seems, its appearance, (what Kant called *phenomena*) and how the world is in itself (what he called *noumena*).

Kant held that the mind organizes objects and experience by a series of inbuilt concepts, which are part of the structure of our minds. He called these the categories of understanding. They act as a built-in operating system already installed within our minds and without them we could not organize sense-data or realize we were having experiences.

But Kant went further. He also claimed that there are categories of moral thought, which involved reasoning about what we *ought* to do. Kant called these *imperatives.*

They are obligations which are valid for everybody. In particular he stated what he called the *categorical imperative,* which is a universal moral law. We know that any given action is correct if we can say that such an action would be right for everybody.

This categorical imperative is an *a priori* concept. That is to say, we know it comes into play before experience does; we know it because of the structure of our mind and it is an objective moral duty.

Kant makes all morality quite independent of God. His notion of duty has force whether one believes in God or not, and the notion of God is not invoked to justify it.

## Romanticism

The Romantic Movement may be characterized as a way of feeling. Rousseau (1712–1778) was a founding figure and its fundamental notion centres round the French word *la sensibilité*, which means being sensitive. Romantics were prone to strong emotions, which they thought were of greater value than any sort of well thought out plan. Feelings had to be strong to have value.

Nature was prized above civilization, the lonely being above the clubbable individual; the savage was noble and society was corrupt. The dark and brooding poet was the ideal person, the wild forest or the thundering ocean the superlative setting; living as a poor peasant was the perfect situation to be in. But did any Romantic ever end up life as a peasant?

Obviously it was another movement of revolt – against the social order, against the mass organization of the industrial revolution, against the transformation of the huge industrial cities and the debasement of their slums. It did not, however, provide a basis on which to reform society, since society was corrupt. Feeling was more important than reason, therefore any reform programme (a product of reason) was bound to be suspect. The individual acting alone was more important than cohesive political or moral action.

The Romantic Movement had its most important and enduring effect in the appreciation of landscape, the desire to preserve the wilderness and the protection of wildlife. In the field of education, following Rousseau's *Emile,* children were perceived as possessing their own individuality and their own needs and requiring the freedom to develop in accordance with their own nature: play was in fact a learning activity. In theological terms, the Romantic influence gave thrust to the demand for strong and sincere feeling in religious practice; there was a new stress on individual action, conversion and responsibility.

## Liberalism

Liberalism is the political and intellectual opinion that individuals should be free to make all important personal decisions, particularly involving political and religious belief. It stands for the freedom of individual conscience. Its theoretical underpinning comes from the work of Locke (1632–1704) and Montesquieu (1689–1755).

Their theories of the liberal state proposed that government should be shared between three 'powers': the legislative power to make laws; the executive power to carry out the day-to-day running of government and the judicial power to deliver judgement when disputes arise. These powers are all constrained by each other as each power acts as a watchdog against the excessive rule of the other two, thus providing checks and balances for each one.

Liberalism was originally intended to act as a check against the absolute power of kings; it later came to mean the defence of individual rights against the powers of the State. In economic terms it originally meant free enterprise: the State should not use its power to interfere with the free play between business competitors. In some areas it has sometimes come to mean the duty of the State to manage the economy and to improve the position of all minorities which may suffer discrimination.

Where liberalism suggests the notion that 'you can't buck the market', economic effectiveness and the successful creation of wealth have become determining standards for moral choices. In others it has led to the notion that what is good for an individual always takes precedence over what might be good for a social grouping.

## Marx

Marx accepted Hegel's view that all change takes place by means of a constant process where an idea (thesis) is produced, an idea develops in opposition to it (antithesis) and the conflict between the two is resolved by a synthesis including both thesis and antithesis. Marx believed that this dialectical process was an unchangeable process of history involving economic factors. Modern capitalism was born out of a continuous interplay of economic opposites, involving struggles over who controls the means of creating wealth.

This notion of opposites reveals itself in differing classes, particularly those who control the means of production and those who work to create the wealth for them. The organization of classes and the mindsets that spring from those economic roles create what Marx called the class system. Each of us belongs to an economic class and is blinkered by the outlook typical of that class; so our ideological outlook is ultimately controlled by the role we play in the means of production.

Technological advances increased wealth for those owning the means of production, but inevitably the conditions of the working class worsened. Marx's solution was to impose, through revolution, a classless society where the proletariat, those who created the wealth, would also own the means of production. Indeed he saw this as an inevitable part of the capital – labour clash: the working out of the economic dialectic in history.

Ordinary workers have no capital and are therefore forced to sell their labour as a commodity. In a way, according to Marx, when they do this, they sell themselves. In this process the workers never get the full value for the wealth their efforts have created. Capitalists, on the other hand, seek to get the highest possible amount of money for their investment. This is a source of conflict between capital and labour which can only be resolved through revolution and the dictatorship of the proletariat.

Marx also held that industrial and technological innovation was always going to be so rapid that it would outstrip the speed at which methods for controlling them were devised. So in the modern industrial world, human beings are cut off from true, creative fellowship with others and suffer from self-alienation; they become isolated, insecure and fearful in the world which they inhabit. Things are given value; little value is placed on the people who create them.

Marx's thought is classified as dialectical materialism and materialism holds that all thought and values arise from material sources. Marx's thought also stresses ethical obligation; though it is difficult to see how notions of obligation and duty can arise from a purely materialistic discourse. Materialism evidently involves a rejection of all 'spiritual' concepts and, thus, a rejection of God.

In addition Marx saw the Church as the tool of the ruling class and therefore as an agent of capitalism. The wide acceptance of this viewpoint has contributed to the de-Christianization of the working class populations of Europe.

With regard to capitalism itself, there is no doubt that many of Marx's criticisms were taken on board, and capitalist systems showed enough flexibility to adapt and improve the economic conditions of many working-class populations.

The fall of communism in the late 1980s was, however, seen as a vindication of capitalism and as a permanent indictment of Marxism. Yet, since that fall, and the subsequent exaltation of the free market, many of the tendencies Marx criticized, appear once again to be on the rise. Increasingly one finds that the Welfare State is under-funded; the provisions made for health, social welfare and pensions are considered to impede economic progress and economic effectiveness is seen as the only thing justifying action. Possessions and the creation of wealth are again more highly regarded than the people who operate the economy.

Trends are not yet clear, but will capitalism return to something like the value system it paraded when Marx first penned his critique of it? Obviously much has changed; heavy industry no longer creates the mass of wealth, but other agents of the capitalistic system do. Will a new Marx be needed to evaluate the new Capitalism? And what is the role of Christian Theology as a critique of contemporary society?

## Freud

Sigmund Freud (1856–1939) was a young Viennese doctor who set out to treat nervous ailments. He experimented with hypnosis and found it produced some striking results. He concluded that mental processes are essentially unconscious and that sexual impulses play a large and unappreciated role in causing nervous and mental disorder. Freud used his study of patients' dreams to further develop his 'sexual hypothesis'.

He considered that the unconscious is revealed in everyday life, in slips of the tongue, in mishearing and failing to remember correctly. He is credited with inventing psychoanalysis which he considered to be an exacting and universal application of the principles of determinism to mental life. He also considered that psychoanalysis can reveal much about the process of artistic and literary creation and that sexual impulses have made a huge contribution to all spheres of cultural, artistic and social endeavour.

Christian puritanism had largely ignored sex. It was obviously necessary for the survival of the human species. But, in personal terms, it was an unfortunate necessity for men, which women had to tolerate, but not to enjoy. Freud's thought was regarded with deep suspicion in Christian circles. It was considered to be 'filthy' and degenerate, insisting on discussing an aspect of human behaviour which had to do with human sinfulness rather than the Christian's redeemed state.

A new attitude to human erotic feeling was emerging. People were becoming more open and more understanding about sex. Christian puritanism and repressiveness in matters of sexual practice were being rejected. Maintaining traditional religious attitudes in this field was increasingly seen as unhealthy and limiting.

So, by delving into the darker recesses of the mind, Freud demonstrated the importance of dreams, fantasy and psychopathological signs. He showed sex to be at the heart of neurosis, stressed the importance of childhood experiences, showed how mythology and symbolism were relevant to living and revealed many of the mind's dynamics.

Yet even as he brought the mind under rational investigation, he demonstrated that beneath the rational veil there is, in our being, a vast reservoir of non-rational forces. In this way Freud's thought undermined the image of the human being as the pinnacle of creation, a view which the Enlightenment had inherited from medieval Christianity. But he also undermined the notion that we are purely rational beings.

## Feminism

The central belief of feminism is that, throughout history, women have been discriminated against.

Feminism has many different forms of expression and different feminists emphasize a wide variety of concerns. There are various theoretical forms of feminism, concentrating on abstract issues and the timeless truths about reality. Social forms of feminism concentrate on seeking to have all women treated equally with men in society. There are important political agendas labelled feminist.

Feminist ideas came to greater prominence in the 1960s and 1970s. At this time there were more women in the workforce, more women in secondary and third-level education, and greater access for all to the mass media. It was a time when old restraints and cultural assumptions were being cast off and when there was greater availability of inexpensive methods of birth control.

Why are we the way we are? Is it because we are biologically programmed? Or is it the result of a long conditioning by powerful social influences? Are women the way they are because of biological factors or have they been conditioned by a powerful male establishment which is both social and political?

Some say that the difference between men and women is not innate, but is constructed; others say that the experience of motherhood has a deep significance in shaping how women understand themselves and relate to the world around them. According to this model, male thinking emphasizes the separateness of individuals; female thinking emphasises connectedness because, in pregnancy, women experience the sharing of their bodies with another human being.

Yet other feminists react violently against any attempt to reduce women to their motherhood role. Another group of feminists contends that women's freedom will only come about when all dependency upon men, including a dependency on them for sexual fulfilment, is broken.

Mary Daly (1928– ), a radical feminist theologian, has scorned the idea of referring to God as 'Father'. She has refused to admit men to some of her lectures on the grounds that it would inhibit free discussion.

Feminism has been a powerful factor in undermining the assumptions of authority and power which have been widely imposed and accepted since the beginnings of the Western European cultural model.

## Liberation Theology

Liberation Theology is criticism from within. The Christian commandment to love one another, the Christian insistence that the message of Christ was for all people, was a powerful critique of the way power was actually exercised within Christendom, the industrialized West and its colonies. The scandal is that nobody noticed for nearly 2,000 years.

Europe had been obsessed with itself. Christianity wore very European blinkers. As the nineteenth century progressed, there was an increasing awareness of the much wider canvas of human history and cultures, together with a growth in social awareness and social conscience.

People started to realize that such a conscience stood in sharp contrast to historical Christian attitudes. They were coming to see that Christian practice had, for many centuries, been shaped by class and racial prejudice.

Without any theological justification the Christian Church had ruthlessly put into practice an implied doctrine of the superiority of the white man. Liberation Theology struggled to place the 'preferential option for the poor' at the top of the social, political and theological agenda.

## Mysticism

Together with the secularizing tendencies of the last few centuries, there have been two opposing constants which I propose to call mysticism and 'fundamentalism'. The mystical contribution to modern life has been almost totally confined to the sphere of religious faith. The tendency which I call fundamentalism has found expression within the community of faith but it has also had interesting and, at times alarming, political parallels.

Mysticism makes a very particular claim. It is that certain individuals come, on occasion, to a direct awareness of God without any intermediary. At times this awareness of God is so close that we may talk of direct union with God. Mysticism is not confined to Christianity; it exists in other religious traditions.

Mysticism is very definitely an individual experience; yet the claims made by mystics have a degree of consistency which allows us to suppose that mysticism takes similar forms and that those who experience the mystical state pass through similar stages. What is more, the individuals concerned appear to have a special receptiveness and to make special preparation for the experience. Nevertheless the evidence is persuasive: one cannot induce the state; the mystical experience seizes the individual.

The mystical experience is a form of prayer and the individual being taken into mystical union passes through many stages, although the stages have continuity. While there is no cast-iron agreement as to what they are, there is enough accord for them to be briefly listed here as vocal prayer, discursive prayer, affective prayer, the prayer of simplicity, the prayer of quiet, the prayer of union, ecstasy and, finally, spiritual marriage.

It is difficult to discuss mysticism because the states described by mystics are outside the experience of most people. There is no way ordinary believers can confirm what is thus described, no way of repeating the experiment for themselves or even of understanding what is being described. The mystical experience may be given a systematic description, but it cannot be rationally critiqued.

Nevertheless many people look to the mystics as the very best evidence we may have for the claims of religious faith. Furthermore, mystics are not necessarily dreamy, impractical people. Some of the best known mystics have been people of vast, realistic and effective energy. The evidence of such people reminds us that the claims of mystery and transcendence have their place in modern living.

## Fundamentalism

Let us turn to 'fundamentalism'. This is not at all the same as mysticism and has nothing to do with the gradations of the mystical experience towards union with God. Rather it has to do with the conscious or partially conscious adoption of a form of belief from which one is either unwilling or unable to move.

'Fundamentalism' arises when individuals or communities experience the need for a firm foundation for identity, values or action. 'Fundamentalism' is 'adopted'; it arises out of an inner need for some form of guaranteed security. The individual is not, as in mysticism, 'grasped' by the holy. 'Fundamentalism' can undergo rational critique. But it refuses, rather than is unable, to submit itself to such judgement. At its most ruthless, fundamentalism has affected whole institutions; it has persecuted and burned heretics. It has its most acute and disturbing expression today when individuals, or whole communities, commit some awful deed in the name of a core value. The best example one might give is the suicide pacts that have been discovered in some enclosed religious communes.

Such examples are not confined to the religious sphere. Unlike mysticism, 'fundamentalism' has entered the political sphere and there have been dreadful results: the Nazi extermination camps, the Gulag in Russia, the Killing Fields of the Khmer Rouge.

## Modernism

Modernism is a particular way of organizing the contemporary world. It arises from a number of influences and expresses a variety of convictions.

It has been influenced by the Industrial Revolution and by the development of technology. The labour that used to be done by human beings is now done by machines. Contrary to early fears, this did not mean that human workers became redundant; rather it meant that they had to be organized in vast numbers, in a comparatively small space, to oversee and connect the work done by a series of machines.

Humans no longer worked outdoors, aware of the rhythms of nature, but indoors, in artificial light; they did not follow the rhythms of their bodies but the rhythms of the machines they operated. They did not work in small isolated communities but on assembly lines. They did not produce a complete product but were only involved in a part of the process. Their lives were not varied; their work was boringly repetitive. Modernity was, in part, an attempt to organize human beings as if they were machines.

The second influence has been that time had become absolute. In an agricultural economy, workers followed the rhythm of the sun; they got up early in summer, later in winter. They worked and went to bed late in summer; they socialized more in winter. They stopped to eat when the sun was high. They rested in winter; they worked hard in summer. They worked at home or near home and family.

With the coming of modernity, they got up at 7 o'clock, summer and winter; they went to bed at 11 o'clock, summer and winter. They stopped for lunch at 1 o'clock. What is more, those hours of the day had nothing to do with when the sun rose or set. Time had become harmonized and standardized. Midday could be varied, as in Daylight Saving Acts, to suit economic need. Work was pre-planned; it no longer depended on the weather. One worked the same length of time every day, summer or winter. Summer, rather than winter, became the time for leisure. The place of work became a built and controlled environment, divorced from home and family. Time was absolute and the needs of the workplace determined how it was organized and used. A worker's needs or a worker's family were no longer determining factors.

The third influence is the means of mass communication, first newspapers, then radio and television, now the internet. Culture is now handed down from central authoritative sources; it is no longer in the hands of the local story teller, local woodcarver or local artist who plaited dried grasses; culture is no longer a local product. Where culture had once been the expression of local needs and longings, it is now a form of influence and control by a centralized source. Out went the king; in came the television magnate!

Modernism was not without its benefits. Houses were better built, drier and better heated. People were better clothed and had a greater variety of household goods. Standards of living rose. Engineering brought better roads, bridges, clean water and efficient and safe waste disposal. Modern forms of transport meant a greater variety of foods. Schools raised the awareness of the population; hospitals looked after their health and hygiene improved.

The way the great majority of the population viewed the world also changed. Reality was reduced to be what could be observed. The scientific method became the only method for deciding truth and, through it, humans could at last achieve certainty. People believed in progress; it would inevitably overcome all the problems facing the human race. Nature was no longer something fixed and static, but dynamic and developing.

What happened in the universe arose from fixed causes; therefore all life was in some way determined. The lone individual pondering reality, observing and carefully weighing evidence was the ideal of the inventor, the thinker or the scholar. Individualism took on greater value. The human being was capable of arriving at truth and was therefore the final authority in all matters. All external or imposed authority was suspect.

## Postmodernism

Most people living in the early twenty-first century hold many, if not all, of the views outlined in the paragraph above. Yet, at the same time, doubts as to their validity or value are beginning to arise. What is more, many people increasingly hold both a given view and its apparent contradiction at the same time. This outlook has been characterized as postmodern.

The postmodern person denies the objectivity of human knowledge. Individuals are often aware that they are conditioned by the special circumstances of their situation which do not hold good for all time or for every place. Postmodern individuals increasingly doubt that there are absolutely basic and indubitable first principles on which systems of knowledge can be erected. All-inclusive systems of explanation, holding good for all time and every place, are distrusted.

People no longer believe that knowledge is a good thing in itself. The destructive uses found for many of the most exciting discoveries of science have stirred up profound distrust, if not despair. The inevitability of progress is increasingly denied. Individuals are no longer seen as the ideal persons to discern objective truth and, increasingly, teams of workers, community-based knowledge and working on projects for restricted groups are valued. Truth is not necessarily known by reason but often by intuition. My meaning and your meaning now have an equal claim on the respect of all.

## Appraisal

The paragraphs above describe some of the influences and outline some of the results that accompanied the shift from a God-centred to a human-centred worldview. The transition was not sudden. It had been evident from the late Middle Ages. It gathered pace at the Renaissance and went into overdrive during the nineteenth century.

The changes may be seen as coming from the contradictions between scientific discovery and biblical revelation and the decline of the metaphysical outlook following the criticism of empiricism. Political and social criticisms have been levelled against religion and in particular against the way the Church has wielded or influenced political power. Finally, people have acquired growing psychological awareness and insight, and the notion of pleasure has become an acceptable and desirable value.

None of these values is fatal to religious belief, but it is evident that once they were accommodated, religious belief could no longer continue as before. Many believers have come to terms with many, if not all, of these trends. Yet they have also functioned as an excuse to avoid commitment to religious faith, which was now inevitably more difficult and more challenging than it had once been.

It is no longer possible to state a religious proposition and expect to have it accepted because it is just that: an element of the dominant culture of the society in which one lives. It is no longer possible to be a religious believer and belong to a dominant grouping; religious communities are increasingly thinly scattered among an indifferent population. It is no longer possible to be a religious believer on a basis of unthinking custom; religious adherence is increasingly a question of carefully considered, critical responses, often at some cost.

Nevertheless beneath all the appearances to the contrary there is a bedrock of concealed continuity. The secular outlook of Western Europe still values many principles which derive from its Christian foundations. Christian ethical terms and values, the value of the individual human being, the belief in the human as a rational being, the conviction that reason is a fundamental tool for discovering knowledge, concern for the less well-off, the intelligibility of the empirical universe, the necessity of and responsibility for exercising dominion over the natural world, the moral responsibility of each individual and a belief in the inevitable progression of human beings towards self-fulfilment have all got Christian roots. In every one of the features listed above, secular terms may have replaced specific religious language; but the religious language can still be heard quite clearly by those who know what it is.

Indeed, the Western world would not be what it is today without the Christian theological enterprise. How does that theological enterprise continue its mission in the context of the world that it has shaped?

In the pre-modern period Theology had expressed the dominant cultural values of the day. The modern shift in cultural expression has meant that Christian Theology is now counter-cultural, as it was in its earliest days. Theology now functions as a critique of dominant values. It does so in a number of ways. For instance, where Theology expresses conservative feeling, it criticizes moral outlooks which promote personal freedom and hedonism at the expense of community responsibility. Where Theology promotes radical, social and political activism, it criticizes the self-interest, sectionalism and greed of contemporary economic activity. In other contexts it criticizes the dehumanizing treatment which human beings mete out to fellow humans, made in the image of God. You might care to note other examples and instances.

# 9 Friedrich Schleiermacher and Religious Feeling

Schleiermacher is considered to be the first modern theologian. He influenced all the great theological thinkers of the twentieth century. All those who followed him were either in dispute or in dialogue with him.

He had close contacts with the Romantic Movement, indeed, was a product of it. He was the first Calvinist to teach at the University of Halle. He was the first Professor of Theology at the new University of Berlin. As a preacher at the Charity Hospital in Berlin he set out to win the educated middle classes back to religious practice.

He defined religion as a 'sense and taste for the infinite'. He held religion to be a matter of intuition and feeling and played down the notion of religious dogma. His scholarly work covered a wide range of theological subjects.

When he placed a very strong emphasis on the role of feeling as the basis for religious thought and practice, he was reacting strongly against the rationalism of the eighteenth century. In time there would be a reaction against him, led by Karl Barth (1886–1968) and Emil Brunner (1889–1966), who stressed once more the authority of Scripture, the dependable standard promoted by the sixteenth century reformers.

## Life (1768–1834)

Friedrich Daniel Ernst Schleiermacher was born in 1768 in Breslau in Prussia. His father was a Calvinist minister and a court chaplain; his mother also came from a clerical family. He was born during the Enlightenment and was thus taught to believe in the power of human reason, to be confident that natural, rational methods can discover truth in all fields of enquiry and to see if he could discover the natural religion of all humanity. So two rather contradictory tendencies – pietism and natural reason – contributed to his thought and development.

He started his theological education in 1785 under the influence of the Moravian Brethren but he soon had difficulties with their teachings.

He objected in particular to their teachings about Christ's atoning sacrifice. He went to study Philosophy at the University of Halle in 1787. Here he came into contact with Enlightenment thought, with the Romantic Movement and with the philosophy of Kant. He also had moods of religious scepticism.

**Romanticism** A literary and artistic movement of the late eighteenth and early nineteenth centuries. It promoted subjective feeling, strong emotions and escape from established classical forms.
**Enlightenment** The critical mindset of the eighteenth century: the rational examination of previously accepted ideas and institutions.
**Pietism** A seventeenth and eighteenth century reform movement within German Lutheranism seeking to reform and intensify devotional life.
**Atonement** The reconciliation of God and the human race brought about by Jesus Christ.
**Scepticism** Doubting, questioning or disbelieving: particularly the teachings of religion.
**Dogmatics** Dogma is the system of religious teaching authoritatively considered to be absolute truth. Dogmatics is the study of dogma.

Schleiermacher became a clerical student and did well in his early theological examinations, except for dogmatics. He spent 1790 to 1793 as tutor to an aristocratic family. Here he was introduced to the notion of a faith which unites people of different doctrinal outlooks. He undertook his first post as an assistant pastor, also becoming a chaplain at the Charity Hospital in 1796.

He now became friendly with thinkers involved in the Romantic Movement; he started to translate Plato and in 1799 published his first book *On Religion: Speeches to Its Cultured Despisers*. The central idea was that feeling was more important to religion than the fashionable Enlightenment rationalism of his day.

Schleiermacher became a university teacher and preacher at the University of Halle in 1804. In 1806, following the defeat of Prussia by Napoleon, Halle was no longer a Prussian city. Schleiermacher was a passionate patriot, so needed little persuading to come to Berlin where Friedrich Wilhelm III was founding the new University of Berlin, seeking to make the city a centre of intellectual excellence. In 1809 he took up the post of pastor to the Trinity Church. That was the year he married Henriette von Mühlenfels. They had a son who died in infancy.

The next year he also became Professor of Theology and Dean of the Theological Faculty at the University. His *Brief Outline of the Study of Theology* was the programme of theological studies he designed for his students; it was published in 1810. His book *The Christian Faith, presented systematically according to the Principles of the Evangelical Church* was published in 1821. It is highly regarded as a great work of Protestant dogmatics.

During the course of his life he was to lecture extensively on language, translation, psychology and hermeneutics, as well as on theology.

In his latter years he was active in the movement to merge the Evangelical (Lutheran) and Reformed (Calvinist) churches, thus creating the United Church of Prussia. He died in 1834 following a brief illness.

### Timeline

1765 Watt improves the steam engine
1768 Birth of Schleiermacher
1770–1775 The *Sturm und Drang* movement in Germany
1775 American War of Independence
1781 Kant's *Critique of Pure Reason*
1785 Schleiermacher studies Moravian Theology
1786 Mozart's *Marriage of Figaro*
1787 Schleiermacher studies at the University of Halle
1789 The French Revolution
1796 Schleiermacher at the Charity Hospital
1799 Schleiermacher's *On Religion: Speeches to Its Cultured Despisers*
1804 Napoleon is crowned Emperor
Schleiermacher lecturing at Halle
1809 Schleiermacher pastor at the Trinity Church
1810 Schleiermacher Professor and Dean of Theology at Berlin University
Schleiermacher's *Brief Outline of the Study of Theology*
1815 Napoleon defeated at Waterloo
1821 Schleiermacher's *The Christian Faith*
1823 The Munroe doctrine is published: The United States has special authority over the American continent

1832 von Clausewitz's *On War*
1834 Death of Schleiermacher
1837 Queen Victoria comes to the throne in Britain

## Thought

Schleiermacher addressed two audiences; on the one hand the educated and self-confident classes who felt that humanity had developed to the point where it no longer needed religion; on the other hand questioning believers who sought a new way of understanding faith in the light of new Enlightenment thinking. *On Religion* addressed the first audience: it set out to persuade. *The Christian Faith* was addressed to the second group; it set out to be systematic and coherent and was written for the Church. Schleiermacher insisted that some things are covered in mystery and cannot be known.

### *Influences upon Schleiermacher*

Schleiermacher admired the thought of Immanuel Kant and studied him closely at university. He did not, however, agree with Kant that religion is the same as morality. This view is particularly strong in Kant's *Critique of Practical Reason.* Schleiermacher was more impressed with Kant's study of aesthetics in the *Critique of Judgement.* So he stressed aesthetic feeling as the underpinning of religion.

Schleiermacher was also influenced by the Romantic Movement, particularly the importance of the individual. Traditional thought held that individuals related to the world through the power of reason. The new movement stressed that individuals relate to the world through the power of feeling and the intensity of their awareness. Romanticism was also aware of the weight of history. Religion, for Schleiermacher, is a historical occurrence; to be alive and active, religion must become living history. God existed in a relationship with humans throughout the flow of history. Romanticism was not content with the conformity to social standards which society imposed. It stressed the rebellious and original quality of individual being and striving: the artist as brooding outcast.

*Schleiermacher and religious feeling*

Schleiermacher tried to rethink the meaning of religion. He disagreed with Kant; religion was more than morality. He also disagreed with Hegel; religion, he claimed, was more than knowledge or reason. The important element in religion is urgent self-consciousness – absolute dependence upon God. The roots of this religious awareness come before impressions of right and wrong and before our ability to experience and process thought. All peoples possess this religious awareness.

For Schleiermacher, God is a powerful force, a relationship which grasps our whole being. Schleiermacher is not against morality or thought. He just finds the primary urge to faith elsewhere: in the experience of absolute dependence.

This experience is transmitted to individuals through faith communities. Christianity is one such community. Here our awareness of God is shaped through Jesus Christ. Christian life is worked out as we lead lives of ethical responsibility and love. The validity of such a faith had its roots in feeling, yet was reflected upon in theology and experienced in thoughtful and faithful practical living.

**Aesthetics** Theory concerning what is beautiful; principles of artistic expression.

**Ethics** Concerning the principles of right and wrong.

**Anthropology** The study of human beings, particularly their social characteristics.

**Rationalism** The belief that human reason is the main source of all human knowledge and action.

**Orthodox** Adhering to accepted, established religious faith.

**Deism** A form of belief in God based only on reason, rejecting all supernatural revelation. God does not intervene in the universe, but created it and then left it to function according to its own laws.

*How Schleiermacher saw the role of theology*

Schleiermacher wanted to draw out and reflect upon this foundational feeling of absolute dependence. He did so using three disciplines:

philosophy, history and pastoral practice. His theology, therefore, had three subsections: philosophical theology, historical theology and practical theology. This model of the university teaching of theology was to be widely copied all over the world.

Philosophy of religion was to replace Natural Theology and act as an introduction to Systematic Theology. Schleiermacher was criticized for having Catholic tendencies but never intended to replace theological truth with philosophical categories and thought processes. It was a change that would, in time, allow the application of traditional theological thinking to the study of world religions.

Historical–critical study was new, important and exciting in the early nineteenth century. Schleiermacher wanted it to be the intellectual tool for theological studies, allowing us to interpret theological thought with greater insight. Theology, for him, was the life of the community of faith developing throughout history. He stressed the importance of studying the Bible, the history of Christianity and the dogmatic outlook of the present-day Church. He wanted to be able to pick out the defining essence of Christianity and apply it in theological studies and practical living. Pastors could not minister to the present if they did not understand the past. This historical awareness was necessary in order to preach, to teach and to act as shepherds to the flock.

### *Schleiermacher's theological method*

Schleiermacher wanted his book, *The Christian Faith*, to be a statement of dogmatic theology for both the Calvinist (Reformed) and Lutheran (Evangelical) traditions. His originality was to start with religious experience, the feeling of absolute dependence, and gradually think his way towards God. This is why, in *On Religion*, he started with anthropology: the study of what it is to be human. He tried to show his cultured and cynical friends that without religion, and in particular without Christianity, there is no human fulfilment.

The problem of Schleiermacher's day was the gulf between rationalism and orthodoxy. Orthodox religion promoted a 'religion from above'; the fashionable Deism of the eighteenth century advocated a 'religion from below'. Schleiermacher believed that it was right to reject an authoritative theological outlook which suppressed human creativity. However the natural religion of reason promoted by the Deists was insipid and barren. So Schleiermacher set out to describe a new vision of God which was a vision of humanity's experience of God – the human contemplation of human experience.

Given the audience he was addressing, cultured and cynical sophisticates, there was little point in starting with dogmatic and authoritative pronouncements about God; one had to start with something more immediate, something that had a better chance of being accepted as a given: religious feeling.

## On Religion: Speeches to Its Cultured Despisers

Schleiermacher suggests that religion is neither knowing (rational doctrinal orthodoxy) nor doing (morality); religion arises out of feeling. It is an inner experience. It is unfathomable and beyond understanding. Feeling, knowing and doing belong together, but we come to awareness of God through feeling our absolute dependence upon God.

Schleiermacher argued in his first speech that nobody could be fully human without being religious. Schleiermacher agreed with the cultured despisers to the extent that blind following of religious orthodoxy had been a cause of suffering. But religion did not begin with doctrine; it began as an internal feeling of 'the infinite' and 'the eternal'. If one did not recognize this there could be no self-improvement. Society had to recover the ability to listen to God speaking to the heart.

In the second speech, Schleiermacher suggests that knowledge which is based on memories and assumptions damages religious feeling. God is not to be found in right actions, right thinking or in science. Religion is sparked when finite creatures become aware of the infinite which is so different from them. Only when there is harmony between knowledge, action and piety can human potential be realized.

**Doctrine** A set of principles presented for belief by a religious group: the teachings of a church.
**Proselytizing** Seeking to convert a person from one belief to another.

**Mediator** One who seeks to bring about a peaceful settlement between opposing parties. In Christian theology it refers to the work of Christ reconciling God and the human race.

Schleiermacher asks his readers to consider a given moment in their lives. Feeling comes from sensations of the world. These feelings are the domain of religion. Knowledge comes when we think about them. Morality arises when we try to act on those feelings.

Science may investigate religion. There are many religions, each an expression of the one religion. Schleiermacher tended to regard Scripture as sacred legend rather than literal truth.

In the third speech Schleiermacher explored how we might receive a hint of religion in the material world. Children coming face to face with the marvels of the world experience joy. Such a feeling is religious; if the child were allowed to cultivate this feeling, religion would blossom.

But such beginnings are often crushed and individuals are separated from the infinite. This is the fault of hard-nosed middle-class common sense and caution. Such an outlook reduces our horizons and makes us imaginatively barren and less than human. Religion can only be cultivated by quiet reflection.

In the fourth speech Schleiermacher tells us that religion must be social. We are finite beings and must communicate our experiences to others and be open to their experiences. Schleiermacher rejected the idea of proselytizing or the notion that salvation is only offered to insiders. There must be no limits placed on religious self-expression; people should not be forced to subscribe to creeds.

In the fifth speech Schleiermacher suggests that the religion people need is Christianity. Up to now he had suggested a wide range of religious expression and had denounced the practice of enforcing belief in certain doctrines.

He denounces natural religion. It denies people's true individuality. It is easily corrupted by the State. True religion is historical religion and religious culture will always be greater than the possibilities of any one individual. Individuals, even pious individuals, cannot have a full picture of the infinite.

Finite creatures need a mediator and for Christians that is Jesus Christ. Jesus Christ is the last mediator; not the only mediator.

## The Christian Faith

In his Introduction to *The Christian Faith* Schleiermacher explains his religious methodology. In Part I he suggests theological themes common to all religions; the awareness of God through 'absolute dependence'.

Piety is at the heart of all church life. It is neither a question of knowing nor of doing. It concerns how our feelings are changed when we become aware of our absolute dependence, of how we stand in a relationship with God. It is not something which happens by chance. It is not something which is different in each individual. It is a universal experience. When we recognize that fact, this feeling takes the place of all the so-called proofs of the existence of God.

In Part II Schleiermacher develops his understanding of revealed Christian Theology. This reflects the 'antithesis of sin and grace' and moves from a very general and abstract relationship between God and the world to a clear and open relationship in Jesus Christ.

**Antithesis** Direct contrast; exact opposite.
**Speculative** Resulting from meditation and reflection. Often referring to conclusions based on conjecture rather than hard evidence.
**Christology** The study of the Person of Christ, particularly the union of the divine and human natures in Christ.
**Monotheism** The belief that there is only one God.
**Teleological** Relating to ends and goals.
**Redemption** This is the act of freeing humanity from the power of sin and restoring the world and its inhabitants to communion with God. In Christianity, redemption became effective with the dwelling of Jesus on earth and his death on behalf of others.

At a first level, faith is a lived experience in the world. At a second level, Theology is the activity of reflecting on that faith. Theology started with practical matters, not with God. It was 'empirical' not 'speculative'.

Feeling allowed Schleiermacher to restate Christian faith at a period when thinking people influenced by the Enlightenment thought they had done away with it. He also wanted to unite the practical and the theoretical.

*The Christian Faith* was Schleiermacher's attempt to express human religious feeling and affections in words. For him all the traditional Christian doctrines correspond to human ways of experiencing God. So Christology was very important; but he held the doctrine of the Trinity in low esteem.

He taught that Christianity is a monotheistic religion of the teleological kind. Everything in it is related to the redemption brought about by Jesus Christ. It is this single fact that sets it apart from all other religions. Faith in Jesus Christ as redeemer is the only way to share in Christian communion.

In a controversial contribution to modern theology Schleiermacher rewrote the doctrine of God. The starting point is how Christian people are aware of God in feelings of absolute dependence. If we try to describe God, we end up, in fact, by limiting God. We no longer pay due attention to the all-powerfulness of God and instead make God dependent upon the world: dependent upon us and upon our analytical insights.

So Schleiermacher taught that all the attributes we ascribe to God do not describe something special about God; rather they indicate the ways in which we experience our feelings of absolute dependence upon God. When we talk about God we are really talking about the way we experience God. By emphasizing the notion of total dependence upon God, Schleiermacher concluded that God is the reality that determines everything, including good and evil.

### *Schleiermacher's dogmatic theology*

Schleiermacher believed that Christian doctrines are how we express Christian religious feelings through language. Dogmatic theology, then, is the way we organize the prevailing way of expressing doctrine at any given time.

The role of Schleiermacher's dogmatic theology was to demonstrate the Christian faith using the 'dialectics of language'. Dogmatics arise out of Church. Theology cannot begin with natural reason because Christian religious feelings only arise when Christianity is experienced. The first point must be the experience of Christian redemption in Jesus Christ.

We cannot know God as God really is. We can only know God in relation to ourselves. On the one hand we know we are absolutely dependent upon God. In our experience of nature, we become aware of the fact that we are creatures. On the other hand we become aware of God when we experience the contradiction between sin and grace.

This opposition of sin and grace is of vital importance in building up our religious self-awareness. Sin is the present state of human beings. It is a conflict dividing our sensuous nature from our spiritual nature. It separates us from God.

On the other hand we experience some form of communication from God, some sort of fellowship with God. That is grace. We can only know sin because we experience grace. This explains our religious self-awareness. Human blessedness is a matter of reinforcing our awareness of God. Sin is a matter of covering over our awareness of God.

**Dialectic** Working out contradictions through the interplay of opposing ideas.
**Grace** Supernatural gift freely bestowed by God.
**Sin** is a deliberate missing of the mark; the intentional disobedience to God's known desire; the state of humanity which, in its weakness, cannot attain divine perfection.
**Trinity** The Christian understanding of God: the unity of Father, Son and Holy Spirit in a single Godhead.

### *Schleiermacher's Christology*

When Schleiermacher comes to consider Jesus Christ he starts from the human angle. We see in Jesus Christ the perfect awareness of God. This allows us to see how we have allowed sin to block out our awareness of God. Traditional theology held that sin came from Adam. Schleiermacher tells us that the power to recognize sin comes from Jesus. In this way grace comes from the person and work of Jesus Christ.

Jesus was sinless because he came to a perfect awareness of God while on earth. He demonstrates to us what ideal humanity is like. In Jesus we see our true reflection. Jesus brought something new to humanity and to the world. Jesus is our great example.

Of course we cannot perfect our own humanity by ourselves. Our religious awareness has become corrupted through sin. We need a mediator who communicates God's redemptive power to us. Jesus is our great redeemer.

The redeemer draws us into the power of his awareness of God and reconciles us with God. Jesus shared the same humanity as all human beings but was exceptional because his awareness of God was so powerful. His redeeming work is a question of bestowing that awareness of God upon all believers.

This means that the event where the redeeming and reconciling work of Christ is done is not the crucifixion but the incarnation. It was at the incarnation that something new entered human history and that a new humanity was formed and a new world announced.

### *The Trinity*

In Schleiermacher's thought the Trinity is not something which can be derived from his foundational experience of God as a feeling of absolute dependence. It seems to arise when we place two doctrines side by side: the doctrine of Christ and the doctrine of the Holy Spirit working in the Church. It demonstrates the union of the divine being with human nature. This is visible in the personality of Christ and also in the way the members of the Church become a common believing and worshiping body.

Schleiermacher examines the Holy Spirit in the setting of the worshipping community. Through the Holy Spirit, believers have communion with Christ. The Holy Spirit energizes the corporate life of believers.

### *Schleiermacher's view of language*

Schleiermacher declared that when we think we rely upon language, and our thinking is limited by language. Meaning depends upon the way we use words. In addition, there are profound differences between individuals in the way they use language and consequently in the way they form concepts.

Not only are there differences between the way individuals use words, but there are differences between the way words are used between one historical period and another. We use the word 'presently' to mean 'soon'. A few hundred years ago it was used to mean 'immediately'. These thoughts are particularly important for translation, and Schleiermacher, as a translator of Plato, spoke from experience. This point is, of course, most important for the interpretation of Scripture.

Schleiermacher's notion of 'semantic holism' suggests that the various senses of any word are kept together by a wider unity of meaning. In ancient times people wrote by cutting letters onto wax tablets with a *stylus*. The word was later used to refer to a gramophone needle; it can now refer to a handheld pointer for use with electronic organizers like a personal digital assistant. These different meanings are held together by the notion of a pencil-shaped object which allows us to convey and organize different sorts of information. We might refer to the different forms of stylus as lower-order concepts and the overall idea suggesting similarity as a higher-order concept.

Higher-order concepts help explain lower-order concepts and new lower-order concepts enrich higher-order concepts. In addition, the grammatical structure of the language has a bearing on the way the words of the language communicate ideas.

**Concept** A thought, an idea, a notion; a way of understanding a situation or occurrence.
**Hermeneutics** The criticism and interpretation of symbols and texts.

### *Schleiermacher's views on hermeneutics*

Hermeneutics is the art of understanding communication by means of language. Schleiermacher understood it to apply to all areas of verbal communication: oral and written, ancient texts and modern texts – Scripture, law, literature and all other forms of text.

Interpreters of the Bible are dependent upon this discipline in exactly the same way as the interpreter of any other type of text. They may not call upon any exceptional circumstances, such as the notion of divine inspiration.

We assume that we understand a text automatically because we speak the language of the text. ('Text' is used here to refer to any unit of language conveying meaning, be it written or oral.) In fact, because every individual uses language and forms concepts differently, misunderstanding is more likely to occur automatically. So understanding must be 'willed and sought' constantly.

The interpreter must seek an understanding of the text's historical background. The interpreter must consult rules for the use of words, indications of meaning. This has to do with how language is shared. The interpreter must pay special attention to how individual authors specifically use words. Not only must one understand the words used and the way they are used but one must also be aware of the intention of the text: a text that sets out to convince you to adopt a certain course of action must not be treated in the same manner as a text giving dispassionate information.

Translation is often a problem because there is a wide gap between the source language, the language of the text to be translated and the target language – the new language one wants the text to be understood in.

Because of these difficulties translators often try to express an idea in a way that is understood not in the source culture but in the target culture. Schleiermacher rejects such a practice, saying it distorts the author's thoughts. He wants the translator to find a means of bringing the reader of the target language text closer to, indeed into, the culture of the source text.

Because of the many problems involved in trying to 'bend' the target language in the direction of the source language, Schleiermacher felt that reading a translation was always second best.

## Appraisal

Schleiermacher wanted to give expression to Christian dogma in such a way that there would be room for independence, diversity and change. He is sometimes thought to value feeling over knowing, so he has been accused of being anti-intellectual. He is not averse to 'knowing'; he thought religious feeling more important. Human knowing is limited and does not allow access to the full scope of being human. When thinking about the human sense of dependence upon God, he emphasizes the notion of relationship. Schleiermacher did not want religion to be reduced to a set of facts.

He is the essence of modernity in that he constantly holds opposites in tension: knowing/doing, feeling/reason, dependence/freedom, experience/tradition. In this, his view of Theology was dynamic rather than static. He tried to lay out the task of Theology as the servant of the Church, where it is now. He tried to place religious belief in the cultural, social and economic setting of his day. He promoted contextual theology.

In this way Schleiermacher felt Theology should reflect the belief of a specific community of faith. In spite of his emphasis on religion as a feeling of absolute dependence, Schleiermacher was quite definitely not promoting Theology as the feelings of isolated individuals. What dogmatic theology does is to state, in systematic form, the doctrines prevalent in the Church at any one time.

The problem of Schleiermacher's day was the gulf between rationalism and orthodoxy. What is the problem of today?

Critics accuse Schleiermacher of trying to take religion out of the range of any criticism. It is a matter of an individual's private feeling therefore others have no right to criticize it. Did Schleiermacher cause Theology to focus on human potential and distract it from the contemplation of the reality, awesomeness and majesty of God?

Is religious feeling a reliable guide to truth?

# 10 John Henry Newman and Catholic Renewal

Continental Catholicism came out of the revolutionary period, in the late eighteenth to early nineteenth centuries, very changed. Wealth had now passed into the hands of the middle class laity. Freedom of worship, including the freedom to stay away from church, was now guaranteed. The Church had lost control of teaching.

Many people were upset by these attacks on the Church. They considered that a return to a strong papacy was the only way to protect the Church against the government. This policy of a strong papacy and centralized Vatican rule was known as 'ultramontanism'. It contrasted with 'erastianism', the pre-eminence of the State in church government.

In Britain the nineteenth century began with the Church of England as the state church in England, Ireland and Wales and the Church of Scotland established in Scotland. The century ended with the Church of Scotland divided, the Church of Ireland disestablished and the Church in Wales about to be. These changes were not introduced as an effort to diminish the Church. State interference had no hostile agenda here. Politicians did, however, see the need to place all citizens on an equal footing, in the religious sphere at least.

When introducing these changes in Britain, Parliament was responding to the need for change rather than being destructive. What is more, it was responding to the need for change which a self-satisfied, established Church should have realized and introduced without outside prompting; it did not. As the century progressed, British religious life and feeling became extremely energetic. The various existing church bodies exhibited astonishing internal dynamism, not to mention rivalry. In addition, because of Britain's colonial spread, that energy was felt almost everywhere in the world.

But this State interference with the structures of the Church caused a crisis of conscience among conservative churchmen. In this crisis of conscience, one of the more powerful religious movements of the nineteenth century found its initial thrust.

The Evangelical Movement had without any doubt been the most vital religious force in British religious life in the early part of the century. This theological tone was about to change. John Henry Newman would play a significant role in this shift of emphasis.

## Life (1801–1890)

John Henry Newman was born in London in 1801 and brought up in the Evangelical wing of the Church of England. While still an adolescent, he had a conversion experience, an accepted part of the Evangelical tradition. He began his studies at Oxford in 1817, where he was a member of Trinity College. He became a Fellow of Oriel College in 1822 and was ordained deacon in 1824.

Newman encountered quite different religious influences at Oxford. He was strongly influenced by Richard Whately (later Archbishop of Dublin) who was a colleague of his at Oriel, vigorously opposed to state control in church matters and also strongly anti-Evangelical. Hurrell Froude was a young and influential friend who admired the Roman Catholic Church; he also venerated the saints, believed in the Real Presence of Christ in the Eucharist and was fascinated by the medieval Church.

Newman was, in time, appointed Vicar of the University Church of St Mary the Virgin in Oxford. He therefore occupied a high-status position within Oxford church circles. He possessed a direct awareness of God and a deep conviction of divine guidance. To these he allied a strong, yet subtle, intellect.

Newman travelled quite extensively in the south of Europe in 1832–1833 during which he appears to have undergone some crisis, possibly involving both health and spirituality. He returned to Oxford, was immediately associated with what would become the Oxford Movement, and soon became one of its leaders. He was a master of flowing prose and widely considered to be a great literary stylist. His preaching strongly influenced many generations of undergraduates: 'He had,' said one, 'the sweetest voice I ever heard'.

Newman and his friends published the *Tracts for the Times* between 1834 and 1842. There were 90 in all and Newman wrote 24 of them. They were popular statements of the religious position adopted by the thinkers of the Oxford Movement, a Catholic party within the Church of England.

*Tract 90*, which interpreted the 39 Articles of the Church of England in such a way as to make them agree with the decrees of the (Roman Catholic) Council of Trent, caused uproar and Newman was silenced by the Bishop of Oxford. He was now beginning to have doubts about the claims of the Church of England to stand in complete continuity with the undivided, pre-Reformation, Western Latin Church. From 1841 he gradually withdrew from his position in Oxford. He resigned his living at St Mary's in September 1843 and preached, a few days later at Littlemore, his sermon on 'The parting of Friends'. He chose as his text, Psalm 104. 23, 'Man goeth forth unto his work and to his labour until the evening.' It was his last sermon as a clergyman of the Church of England. He had preached his very first sermon on that very same text. Newman was received into the Roman Catholic Church in October 1845.

Newman later published his *Essay on the Development of Christian Doctrine* in defence of his change of allegiance. This work was to puzzle those who were responsible for preparing him for ordination in Rome. He set up the order of the Oratorians of St Philip Neri in Birmingham in 1849 and between 1854 and 1858 lived in Dublin, Ireland.

University education had long been a problem in that country. The only third-level institution had been Dublin University, which was restricted to Anglicans. The government had, in 1845, set up three other third-level institutions, in Belfast, Galway and Cork, but had insisted they have no religious affiliation, following the model of the University of London. The Irish Roman Catholic bishops had objected strongly to these 'godless colleges' and had invited Newman to set up a Catholic University in Dublin. His thoughts on Christian education were detailed in his *The Idea of a University* published in 1852.

The *Rambler* was a Roman Catholic review set up to give voice to liberal Roman Catholic opinion in Britain. Newman was editor for a while, but an article he wrote setting out his views of the place of the laity in the Church was viewed with suspicion in Rome and Newman resigned. Newman was also held responsible for the critical review of a book by Cardinal Manning and the two fell out. Manning had been a friend and clerical colleague of Newman's in the Church of England; he too had converted to Catholicism, but his career there was more spectacular than Newman's. Finally, a dispute with Charles Kingsley led to Newman's writing *Apologia pro vita sua*, his spiritual autobiography, one of the religious classics of the nineteenth century.

For much of Newman's career as a Roman Catholic priest, he was regarded with suspicion by his own church authorities, and this must have been a great disappointment to him. Some authorities have suggested that the reason for this was that the Roman Catholic theological tradition was strongly dependent upon the Latin tradition of the church and the medieval schoolmen, Thomas Aquinas in particular. Newman, on the other hand had been steeped in the Church Fathers, who were mainly Greek and who had a subtly different temper of mind. However Newman was finally made a cardinal in 1879.

Since Newman's death there has been a gradual but positive appreciation of the power and subtlety of his mind, and of the authority of his spiritual insight. He played a role in the restoration of Roman Catholicism in England but also particularly in the growth of the Catholic tradition within the Church of England.

He was a highly disciplined, well-read and learned scholar, yet Newman's outlook was firmly based on the idea of Christianity as a religion of the heart and of the mind. He chose *cor ad cor loquitur* (heart speaks to heart) for his motto as a cardinal. He was always realistic and his preaching related to the practical lives of ordinary people. Prayer was not for him a duty but a privilege.

Even though his religion stressed the importance of personal commitment, Newman's discipline of prayer and meditation centred on the communal worship of the church within the framework of the liturgical year.

He was well read not only in the early Greek Fathers but also in the Anglican Caroline Divines (High Church theologians of the seventeenth century). From both of these sources he was acquainted with the spirituality of the Eastern Church. He had a deep sense of the presence of God with Christians as they learned to pray, to intercede for others and to become aware of the needs of others and are attentive to their moral responsibilities.

### Timeline

1791 Death of Charles Wesley

1793 Execution of Louis XVI of France

1800 Union of Ireland with Great Britain

1801 Birth of John Henry Newman

1807 Wordsworth's *Ode on Intimations of Immortality*

1815 Defeat of Napoleon at the Battle of Waterloo

1819 Singapore comes under British administration

1829 Stephenson's steam engine

1833 Newman's *The Arians of the Fourth Century*

1834–1842 Newman's *Parochial and Plain Sermons*

1837 Queen Victoria comes to the throne in England
Chopin's *Preludes*

1841 Newman publishes *Tract 90*

1842 Hong Kong under British administration

1845 First edition of Newman's *Essay on the Development of Christian Doctrine*

1848 Insurrections in many European countries

1851 First Universal Exhibition in the Crystal Palace in London

1852 Newman's *The Idea of a University*

1854–1855 Crimean War

1857–1858 India comes under British administration

1859 Darwin's *The Origin of Species*

1861–1865 Civil War in the United States

1864 First Workers' International in London
Newman's *Apologia pro vita sua*

1867 First book of Marx's *Das Kapital*

1870 Vatican Council proclaims the doctrine of Papal Infallibility
Newman's *A Grammar of Assent*

1890 London's first underground tube line opened
Death of Newman

1896 Discovery of uranium

## Thought

Newman's major academic work, The *Arians of the Fourth Century*, was published in 1833. This work was a systematic study of the Church Fathers. Newman's sermons in St Mary's Church were published under the title *Parochial and Plain Sermons*, in 1834. This book was widely known beyond Oxford and is said to have had a profound influence on the religious life of England. Once again the influence of the Church Fathers is evident.

### *The Oxford Movement*

The Church of England was an established, that is to say it was a state church. While governed by bishops it was subject to Parliament. The government of the day could regulate it. The Oxford Movement arose out of a feeling that the mission of the Church was divine; all churchmen owed a duty to a higher authority than government, parliament or even the king. The immediate cause of the protest was a proposal to restrict the number of Irish bishops and, given the situation of the Irish Church, the proposal was not unreasonable.

John Keble (1792–1866), in an Assize sermon, denounced this move as National Apostasy, for the Church was not the creation of the State but of a higher authority. It was a condemnation that caught the mood of the times and soon Anglican clergymen everywhere were being called upon to 'magnify their office'; they were, after all, the successors of the Apostles, not civil servants.

The vehicle Keble, Pusey, Williams and Newman used to spread their views was a series of tracts – articles which were distributed all over the land, often by volunteers. The tracts were scholarly, but were nevertheless easily understood.

The services of the Church of England, which had, on the whole, been dull, bald and pedestrian, gradually became more formal, more solemn and stately. There was more colour and more movement; there was greater emphasis upon symbol and upon sacramental worship. There was also bitterness and small-minded backbiting. The Anglo-Catholic school scorned people of Evangelical outlook. Relations with the Free

Churches, which many Evangelical clergy had been encouraging, were severely damaged.

However, at the same time as the Oxford Movement was developing, another movement of quite different temper was making its presence felt. This was the 'Broad Church', a tendency to interpret the church's formularies in a liberal, rather than a literal fashion. Thus many of this Broad Church school rejected the Virgin Birth, denied eternal punishment, welcomed Biblical criticism, and some went as far as proclaiming that the state church should welcome all Dissenters, nation and church becoming virtually synonymous. Evangelicals, Broad Church and Anglo-Catholics all tended to dislike each other with equal energy.

## Tracts for the Times

Many controversial subjects were supported in the *Tracts for the Times.* The Holy Catholic Church was promoted as the only way to eternal life. They opposed any alteration in the *Book of Common Prayer*, seeing the Prayer Book liturgy as in continuity with traditional, pre-Reformation, Catholic worship. The Prayer Book urged Fridays as days of fasting and this practice was encouraged by the *Tracts.* The apostolic succession was taught and the bishop of Rome was described as having a primacy of dignity in the Church. He was not however entitled to interfere in the dioceses of other bishops. The *Tracts* energetically promoted what they believed were the practices and beliefs of the Apostles and the early church.

The *Tracts* declared the Church of England to be a true branch of the One, Holy, Catholic and Apostolic Church founded by Christ. Non-conformists were described as teaching only part of the apostolic truth, and the Roman Catholic Church, as teaching more than the sum of catholic truth. The *Tracts* wished to reintroduce to the Church of England practices which were required by the rubrics but which had been neglected as a consequence of both the Puritan revolution and the laxity of the eighteenth century.

The *Tracts* encouraged the daily recitation of Morning and Evening Prayer and the frequent celebration of the Eucharist. They taught Baptismal regeneration: both baptism and faith were necessary for salvation.

They supported the Apostles', Nicene and Athanasian Creeds as compelling statements of Catholic truth. They admitted that some of the doctrines taught in them were not to be found in Scripture, but instead were indirectly present in the Bible.

**Fathers** A restricted group of early church writers whose influence on doctrine was vital.
**Rubrics** Instructions concerning the conduct of church services, usually printed in red.
**Creed** A statement of what one believes. In particular the Apostles', Nicene and Athanasian Creeds which have high status amongst almost all Christian churches.

The *Tracts* caused much excitement and comment. They gradually became more scholarly. They promoted a vision of the Church of England directed by studious and learned men, living simply and working hard. The views promoted in the *Tracts* were complemented by Newman's preaching in St Mary's, where he attracted large congregations from all over the university.

The *Tracts*, however, promoted an elitist, 'Oxbridge' view of the Church. The outlook of the Tractarians has been criticized as appealing to a small intellectual class but largely ignoring contemporary reality – the growing horror of the huge industrial cities, their slums, the Irish famine and other social problems. If this criticism could be directed at the first generation of Tractarians, it was one to which a second generation responded with energy and verve.

The *Tracts for the Times* had an influence beyond the time of their writers and the Anglo-Catholic Movement gradually took off. A theological college was soon opened to train clergy in Tractarian principles. But not everybody supported them. Many people throughout 'Protestant' England were offended by calls to fasting, frequent communion, a high view of the priesthood and other 'Romish' tendencies.

Nevertheless the Anglo-Catholic movement was to result in practices now considered normal: candles on the altar, choirs wearing surplices, intoned services, crucifixes in church, the use of Eucharistic vestments and preaching in a surplice rather than in a black gown. In addition there was a rapid increase in the number of monastic communities. In time, attention also focused on ministry to the underprivileged and in the slums of the industrialized cities.

## *The* Via Media

The early Tracts held out a view of the Church of England as both Catholic and Reformed. This was a middle way (*via media*) between what they saw as the abuses which had grown up in Rome and the errors of the extreme pruning which had been forced by seventeenth century Puritanism. This minimalism had continued to be a feature of the Dissenters' outlook and worship and was reinforced by Methodism.

The *via media* was a view which was particularly promoted by the early Newman but had been suggested by earlier theological thinkers. It has undertones of the well-read clergyman, temperate in habit and speech, living a simple life and devoted to his parishioners. It was the essence of 'moderation in all things'.

## Tract 90

This tract, the last of the *Tracts for the Times*, was written in 1841 by John Henry Newman. It caused a major controversy and was responsible for bringing the publication of the *Tracts* to an end. The Thirty-nine Articles of the Church of England were an attempt by the Church of England to regulate its doctrinal position with respect to the theological controversies of the sixteenth century. They were concerned to counter both Roman Catholic and Calvinist viewpoints. In *Tract 90* Newman declared that the Articles did not contradict the Catholic faith – that they could be read in a Catholic manner.

The articles did not condemn Catholic faith and doctrine; they condemned their abuse by Rome. But the tract raised a storm as it appeared to make possible the invocation of saints, purgatory, the use of images and other practices traditionally rejected by moderate, undemonstrative, English churchgoers.

Newman stated that his aim was to show that while the *Book of Common Prayer* was readily admitted to be of Catholic origin the

Thirty-nine Articles were the product of an un-Catholic age but were not un-Catholic. They could be accepted by those who aim at being Catholic in heart and doctrine. Let us look at some of the ideas in this tract.

The section do not declare that Scripture is the sole rule of faith. It had always been the case that Scripture, along with the decisions of the first four General Councils and the tradition of the Church together form the Rule of Faith.

With regard to purgatory, pardons, images, relics and invocation of the saints, only the 'Romish' doctrine is condemned; the practice of the early church is not condemned. Furthermore the doctrines condemned are those widely in vogue before the reforms of the Council of Trent. Newman was at pains to stress that he was not recommending doctrines not condemned under this article. His aim was to make clear what the article did not condemn and that such practices could be held as matters of private belief. In addition he wished to support the Christian liberty of the believer where the Church had not restricted it.

Similarly with the doctrine of transubstantiation, Newman held that the Articles did not oppose every kind of change, nor did it seek to tie down the meaning of the word 'substance'. What the Articles opposed were certain exaggerated claims of material change common at the time the Articles were written.

**Doctrine** A set of principles presented for belief by a religious group: the teachings of a church.
**Invocation of saints** is the practice of requesting saints to pray to God for the living. The saints are holy and therefore close to God but also understand humans because they are human.
**Purgatory** A state of purification, following death, before being admitted to heaven.
**Pardons** Here a form of Indulgence by which sins are forgiven following the payment of money to a church cause.
**Relics** Can refer to both the bodily remains of saintly individuals as well as their remaining possessions. They were honoured as having served as temples of the Holy Spirit.

**Transubstantiation** The official Roman Catholic doctrine of Eucharistic change. The substance of the bread and wine changes to become the substance of the body and blood of Christ, even though there is no change in outward appearance.
**Mass** Word commonly used in the Roman Catholic and High Church Anglican traditions for the celebration of the Eucharist.
**Limbo** The opinion, now largely abandoned, that the unbaptized, particularly children who died before they could be baptized, are excluded from heaven, but not kept in a place of torment.

The section on masses was not written to condemn the mass. Rather it condemned exaggerated errors about it. In particular the article condemned false teaching about the benefits of multiplying masses. This referred to a common superstition that the more masses were said for an intention, the greater the hope of that prayer being answered. Moreover, the article condemned any attempt to see the mass as independent of the sacrifice of the Cross. Thirdly, the article condemned using the mass as a means of increasing a priest's earnings.

At that time, the common view was that since the Articles were drawn up by Protestants, and were done so to establish Protestant teaching, the Articles should only be interpreted in a Protestant manner. Newman, however, held that it was his duty to take reformed confessions of faith in the most Catholic sense they allowed. When he did this he brought them into harmony with the Prayer Book. He reminded his readers that, as clergymen, they had given assent to both.

He was interpreting the Articles in a literal and grammatical sense and this was the recommendation of the Declaration prefixed to the Articles. Finally, the Articles were framed in such a way as to include moderate reformers and, at the time, that included Catholics; so Newman rejected the attempts then being made to use the Articles to exclude Catholics.

*Tract 90* created a storm of controversy. Its apparent logical hair-splitting drew accusations of 'jesuitry'. The Heads of Oxford colleges condemned it, questions were asked in Parliament. Finally, the Bishop of Oxford intervened and requested that no more *Tracts* be published. Newman and his friends had long preached the Apostolic Succession and the authority of the Church; they were now caught by the logic of their own position and had to submit to ecclesiastical authority.

### *Newman's* An Essay on the Development of Christian Doctrine

The development of Christian doctrine is a term used by Newman to give an idea of the way statements of Christian doctrine inevitably become more detailed and precise over time. The central principle is that later statements of doctrine must remain consistent with earlier statements. The later statement must be contained in germ in the earlier, must be a development of it and not a contradiction of it. The idea was put forward in Newman's book *An Essay on the Development of Christian Doctrine* and was particularly used by him to defend Roman Catholic teachings from attack by thinkers influenced by the Reformation.

Protestant theologians had often denounced Roman Catholic doctrines as developments or corruptions of pure, original, scriptural, Christian teaching. Among such teachings, Newman's opponents numbered devotion to the Blessed Virgin Mary, the invocation and intercession of the saints, and teachings on purgatory and limbo.

Newman objected that Protestants also held doctrines which, while they were classical, orthodox theology, were in fact developments. He cited teachings about the Trinity and the divine and human natures of Christ. He argued that they arose because of the slow, careful and mature reflection of reason on Christian belief, drawing out consequences which had not been obvious at first.

Newman wrote his *Essay on Development* to express three convictions about the Roman Catholic Church: first, that Rome was the legitimate inheritor of the church of the Apostles and of the early Fathers; secondly, that Rome stood in a direct and valid line of descent from the primitive church and, thirdly, that Anglican and Protestant objections to that claim had no basis.

Newman viewed the *Essay on Development* as a negative book, standing against an earlier position, written to confront a contrary viewpoint. It is the work of Newman the controversialist as opposed to Newman the creative theologian. He revised it massively. It was first published in 1845, and he did not produce a final version until 1878.

## *Newman's* Grammar of Assent

This work contains Newman's most mature reflections and is especially known for the way Newman makes a distinction between notional and real assent. Notional assent comes when we apprehend propositions as notions or abstractions. The mind contemplates its own creations instead of things. Real assent comes when the mind is directed to things, represented by the impressions they have made upon the imagination. Real assent has power and conviction in a way that notional assent cannot produce.

The book analyses the role of conscience in our knowledge of God and how we use the 'illative' sense. The illative sense is our ability to judge from given facts as we move towards religious certainty. When we use the illative sense, however, we use processes outside the limits of strict logic. Assent to religious truth comes about through the promptings of grace. The will allows the intellect to agree to faith and allows the whole person to submit to God.

Knowledge in the religious sphere comes through personal participation, involvement and input. The truths of religion will become obvious to those who commit their whole existence to it but will always be difficult for those who continue to judge it neutrally from the outside.

In his *Grammar of Assent* Newman wants to show how reasonable it is to profess Christian faith. He wants to explain how, in all spheres of knowledge, the human mind moves from an act of inference to an act of assent. The conditional acceptance of a proposition is an act of inference; the unconditional acceptance of a proposition is an act of assent.

Newman lived at a period when philosophers were coming to believe that propositions concerning knowledge and the operation of logical operations upon them could be seen in terms of a 'calculation' and that logicians would soon be able to construct a 'universal language'.

Newman believed that such a position was far too reductionist. It tried to limit what could be said and to invalidate a whole range of subjects which are subjects of normal human communication. He held that the human spirit was capable of, and should give itself to, great and wide sweeps of thought.

All human beings acquire and develop knowledge by means of inference and assent, and Newman believed that, if developed, such operations could, and should, lead to spiritual growth and advantage. He did not wish to abolish the use of rules and logic. He believed that knowledge and human communication should not be reduced to the mere application of logical rules upon given propositions in restricted circumstances. He thought the human mind capable of great nuance and that its mental capacity and subtlety were both given by God.

The rules of logic are the tools which God has given to human beings in order that they may come to a clear understanding of reality. But Newman saw that the movement of the human mind from inference to assent is not a simple process. It involves two steps. In the first phase it operates logically and mechanically. But in the second phase, it introduces a subjective element which gives to each individual's thought process a personal flavour.

This intimate core cannot be tied down by linguistic description. Here the mind seeks to reach out, to grasp, in its own way, the truth being suggested by the 'accumulation of probabilities' which had been offered by the first, more mechanistic, phase.

Proof is thus defined as the point where converging probabilities meet and where adverse explanations and difficulties are cleared away. The experienced mind becomes convinced that certain conclusions are inevitable, although it has not yet come to the stage of proof. Newman referred to this spontaneous way of reasoning as the 'illative sense'.

Individuals move from inference to assent using a logical process that is nourished by a personal ability to discover truth. In describing how this illative sense works, Newman saw it as operating in a manner parallel to the way conscience works as we seek to discover good. It is only because we possess this illative sense that we are capable of coming to an apprehension of truth in matters of religious faith.

Newman himself saw that the weakness of his work was the lack of any test for a 'false certitude'.

## *Newman's* The Idea of a University

Shortly after arriving in Dublin to set up the Catholic University in that city, Newman gave a series of public lectures, later published as a book, *The Idea of a University*. This book expressed his thoughts on what the university was and what it should set out to achieve. It was a statement of what the defining principles and general aims of the university should be; it was not a statement of its courses and curriculum.

A university is a place where all may meet and exchange ideas. It is there that many different people, from different backgrounds and countries, meet to discuss, share and exchange many forms of knowledge and discipline. Knowledge may be mined from books, but the tone, the spirit, the life and the colour can only be experienced, caught and in-breathed where people interrelate and co-operate. To learn, one needs interaction and debate.

The Church founds a university for the spiritual welfare of its members, to enhance their usefulness and their religious influence. It wants them to be better able to live their lives and do their work, turning them into better, and more intelligent, more capable, more active members of society. Its aim is the intellectual education of the whole personality. The university seeks to develop intellect, to give it superior power and versatility, to equip it with greater command over its own strength and to enhance its judgement.

The purpose of a university, then, is to prepare good members of society. This is to be achieved by schooling in the art of social life. Genius and heroism are not produced by narrowly focussed training. The function of the university is not to train for any particular profession, be it scientist, economist or engineer.

The purpose of university education is to raise the intellectual tone of society, to improve the national taste and to cultivate the public mind generally. It is to raise intellectual and moral standards. It allows individuals to have a certain and well prepared view of their opinions and judgements. These should be developed in deep concern for truth. University education also gives the skills to assert and defend them publicly.

The university naturally sets out to teach universal knowledge, of which Theology is as important as any other. This is, of course, a reference to the polemics of the day, since the government wished to set up non-religious universities. Newman disagreed. He considered that a university without history, ethics or reason would involve a shrinking of universal knowledge and offer a deficient discipline. Therefore the considerations of Theology, which were handed down by testimony, inferred by reason and which convince us by metaphysical necessity, would be as necessary as any other discipline.

If God is more than nature, Theology claims a place among the sciences. Truth, Newman held, was the result of mental processes bearing upon the same subject matter viewed under different aspects. The mind must do more than just concentrate on an extremely reduced set of data. It must seek a wider understanding, which is the result of the interaction of many forms of discipline upon each other.

## Appraisal

During the eighteenth and nineteenth centuries the Roman Catholic Church encountered conditions, particularly in Europe, which did not make for a great deal of calm theological reflection. The Protestant Churches, particularly those in Northern Europe, did not always meet the same degree of violent opposition, yet they were placed on the defensive by the challenges of the intellectual and political climates of the day. The consequence was that polemical theology, rather than constructive theology, was often the flavour of the day. That flavour certainly may be found in Newman, and he was a dogged and subtle controversialist but it would be unfair to limit him with such an assessment.

The Roman Catholic tradition had persistently emphasized the constancy of the Catholic position, had promoted authoritative pronouncements and tightly supervised all theological work. Theologians had been nudged towards a habit of repetition rather than of originality. This trend was strong during the conservative First Vatican Council. In addition Pope Leo XIII gave the works of Thomas Aquinas special status, making his thought normative for all orthodox Catholic thinkers. This tendency was defensive and unadventurous.

Nevertheless signs of renewal can be discerned at this time, and a thinker such as Newman, who saw the tradition as the living, vibrant, renewing voice of the Church, is a herald of future development. Here two ideas of Newman's have been richly productive – his ideas on the development of doctrine coupled with his doctrine of 'reserve' – whatever we can come to know of God, there is always more to be known.

Newman may not have been a versatile and inventive theologian, but he was a sensitive psychological analyst and a sharply aware moral thinker. He had telling insights into the nature of religious faith and the drives that produced it.

Newman thought and wrote under the influence of many of the pressures that we have described as creating the contexts of modern theology. Yet his approach was still a cautious one; his search was still for authentic, authoritative, divinely guaranteed pronouncements. He had a foot in the old world and a foot in the new.

As can be seen, Newman was not a doctrinal innovator. His romantic sensibility gave him also a certain path to follow. His call was to embrace a certain type of church community and church practice. But the temper of his mind was conservative rather than liberal. He promoted a certain type of discourse against the trends of his time. He was concerned with making his theological stand among the controversies of his day, in mid-to-late nineteenth-century Britain. Newman did his theology contextually. Where others had embraced modernity, Newman demurred, but with nuance.

To what extent is theological fashion the form of discourse that is most capable of being heard in its setting?

# 11 Karl Barth and a Theology of the Word

Barth was born into the era of Liberal Theology, which is judged to have started with the publication in 1799 of Schleiermacher's *On Religion: Speeches to Its Cultured Despisers*. It ended when Barth's *Commentary on Romans*, an interpretation of St Paul's great letter, was published in 1919. Barth lived through some of the most distressing years of European history, experiencing both World Wars.

## Life (1886–1968)

Karl Barth was born in Basel in Switzerland, the son of a teacher of New Testament Theology. When he was two, his father moved to a prestigious post at the University of Berne. The home background was theologically conservative and strict. Barth studied at the Universities of Berne, Berlin, Tübingen and Marbourg. He had decided to become a theologian at an early age, in order to clarify his thoughts on religious matters. In his early years he adopted a liberal position, served for a brief time as a pastor in the Jura region and worked for a short period in publishing. At the age of 25 he took up a pastoral post at Geneva, where he met his wife, Nelly.

Two years later he started a ten-year stint of pastoral work in the border region between Switzerland and Germany. He stayed here during the period of the First World War. He quickly came to the conclusion that Liberal Theology was of little use in his weekly task of preaching to the working-class people of his village. He decided to undertake a painstaking study of the Bible. Here he discovered not Theology but 'Word of God'. He was to continue to be a fervent supporter of the verbal inspiration of Scripture.

**Transcendence** Above, independent of, surpassing the material universe.
**Word (The)** is a translation of the Greek word *Logos*, meaning word or reason. It was seen in the Old Testament and in Greek thought as referring to the universal reason which ordered everything in the cosmos. In Christianity it refers to the second person of the Trinity. Jesus was identified as The Word.

It was during that village pastorate that he wrote his famous *Commentary on Romans* which attracted a wide readership, particularly in German-speaking Protestant circles. Barth was conscious of the profound shadow of pessimism which continued to hang over Europe following the Great War. His aim was to write in full awareness of that cultural pessimism and furthermore to take complete account of the pastoral needs he encountered. These led him to a fundamental questioning of the established trends of academic theology. His readers felt that his message had creativity, power and authenticity.

In 1921 Barth took up a professorship in Göttingen, later moving to Münster, arriving in Bonn in 1930. He soon came into conflict with the supporters of Liberal Theology. Barth always maintained that God's Word was in greatest danger when it was made accepted and harmless as just another expression of human culture. He was soon to throw in his lot with the 'Confessing Church'. He was a Swiss citizen, so he had freedoms denied Germans.

Hitler had come to power in 1933 and there was immediate confrontation between the Nazi regime and the Lutheran Church. The 'German Christian Church' was a movement sponsored by the Nazis. It tried to promote a blend of Nazi ideology and Christian doctrine.

This movement of Nazi sympathizers soon won majorities at church elections. They were opposed by the 'Confessing Church' movement. This opposition movement set up its own authorities and resisted all attempts to make the Evangelical Church a tool of Nazi rule. Both clergy and laity were persecuted and open opposition ceased on the outbreak of the Second World War. They called themselves the 'Confessing Church' to express their sense of being a church of confessors for the faith.

Barth was actively involved in drawing up many of the doctrinal statements of the Confessing Church. During the early stages of the struggle he held that Nazi thought was a purely political matter, of no concern to the Christian as long as the Christian's freedom to proclaim the gospel was maintained. He later hardened his position to outright condemnation of Nazism. He refused to take an oath of allegiance to Hitler and was deprived of his chair. He returned to Switzerland in 1935, taking up a chair of Theology at Basle, where he remained until he retired in 1962.

His central thought was the transcendence and supremacy of God. During the course of Christian history, every time theologians had shifted their attention from that vital and demanding fact, they had fallen into error. They had trusted human reason in all its worthlessness. Barth held the sixteenth-century Reformers to be the most genuine exponents of the prophetic teaching of the Bible. He placed a special emphasis on the notion of confrontation between God and humanity. His thought was sometimes referred to as 'theology of crisis' or 'dialectical theology'.

He condemned all religion founded on experience, distrusted mysticism and had little sympathy with positive attitudes to science, art and contemporary culture. All human cultural attainments are established in sin. He condemned all thought that issued from the Scholastics, Schleiermacher (1768–1834) or Hegel (1770–1831) but was deeply influenced by both Kierkegaard (1813–1855) and Dostoevsky (1821–1881). God's only revelation of divine being was in Jesus Christ. The only authentic witness to that core fact was the Word of God.

In 1927 he started writing a vast systematic work of Theology and after several false starts the first volume of his *Church Dogmatics* was published in 1932. He would continue to work on this for the remainder of his life. The thirteenth volume was published in 1967, the year before he died. The work was never finished. It is a vast and ambitious piece of dogmatic teaching.

After the war his attitude to Communism was roughly similar to his early attitude towards Nazism: the Church must be detached from politics and cannot in advance adopt the view that Communism is necessarily evil. He attended the Second Vatican Council (1962–1965) as an observer. For the remainder of his life he would be a sharply critical figure in Protestant Church circles, often adopting confrontational and surprising viewpoints. Towards the end of his life his health deteriorated, and he was the butt of increasingly harsh criticism from all points of the theological spectrum.

### Timeline

1884 Mark Twain's *The Adventures of Huckleberry Finn*
Berlin international conference on Africa: the 'Scramble for Africa'
1886 Birth of Karl Barth

1889 The Second Workers' International
1896 Marconi's wireless telegraphy
1914–1918 First World War
1917 The Russian Revolution
1919 Bertrand Russell's *Introduction to Mathematical Philosophy*
Barth's *Commentary on Romans*
1921 Ludwig Wittgenstein's *Tractatus Logico Philosophicus*
1931 Economic crisis reaches Europe
First volume of Barth's *Church Dogmatics*
1933 Hitler becomes German Chancellor; Roosevelt becomes President of the United States
1934 Mao Zedong leads the Long March
1937 Stalinist purges in the Soviet Union
1939–1945 Second World War
1945 Atom bombs dropped on Hiroshima and Nagasaki
Founding of the United Nations
1947 Marshall Plan
1948 Berlin blockade
First Arab–Israeli War
1949 Simone de Beauvoir's *The Second Sex*
1950–1953 Korean War
1953 Death of Stalin; discovery of the structure of DNA
1958 Election of Pope John XXIII
1960s Decolonization in Africa and Asia
1962–1965 Second Vatican Council
1967 Last volume of Barth's unfinished *Church Dogmatics*
1968 Death of Karl Barth

## Thought

### *Liberal Theology*

The term 'Liberal' usually means freedom from bias or intolerance and readiness to adopt new ideas. It suggests openness to reform. Within Protestant circles it developed into an anti-dogmatic way of holding the Christian faith; it had a strong humanitarian emphasis. Liberals felt that theology needed to be restated in the light of up-to-date scientific knowledge; so theological liberalism was dedicated to bridging the gap between Christian faith and contemporary culture.

Some doctrines were abandoned; original sin is a case in point. Others were reinterpreted in the light of current understanding. Liberalism found it difficult to base faith solely on Scripture and sought to secure it more solidly in common human experience. Liberalism was an expression of optimism in the human future.

Liberals had a particular interest in ethical thought. Outstanding Liberal theologians were Schleiermacher, Ritschl and Paul Tillich. Critics like Barth and Reinhold Niebuhr believed their optimism to have been permanently shattered by the carnage of the First World War.

### *Neo-Orthodoxy*

The horrors of The First World War produced deep disillusion in many individuals who believed in progress. Schleiermacher and Liberal Theology, in general, were accused of making religion human-centred rather than God-centred. Karl Barth and writers following him emphasized the 'otherness' of God, believing that Theology could thus escape from the dead end where Liberal Theology seemed to be stuck.

The clarion call that issued from Barth's works stresses the self-revelation of God in Jesus Christ through the Bible.

Barth's repetition of themes, which had already been given clear voice by writers of the Protestant Reformation, was given a 'dialectical' structure. Barth talked of a 'dialectic between time and eternity' and of a 'dialectic between God and humanity'. He was here stressing the discontinuity between us and God. Barth appeared to be entering into dialogue with the writers of reformed orthodoxy (Luther and Calvin), so his outlook was termed 'Neo-Orthodox'.

Barth's central point was that Christian Theology must be a 'Theology of the Word of God'. Theology was not a response to a human predicament or situation. The believer's eyes must be constantly fixed on Jesus Christ as the foundation of the Church.

**Dogma** A system of religious teaching authoritatively considered to be absolute truth.
**Humanitarian** The belief that all humans have a moral duty to work for the continued improvement and well-being of humanity.
**Dialectic** Working out contradictions through the interplay of opposing ideas.
**Orthodox** Adhering to accepted, established religious faith.
**Doctrinaire** Obstinately attached to Church doctrines.

## *The* Commentary on Romans

Barth had grown up in a religious and intellectual tradition where the theme of the Bible was human religion, religious morality and, perhaps, the hidden hope that humans might in some way become immortal, possessing a share of divinity. He came to see the theme of the Bible as the divine nature of God, the totally unique quality of the power, initiative and being of God.

He first boldly expressed such an outlook in his *Commentary on Romans*. His readers were shocked by his doctrinaire tone and by his total indifference to the questions posed by Biblical criticism.

The great theme of St Paul's *Letter to the Romans* is the righteousness of God. We, through faith, as a gift of grace, are given a share in that righteousness. We do not, however, in any way merit such treatment.

Barth wanted to turn Theology on its head. Up to now it had moved from the human to the divine. He wanted it to move from the divine to the human. Human religious thought, feeling and outlook cannot bring us to knowledge of God. Barth wanted to speak of God as totally distinct from everything that had been created.

What Barth saw was not the humanity of God, but the *deity* of God, the distance of God and the mystery of God. He referred to this as the 'pathos of distance'. It included the gap between revelation and culture, between time and eternity: God beyond reason and spirituality. All Theology must start with the reality of God.

'Righteousness' was not human righteousness but the righteousness of God. 'Faith' was not the human response of faith but God's faithfulness to his intentions and undertakings. If humans find it at all possible to know God, it has nothing to do with their capabilities; it is, in fact, the miracle of grace. All human possibilities, history, religion, ethics, ideas and relations must be made subordinate to the sovereignty of God. That is the only sure and certain reality. The communication between the two depends upon, and only upon, the divine decision.

Barth appears to have grounded his thoughts on revelation in what he called the 'infinite qualitative distinction'. God and humans are not in a relationship, either naturally or through religion. God is wholly other. God can only be known through God, if indeed God is knowable at all. The only knowledge of God open to us is God's knowledge of us. We can merely accept that divine knowledge. God remains hidden in divine revelation. God does not become the object of human knowledge in a way that can be expressed in propositions.

Revelation can only be the self-disclosure of God and that revelation is located in the person and works of Jesus Christ. Since the death and resurrection of Jesus, that revelation is located in a past event, but its importance persists as time continues and events unfold. The Christ Barth is thinking about is not the Jesus who walked and talked on earth. The Christ Barth is referring to is a Christ reachable only by faith and expressed in the confessions of faith and in Christian proclamation.

### *The Word of God*

The only source for Christian Theology that Barth would allow was God's Word. This Word comes in three ways. In the first place, it comes through Jesus Christ. The history of God's people up to and including the death and resurrection of Jesus are the core of the gospel. Secondly, God's Word comes in Scripture. Scripture is the most important witness to God's revelation to humanity.

Thirdly, God's Word comes in the proclamation of the gospel. By this Barth understood the Church's proclamation. It may be the act of an individual in any one place; but if it is in accordance with the Church's mission, it is part of the whole Church's proclamation of the gospel. Jesus Christ is the essence of God's Word. Bible and communication of the message are Word in so far as God uses them to reveal Jesus Christ.

God's Word is not a hidden message waiting to be revealed. God's Word has the status *of event* or *happening*. The Bible is God's Word. This is not so because believers believe it to be so or because scholarly examination has declared it to be genuine. The Bible is God's Word because *God* repeatedly uses it to bring faith in Jesus Christ into being.

The Church is under the authority of the Bible and must be obedient to it because the only greater authority is Jesus himself.

In his writings Barth seems to have treated the Bible as divinely inspired.

**Resurrection** is the theological teaching that God would raise up each individual after death to stand in the divine presence and be judged fit for the company of heaven (or not). The early Christians believed that the experiences they had of the presence of Jesus after his death were proof of resurrection teaching and a promise of such a hope and destiny for all committed to Jesus.

**Proclamation** The 'telling out', the publicizing of the Christian Good News.

**Natural Theology** The notion that genuine knowledge of God can be achieved by rational thought, without appeal to Christian revelation.

### *The Barth–Brunner controversy*

Barth violently rejected the idea that it is possible to construct a Natural Theology. In 1934, Barth's friend, Emil Brunner, published a book called *Nature and Grace* in which he maintained that the task for the theologians of their time was to find a way back to 'a legitimate Natural Theology'. His starting point was that humans are created in the image of God. We may be sinful, but we still have the capacity to discern God. We find God in nature and in the events of history; we are capable of recognizing that we are guilty before God. This allows divine revelation and human nature to make contact with each other.

Barth's stinging reply, which ended their friendship, was entitled *Nein!* (No!). Brunner, he claimed, seemed to suggest that God needed human help to become known, that we co-operate with God in the act of revelation. The only point of contact between the human and the divine was the result of divine action, not an inbuilt feature of human nature.

A recurring thorny problem in Protestant thought is the position of the state in the divine order. St Paul had instructed us to pray for rulers because 'the authorities that exist have been established by God' (Rom. 13.1). This was frequently understood as meaning that the State was part of the divine ordering of affairs, and the State often played a role in the governance of the Church. Barth was, obviously, rejecting the idea that, in Germany, Hitler was part of the divine ordering of affairs. There is no doubt, however, that there was more at stake than that.

Barth was starting from the Word of God. Brunner was starting from anthropology, a view of what it means to be human. Barth gave much more importance to God, the object of faith, than he did to the act of faith, the believer's acceptance and assent. Brunner wished to understand how believers in their act of faith may come into a relationship with God. Barth seemed to keep the two at a distance.

### *Barth's theological method*

Barth's theological outlook was shaped by a negative thrust and a positive thrust. The negative drive centred on his rejection of Natural Theology. Reason had undermined the gospel in all its guises throughout history: Roman Catholic Natural Theology, Liberal Protestant Theology, even the contemporary German Lutheran dalliance with Nazism.

The positive drive came from God's Word. It was only possible to know God's Word because of God's Word and there was no other way. Human beings are unable to know God through nature, reason or history. But God, in an act of sovereign freedom and grace, has revealed himself in history. It has come about through a single event: the event of Jesus Christ. Faith in Jesus Christ, as the authentic revelation of God, is self-authenticating. Faith is a gift; there is no further discussion.

Barth wrote a study of the medieval thinker Anselm of Canterbury (1033–1109). Published in 1931, its title, *Fides quaerens intellectum* (faith seeking understanding), was of course a quotation of Anselm's own famous saying, and many see this text as a useful insight into Barth's theological method. Barth interpreted Anselm as a devout man trying to bring understanding to the gift of faith: faith first, understanding later.

Anselm's lesson to us is that all theology must be done in the context of prayer and obedience. Therefore theology cannot be neutral, detached analysis; it must be the surrender of the intellect to God's self-revelation. There must be a life of faith before there can be truthful Theology. Human reason must never be set against the written testimony of the Bible, against the revealed object of faith who is Jesus Christ.

### *A Christocentric and Trinitarian Theology*

The starting point for all of Barth's theological thought is the Jesus Christ event. No matter what the theological issue, he appears to be saying, 'How can I understand this matter in the light of God's act in Jesus Christ?' We have stressed over and over again that, for Barth, Jesus Christ is the one and only self-revelation of God. Jesus is the Word of God. If Jesus is the one whom faith says he is, then he must, in some way, be identical with God himself, and not merely an agent or messenger. Behind the truth of this revelation in Christ there lies the prospect of God as Trinity.

So when he was asked, 'Who is this self-revealing God?' Barth could only answer, 'God as Trinity'. That is to say, God is as follows:

- the God who reveals
- the revelatory event itself
- the effect it has on human beings.

God's revelation has taken place so Barth then asks, 'What must be true for this to have been possible?' 'What does the fact of God tell us about the nature of God?' Humanity, separated from God by sin, cannot hear the Word of God unaided. So God must work to allow humanity to hear it. God is the one who reveals. What does God reveal? God reveals God. How does God reveal God? God reveals God through the work of God.

The doctrine of the Trinity is what distinguishes Christian teaching about God and revelation from all other theories about God and all other possibilities of revelation. God as Father, Son and Holy Spirit are the divine ways of being God that eternally subsist within God in total unity. Yet it is only because of God as Trinity that we can come to awareness of God's revelation in and through Jesus and of God's presence within the life of the Church and of believers.

Barth's thoughts on the Trinity are the launching pad from which he starts his *Church Dogmatics*. Before Barth's work, the doctrine of the Trinity had been neglected for some centuries.

### *Barth's thoughts on election*

In Theology the term 'election' indicates an act of God's will: God chooses some in preference to others. In the New Testament the elect are the small number chosen by God to do the divine will and to remain faithful to God. It is often used as another word for predestination.

Barth saw the cross of Jesus as the supreme event of history. There Jesus, the Son of God, opens himself to carry the burden of the divine wrath which sinful humanity deserves. Jesus is at once the only elect and damned human being. All other human beings are represented by him and included in him. All human beings should be rejected by God, have brought upon themselves the anger of God and must die the death which God has decreed. But because God loves humanity, that death has been transferred for ever to the one whom God loves and chooses (elects) at their head and in their place.

Barth's sense of predestination is that from eternity God has decided that all members of the human race would be acquitted of the charges of sin laid against them and that this acquittal would be at great cost to God.

The doctrine of universalism means that, no matter what we do, we shall all be saved. Barth's writings are not clear that this is what he means exactly. But he appears to be suggesting that grace is the final and only reality.

Barth insists on God's commitment to a fallen humanity in spite of sin. God has chosen to demonstrate this commitment clearly in the event of Jesus Christ. God bears the pain and cost of this redemption and accepts the human condition, particularly human suffering and death. God has removed the negative consequences of sin from us and directed them towards Jesus Christ.

This is how Barth gets rid of the notion of predestination to damnation. Jesus is the one predestined to condemnation. Barth's emphasis is on the final triumph of grace: predestination to salvation.

Does this mean that all people, Christians and Jews, Muslims and Hindus, Buddhists and animist, saints and sinners will come to salvation? In which case does it matter what we do, think or believe? Barth was adamant that there is no knowledge of God apart from Jesus Christ: salvation is only possible through Christ. However he underscores the final and vital eschatological victory of grace over unbelief.

## *The* Church Dogmatics

The *Church Dogmatics* is a vast work. It is estimated to stand at six million words. The volumes are subdivided. There are 12 such subdivisions. The fifth volume will never appear. The work has four major sections. They are *The Word of God*, *God*, *Creation* and *Reconciliation.* Barth died before he could write the volume on *Redemption.*

The language is direct and strong. The central principle is that everything is dependent upon the action of God. God is sovereign with regard to both divine freedom and divine love. This applies to both God's own being and to God's relationship with humanity. We are not considering set states of being or relationship, Barth allows room for the acting out of the sovereign will of God upon creation. The 'proclamation' of the Church takes place, or is looked for, in a space between the text under consideration and the actuality of the experience being lived by preacher and hearers at that particular time.

God reveals the divine self to Creation. With regard to humanity this is an objective reality, and it allows Theology to be called knowledge. But this knowledge is only available through faith.

Barth does not concentrate on humanity or the Church. He wants to establish what turns speech into proclamation; he seeks to set up a connectedness with God. Word carries past revelation into the future, calling and regulating the Church through empowering Word of God. The Bible is the place where, through the actions of God, the Word is shown.

The Bible demonstrates the fullness of God's Lordship as Revealer, Revelation and the consequences Revelation has on humanity. The Trinity is at the very forefront of Barth's theology. God is Lord of our existence (Father), God is Lord of our estranged condition before God and also of the process which reunites us with God (Son), and God is Lord of how we are freed to respond to God (Holy Spirit).

God moves freely towards humanity, the supreme moment being the event in which the Word becomes human in Jesus Christ. This is the objective side of Revelation.

Barth brings out the true meaning of the life of God's people as he ponders the Holy Spirit. This is the subjective side of Revelation. But Holy Spirit leads to consideration of the authority of Holy Scripture and to how there can be valid proclamation. The Church is directed to speak of God and when it does so authentically, in a way that commands obedience; then God speaks in Word of God.

Barth thought long and hard about how God can be 'God for us'. God is known by self-revelation, but this can only happen in the reality of the response and obedience of faith. God is the one who seeks us out and builds up fellowship with us in love. That love is gracious and holy and also unvarying, eternal and free.

The grace of God is a saving grace, seeking and holding us, claiming our obedience and declaring us righteous and free for eternal life with God.

In Barth's thought, Creation was the setting up of a distinct reality where God shares divine life and glory with the created order. On the human side it is being in grace as we await the final completion of God's work. We know God is creator and that the world exists. That is the reality in which we are set. But the important thing about it is *not* our analysis of it, *nor* our technical control over it.

Important knowledge comes through faith which grows within us through our knowledge of Jesus. The meaning of creation finds its expression in God's purpose. And that is worked out in the new covenant expressed by Jesus Christ and also in the fellowship with God which humanity now gains.

Barth's teaching about the Christian doctrine of Reconciliation centres on the dynamic of the Word of God, focusing on the historic work and office of Jesus. Jesus shows his divinity in the humility of his incarnation and his humanity in the exalted Jesus. The unity of the two is seen in his self-manifestation as mediator between God and humanity: the Lord as servant and the servant as Lord.

Barth is engaged in a constant battle to clear the ground so that Word of God becomes apparent. In this 'allowing-to-be-heard' (my phrase, not Barth's) the Bible is of prime importance. But past theologians and the great Confessions of Faith also have their place. Barth is responsive to what other theologians might call the tradition. Though he rejects all Natural Theology, he affirms that since the Word became flesh there is an objective standard against which all Theology can be measured.

**Covenant** Originally an agreement between two parties, it came to be seen as the faithfulness of God towards Israel in return for the inner righteousness of the people before God. Jesus restated it as humanity receiving a gracious gift from God by which their desire to serve God was made perfect. It requires a response. It has its highest expression in the example of the life and death of Jesus.

**Mediator** One who seeks to bring about a peaceful settlement between opposing parties. In Christian Theology it refers to the work of Christ reconciling God and the human race.

### *Barth and analogy*

Barth was concerned about emphasizing the reasonable quality of faith, and in order to do so, he made use of analogy. What do we mean by analogy?

When I talk of God I use words from ordinary speech, but do not always use them to mean exactly the same thing. If my meaning is the same every time, then I am using a word 'univocally'. If I intend a different meaning each time, then my meaning is 'equivocal'. I am seeking to confuse. 'Equivocal' is sometimes used as a polite term for lying. So am I seeking to confuse, or am I even lying, when I speak of God and use an everyday word in a slightly different sense?

In theological language, we use a word about an everyday object in a way appropriate to that object. But when we use the same word about

God we use it in a way that is appropriate to God. This is what is meant by using a word 'analogically'.

When other theologians had said that God is our Father, they had started from the notion of a human father and appropriately applied the notion to God. But Barth used what he called a 'vertical analogy'. God is our real Father. We only understand the meaning of human fatherhood when we understand the Fatherhood of God as revealed in the coming of Jesus. Human fathers are only fathers by analogy with God's Fatherhood. Barth called this the 'analogy of faith'.

We understand the human condition in the light of God. Barth understood everything in the created order through his understanding of the meaning of Christ. If we really want to understand what it is to be human, we must first understand the Revelation of Christ. This tendency has been referred to as 'Christological concentration'.

### Appraisal

Barth has been attacked from both the liberal left and the conservative right.

On the liberal side he was particularly criticized over his view of Scripture. He was accused of raising the Bible to a position where it was above criticism and ignoring the scholarly and critical work done on the text over the preceding century.

He has also been condemned on the grounds that his Theology is an uncritical expression of faith, that it denies any role for reason in the expression of belief, for Barth refuses to consider any sort of rational justification for Theology. Theology is totally autonomous with regard to other disciplines. Some have seen this as stepping beyond communication of the truths of Theology and into isolation.

Barth's theological outlook emphasizes the otherness of God. It is based on revelation in such a way that it can only be checked against itself and will not allow an outside reference. Some have seen it as a vast belief system that is resistant to criticism.

Conservatives have attacked his definition of revelation as a non-verbal event, a happening rather than a text. They argue that he has undermined the status of the Bible as a document which cannot be in error.

However other conservatives have acclaimed him as the best answer to the Enlightenment's programme which stresses the dominance of unquestionable reason. They welcome the fact that Barth's starting point is revelation and praise its emphasis on proclamation. Barthian Theology is thus a great tool for preaching. Theology is not tied into current philosophical or hermeneutical fashions.

Barth was widely influential, particularly in Protestant circles. Many people from different church traditions were interested in his thought and thus he is credited with fostering ecumenical discussion. The renewal of interest in the idea of 'Church' has much to do with Barth's ideas on the links between Theology and Church. The notion of 'Church' had been neglected in the heyday of Protestant liberal thought.

Some Roman Catholic scholars have viewed Barth's theology as the nearest thing to Catholicism ever to come from the Protestant wing of Christianity, in spite of his rejection of Natural Theology and philosophy. Barth did, however, consider Theology to be a rational quest.

Jesus Christ is the centre of Barth's theology, but other theologians have criticized it as having Jesus Christ only as its subject. Thought concerning God is restricted to thought concerning Jesus Christ. Nevertheless he is also credited with rescuing the doctrine of the Trinity from neglect.

Barth has had an enormous influence on all the theologians of the twentieth century, whether they followed in his footsteps, expanded the scope of his enquiry using his methods to delve into areas he had not touched or broadly agreed with him but pursued other methodologies of enquiry. Even those who disagree with him seem bound to continue the debate in the areas he made his own: Christology, revelation, the Trinity, creation, evil and redemption.

However Barthian Theology has no basis on which to approach other religions which, following its principles, must be condemned as corruptions of faith.

# 12 Dietrich Bonhoeffer and the Cost of Discipleship

Bonhoeffer was one of the most influential theologians of the later twentieth century. This reputation was, in large part, forged because of the radical political stances he adopted towards the end of his life. He was a controversial and original thinker. He was an early enemy of Nazism and as a result took the staggering decision to oppose it, if necessary, by violent means. He was executed in 1945 at the early age of 39.

## Life (1906–1945)

Dietrich Bonhoeffer was born in 1906 in Silesia; the area is now in Poland. His father was a Professor of Psychology at Berlin.

Bonhoeffer studied at both Tübingen and at Berlin. At Berlin he attended lectures by the liberal theologian van Harnack (1851–1930) for whom he had a great regard. He came to reject van Harnack's theological method but continued to admire the liberal tradition. While at Berlin he also came under the influence of Karl Barth (1886–1968).

Bonhoeffer's later thought shows influences from both traditions. The liberal side influenced the sort of question he would ask in his project concerning 'religionless Christianity'. The Barthian side influenced his unwavering conviction that Theology must always keep its focus on the self-disclosure of God in Jesus Christ; it must never become a form of social science. Bonhoeffer graduated in 1927.

He lived and worked for a short time in Barcelona. He then spent a year studying at the Union Theological Seminary in New York. He returned to Berlin in 1931 and was ordained a Lutheran pastor. He worked as an assistant pastor and as a university lecturer in Theology. It was at this time that he began his involvement with the ecumenical movement. He was friendly with members of the Anglican Community of the Resurrection at Mirfield in Yorkshire. He spent some time working in London as chaplain to the Lutheran congregation there.

He opposed Nazism from the very first and was an early member of the Confessing Church – Lutherans who resisted the state church controlled by the Nazis. He was a signatory of the Barmen Declaration in 1934. He returned to Germany in 1935 as head of one of the seminaries of the Confessing Church in Pomerania. It was a more or less underground or secret college. Here he instituted a regime of life and study which was startlingly unusual for Lutherans of the time: community life, common prayer, study, confession to a companion and acceptance of spiritual advice from that companion, and regular Sunday Eucharistic celebrations.

In 1936 he was forbidden to teach by the Nazis, he was banned from Berlin and dismissed from his university post. His seminary was closed by government order in the following year.

He was lecturing in America when the Second World War broke out, but he felt it was his duty to return to Germany. He had friends and family members who were highly placed in the Resistance movement and he was recruited to work with them. With the help of English friends he tried to mediate between Germans opposed to Hitler and the British government. He became engaged to Maria von Wedermeyer early in 1943. She supported him and remained in close contact with him during all the troubles that were to come.

Bonhoeffer was also involved in a plot to assassinate Hitler. He had come to the conclusion that the extreme circumstances of the day demanded an extreme ethical response. He was arrested by the Gestapo in 1943, was imprisoned in Berlin, later at Buchenwald, and killed by the SS in Flossenbürg in 1945 together with General Oster, Admiral Canaris and others. These killings may have been ordered by Hitler, yet they also have all the hallmarks of murder, since they appear to have taken place without judicial process and as a panic reaction to the advance of US troops.

**Liberal** The desire to be free from traditional church teaching and creeds and to be allowed to handle texts and sources in a modern, critical and scientific manner.
**Ecumenical** A movement seeking the unity of all Christian churches.
**Ethics** Concerning the principles of right and wrong.
**Subjectivity** Relating to the person defined as a thinking being; what is personal and individual.

He wrote *Sanctorum Communio* (Communion of Saints), his first theological work on the structure of the Church in 1930. His second work, *Act and Being*, was published the following year. He also wrote *The Cost of Discipleship* in 1937 and *Ethics*, which was not published until 1949.

In addition to the concerns which prompted his actions Bonhoeffer had a deep interest in Martin Luther whom he read closely. He maintained that any concentration on Luther's religious subjectivity was a bad reading; it missed the psychological point. Luther's thought may have contained deep introspection, but it was prompted by a very objective starting point – the foundational revelation of God in Jesus Christ as it was declared in the Scriptures. An ethical being must be consequently grounded in the Word of God in Christ and not in one's own subjectivity.

He is best known for *Letters and Papers from Prison*, which was published in 1951 after his death. His books were gradually translated into English between the late 1940s and very early 1960s.

He was concerned with the growing secularization of the world and wondered how the Church might speak to the world in a secular way.

### Timeline

1900 Publication of Freud's *Interpretation of Dreams*
1903 First motorized flight by the Wright brothers
1906 Birth of Bonhoeffer
1908 Mahler's *Song of the Earth*
1914–1918 First World War
1915 Wegener's Theory of Tectonic Drift
1916 Einstein's Theory of General Relativity
1917 The Russian Revolution
1922 Mussolini's Blackshirts march on Rome
1928 Fleming discovers penicillin
1929 The New York Stock Exchange Crash
1930 Bonhoeffer's *Sanctorum Communio*
1931 Bonhoeffer's *Act and Being*
1933 Hitler becomes German Chancellor
1934–1935 Mao Zedong leads the Long March
1937 Purges in the Soviet Union

Bonhoeffer's *The Cost of Discipleship*
1939–1945 Second World War
1942 First atomic pile
1945 Execution of Bonhoeffer
1949 Bonhoeffer's *Ethics*
1951 Bonhoeffer's *Letters and Papers from Prison*

## Thought

Bonhoeffer's thought is concerned with a search for the beyond which is present with us now and with thorough reform of the Church. His constant question was how Jesus Christ could become Lord for the non-religious in a world come of age, a world where the hypothesis of God was superfluous.

He did not see how the Church, in its present form, could have any message for the modern world. Biblical faith could only be promoted if traditional religion was dispensed with. His notion of 'religionless christianity' has excited interest, but Bonhoeffer did not live long enough to pursue the quest.

### *A world come of age*

A person who has not yet come of age lives under the guidance and protection of somebody older and more experienced. To have come of age is to have lost or broken away from that support, to be autonomous. What might it mean for the world to have come of age?

Bonhoeffer's thought here is rooted in the Enlightenment, when individuals demanded the right to follow their own thoughts without having to answer for them to some authority: each human being is autonomous and must be granted freedom of thought and conscience. In the Middle Ages 'heteronomy' was exercised by clerical control, and Bonhoeffer did not want it to return. Any such loss of autonomy would be an act of despair, obtained by the sacrifice of intellectual honesty.

Bonhoeffer realized that people had become self-sufficient in many areas of their lives, and he felt that this trend was irreversible. People were now tackling many important questions for living without any thought of God. This was almost totally true in science, the arts and ethics. They were also forcefully realizing that the world worked just as well, if not better, without making any reference to the God question. God was gradually, imperceptibly, being pushed back from the forefront of awareness.

So Bonhoeffer set out to analyse this new atheism. It was not so much a question of denying God as ignoring God. The question of whether God exists was now felt to be a pointless one – a waste of energy. It was just not relevant. When the world had not yet come of age, the God question was useful; once they have come of age, individuals can do without God.

This was the world that Bonhoeffer experienced in prison: a context of practical atheism. People were now conscious of themselves, of the world in which they lived, of the laws that governed their existence and of how those laws came to be. The world they lived in was a human construct and not a divine creation.

People speak of God when human knowledge has come up against its limits, when human strength fails. They are looking for *deus ex machina*: the expectation that God will miraculously appear and make things come all right. Such a religious faith is exploitative. It takes advantage of human weakness and ignorance. Bonhoeffer denied that we had, in our human weakness, the right to use God as a stopgap.

We must therefore find God in what we know; God wishes to be understood by us, not found in questions that cannot be answered. In this way God can be related to scientific knowledge and the continuing unveiling of scientific discovery, but also related to the everyday circumstances of life as we confront death, suffering and our imperfections. So Bonhoeffer preferred to speak of God, not in our weakness, but in our strength, not in the face of death and failings, but in the face of human goodness.

Bonhoeffer sets out to make room for God in the centre of reality, in positive circumstances. God has made the world; that creative act is still in progress. The world is held in God's hand, which is the very centre of all reality. Nevertheless Bonhoeffer does not wish the theologian to set out to prove such a theory, for that would be trying to prove to a world come of age that it had not in fact come of age. He would rather understand this world come of age positively and, taking his stand on the gospel and on Christ, make no attempt to hide the atheism of the world but to reveal it.

**Enlightenment** The critical mindset of the eighteenth century: the rational examination of previously accepted ideas and institutions.
**Heteronomy** Being governed by a source outside oneself.
**Autonomy** Self-governing; freedom from outside influence.
***Deus ex machina*** Any unexpected or unlikely device used to untangle a situation.
**Personalism** One of a wide spectrum of philosophical outlooks which stresses the pre-eminence of persons, both human and divine, in the universe.
**I–Thou** The refusal to regard another as a thing, an instrument, a means to an end; granting others the fullest recognition of their personhood and value.
**Metaphysics** is the study of being as being; speculation about the meaning of what is; the study of first principles and first causes; the rational knowledge of those realities that go beyond us; the rational study of things in themselves.

## Sanctorum Communio

Bonhoeffer was influenced by the personalist thought fashionable in the 1920s. He saw the 'I–Thou relationship' as central to all philosophical and theological construction. But the object of Theology is God and in particular the self-revelation of God in Jesus Christ. Bonhoeffer wanted to hold these two tendencies (relationship and revelation) together and sought to do so in his doctoral dissertation, *Sanctorum Communio*, which he successfully defended in 1927.

He argues for a personalism that is fundamentally linked with revelation. Persons only draw their being from a relationship to the divine person which surpasses them. The limit of personhood is where the person (created being) is distinguished from the Creator. This imposes an inescapable ethical duty on all. Transcendence should be seen in ethical rather than in metaphysical terms.

Bonhoeffer's thesis is an attempt to describe the essence of the Church or as the subtitle calls it 'dogmatic research into the sociology of the Church'. He is trying to give expression to a doctrine of Jesus Christ, within the framework of the Church: Christology within ecclesiology.

The Church is a communion because it is a community. But this particular community is a community of the baptized into Jesus Christ, a work of God in Christ: Christ existing as community.

So the Church is, on the one hand, a concrete, visible, social reality and has, on the other hand, a Christological dimension which defies sociological investigation. The Church exists in history as a collective person. Bonhoeffer is close here to the idea of the irruption of God into the world as self-revelation. One cannot understand the Church without the light of faith in the revelation of God.

Like Jesus Christ, Christians take on a representative and substitutionary role. They do so as they build up the capacity to make the suffering of others their own. They do so in the course of concrete living and in the responsibility of prayer for others. Church is a community, a holy gathering, made up of sinners. What makes it different is the presence of Christ where inner conviction and spirituality meet liberal concern for others.

## Act and Being

In 1930 Bonhoeffer successfully defended another thesis; this thesis, entitled *Act and Being*, was to qualify him as a university teacher. Here his concern is not to make clear the foundations of the Church but to see if he can make clear the very being of God. God intervenes from above and so has freedom of action. God dwells with us and so has faithfulness of being. How could God exercise total freedom of action and faithfulness of being at the same time? If God is totally free, God can intervene in the world on God's terms and when God wishes. But in such a case God could go away and forget about the world. Then God would not be faithful.

Bonhoeffer identifies Christ as the one in whom act and being are reconciled. Through Christ, God comes and God dwells. Being is the foundational reality without which there is no act. Act is the irruption of God in the Christ-event: 'Jesus, the man for others'. God reveals himself. But revelation takes place in history. Church and Christianity are not invisible or abstract. Christianity cannot be reduced to religion.

### *Cheap grace*

The phrase 'cheap grace' is a critical and disapproving expression. Luther had famously defined the Church as *simul justa et peccatrix* (at the same time both justified and sinful) and the individual Christian as *simul justus et peccator* (both justified and sinful). Bonhoeffer was afraid that the Church, particularly in Lutheran preaching, had taken an undemanding view of this description. It had ended up preaching grace as something easy to come by, with little cost to self. But Bonhoeffer held that grace was costly; discipleship involves a commitment: grace demands obedience, and we are being asked to do more than give comfortable assent to a doctrine.

## The Cost of Discipleship

This book arose out of Bonhoeffer's experiences while training future pastors of the Confessing Church. He was, in a sense, training pastors 'on the run'. This is not an academic book. The style is closer to preaching.

Here Bonhoeffer's essential thought is that the essence of being Church is following Christ. It is to struggle with the questions: Who is Jesus Christ? What does he command? How do I witness to that? It tries to state a theology of grace, a theology of Christ, a theology of the Church and how they relate to society and to the world.

Luther had taught that we are saved by the grace of God alone and not by works. But if one ignores and despises good works, we could be led to hold grace in contempt. The free grace of Jesus Christ is a call to conversion of life and a call to obedience: to work on behalf of others. The life of the Christian is in the world but not according to the norms of the world.

### *Bonhoeffer's Christology*

Barth had taught that revelation is the result of God's infinite freedom and is a totally contingent act (God was not compelled to make any such revelation). This revelation creates its own response and God is free to withdraw that revelation at any time. God is always outside our knowledge. Any other way of regarding God's revelation was considered by Barth as a human attempt to construct a tame God who satisfies our demands, rather than make demands of us.

Bonhoeffer disapproved of this teaching: it made God appear so utterly free as to be an abstraction. It did not take into account what God had really done in Jesus Christ. Jesus Christ was not an event in God's freedom; Jesus was God being offered on behalf of all humans.

Christology for Bonhoeffer was not a debate about how the transcendent God related to finite mortals; rather it was the puzzle of the identity of the person Jesus who addresses himself to both God and people. Bonhoeffer looked for the answer in the living, breathing conscious man whose story is told in the gospels.

This man is Christ in so far as he lived for others and that was the essence of his being. It was not something which just happened to occur. He cannot be thought of in terms of his being in himself but only in terms of his being for others, in terms of his relationship to me. Thus Christ can only be thought of in community.

### *Religionless Christianity*

It appears that Bonhoeffer intended to write a book on the subject of religionless Christianity but was executed before he could do so. This is a late development of his thought and the outlines of his thinking on the subject are contained in his *Letters and Papers from Prison.*

First, what did Bonhoeffer mean by religion? He considered it to be reliance on God at the margins of life. It involved both individualism and a metaphysical system. There are problems with both. Individualism involves a retreat from the world, an obsession with self; this is unchristian and any attempt to define a metaphysical definition of salvation invariably allows people to escape the challenge of the gospel. Bonhoeffer saw the gospel in strongly ethical terms.

In a world 'come of age' both ideas are challenged: individualism is impossible. First, we inevitably live in a community, which respects our individual uniqueness but demands involvement from us: we cannot remain in an isolated cocoon. Secondly, a world suspicious of metaphysics demands verification of all systems: it looks for reasons for holding any set of ideas, for constructing any value system. If religion is composed of those two elements, then Bonhoeffer saw religion as a barrier to true faith in Jesus Christ.

Bonhoeffer is most famous for his attempts to give a non-religious interpretation to basic Christian ideas and to express them in a way that will impress people who have learned to be in this world without God. He is struggling to come to terms with Christianity's identity in the modern world: 'what Christianity really is, or who Christ really is, for us today'.

This, as we have seen, has now become a problem because the world has 'come of age'. The time when people could be told things by means of word is over. People no longer lived in a world of consciousness or inwardness. This meant they no longer had a religious outlook. It was impossible to be religious anymore.

Is there, Bonhoeffer wondered, a place for Christ in such a world? He wanted to accept the modern world and accept also that Jesus is the Lord of that world. This was a particular theme of reflection while he was in prison. There he met people who never turned to God, yet remained deeply and authentically human, right to the end. His question was, 'How can Christ also become the Lord of religionless people?'

The Church has failed to separate Christianity's message from religious frills, urging people to cultivate an inner life. This is a retreat into subjectivism, into ideas about personal sin, guilt, despair and anxiety. The Church has therefore failed in its duty to the modern world. It has failed to proclaim, has no language in which it is possible to proclaim, the objective work achieved by God in Jesus Christ. As the personal and metaphysical God of the gaps is pushed further and further from the central concerns of people living in the modern world, God is portrayed as a form of weakness rather than as a form of strength.

The task of religionless Christianity is to speak to people at the centre of their lives, both in joy and in suffering. Christianity does not have to presuppose that people are wicked. God must be seen where we are, at every stage of life, not just when we have come to the end of our tether. This is where Jesus met people in the gospels. This, for Bonhoeffer, is what is meant by the revelation of God in Jesus Christ.

**Grace** Supernatural gift freely bestowed by God.
**Contingent** That which can happen or can exist, yet need not.
**Eschatological** Concerned with the last things: death, judgement, heaven and hell. It is concerned with the final destiny and hope both of the individual and of humanity.

*Ethics*

The Nazi-dominated German church had talked of a divided or two-tier reality, an inner world of awareness where the gospel operates and an outer world of reality: the State, the law where the demands of the gospel had no place. This division allowed them to justify ideas concerning the purity of the race and the primacy of devotion to the Fatherland.

Bonhoeffer had a Christological understanding of reality. That is to say he understood everything in terms of the importance and work of Christ. God in Christ had brought everything under divine control. There is no more division into sacred and secular. So the starting point for ethics is not self or the world or how to agree on sets of values. It is God as revealed by Jesus Christ, how Jesus Christ takes form in the world we live in. Ethics is not abstract speculation; it is the need to make concrete judgements and to obey the demands of God.

Bonhoeffer saw the danger in the two-tiered reality argument. It could be used to justify any set of actions in the outer world, which was not subject to Christ's demands. Furthermore he maintained that no sphere of life could be removed from God's healing in Christ. Everything in reality derives its being from Christ's new creation. He referred to this as the 'order of preservation'. But things are only thus defined if they are open to God's revelation in Christ. If they are not open in that way, they may be dissolved. The Hitler regime had closed itself to revelation.

As the Nazi enterprise developed, Bonhoeffer came to adopt a new eschatological ethic – deep-seated obedience to the concrete demands of the crucified Jesus – adopting the teachings of the Sermon on the Mount (Mt. 5, 6 and 7) in a quite literal fashion.

Bonhoeffer made a distinction between ultimate ethics and penultimate ethics. Ultimate ethics, or ethics of the last things, concerns the final completion of God's work. Penultimate ethics, ethics concerning the second last things, has to do with the nitty-gritty of living in the world here and now. Penultimate ethics are vitally important, because they prepare for the reception of the ultimate message: God's work in Christ.

Christianity must preach the Good News but this cannot be separated from the need to feed the hungry, clothe the naked and visit the sick: the difficult, demanding and often unrewarding task of doing good in difficult circumstances.

## Appraisal

Can the inner, spiritual life be separated from the outer necessity of doing good in the world?

Can the religionless person, with no time for God, who continues to do good, for and on behalf of others, be considered a Christian?

Does being baptized and confessing faith in Christ make any difference at all?

Is religion dead? What is one to say about the explosion of religious feeling in the modern world? Why might Bonhoeffer consider much of it to be unauthentic?

Is religious feeling the most important source of inspiration and guidance for living in the modern world? Can religion be trusted to guide us in our lives or is a moral regulator necessary? Would such a moral regulator be set above religious feeling or be obedient to it?

Is the cost of discipleship an indicator of the soundness of that discipleship? How can faith and ethical behaviour be offered to those who live and act from within a secular mindset?

What do you think of Bonhoeffer's belief that the task of Theology is to point to the revelation of God which expresses itself most powerfully in the resurrection of Jesus, demonstrating that the logic of God will inevitably surprise us?

Bonhoeffer presented many faces to the world: visionary, anti-Nazi conspirator, double agent, herald of the Death of God movement, accused of being an atheist and secularizer. The brutal cutting-short of his life has, of course, added to the mystique. The enigma is where later thought might have led.

# 13 Karl Rahner and Human Transcendence

Having considered some of the defining radical and disturbing theological voices of the twentieth century, we now turn to a man who was, in his own way, an innovator, but who was also a faithful and loyal member of the Roman Catholic Church. In his younger days, the Roman Catholic Church was going through one of its more inward looking and ultramontane phases; nevertheless it was a period leading up to the renewal of the Second Vatican Council, at which Rahner was, behind the scenes, one of the most important voices.

## Life (1904–1984)

Karl Rahner was born in 1804 in Freiburg in the Black Forest region of southwestern Germany. He was the fourth child in a family of seven. His father was a secondary school teacher. Rahner describes his family background as normal, hardworking and Christian. As a schoolboy he liked wandering in the countryside and disliked sitting down to do his homework!

In 1919 his elder brother, Hugo Rahner, entered the Jesuit Order and Karl followed 3 years later, at the age of 18. He then began the long period of preparation demanded of trainee Jesuits. Both brothers would be theologians. Hugo specialized in Patristics, the study of the early (mostly Greek) Fathers and Ignatian spirituality. It is said that Hugo once offered to translate his brother's works into German: a reference to Karl's notoriously dense style of writing.

Karl studied Philosophy at Feldkirch then at Pullach. He read Kant (1724–1804) attentively and also discovered the philosophy of Joseph Maréchal (1878–1944). Maréchal was a Belgian Jesuit who held that certain ideas, latent in the thought of Aquinas, could, if given proper attention, be developed to answer some of Kant's critical philosophy. Maréchal started the movement that became known as transcendental

Thomism and contributed to renewed twentieth-century interest in the work of Aquinas (1225–1274).

From 1927 to 1929 Rahner taught Latin to his juniors in the Jesuit novitiate. Between 1929 and 1933 he was pursuing his early theological training in Valkenburg in Holland. One of his teachers here was the future Cardinal Bea, later one of the Vatican's tireless workers for Christian unity. Rahner was ordained priest in Munich in 1932. Between 1933 and 1934 he finished his novitiate in Austria. His superiors wished him to teach philosophy, so he started to prepare a doctoral thesis in his home town of Freiburg, where he also attended the lectures of Martin Heidegger (1889–1976). Rahner denied that the content of his thought he had been influenced by Heidegger but freely recognized a debt when it came to a style of thinking.

His philosophical thesis was on the metaphysics of knowledge in the work of St Thomas Aquinas. He wished to discern the *a priori* conditions of the human mind in the thought of St Thomas. He had difficulties with his supervisor who felt that this study depended too heavily on modern philosophy. He finished his thesis in 1936 and published it in 1939 as *Spirit in the World.*

However, by this time, circumstances required a theology teacher and Rahner was sent off to Innsbruck to prepare a doctoral thesis in Theology. This study would concentrate on how Patristic thought viewed the pierced heart of the Saviour as the source of the Church. Rahner's philosophical training had given him deep insights into Scholastic philosophy; he would now acquire deep insights into another fundamental source of church tradition – the early Fathers.

Rahner began to teach in Innsbruck in 1937 and, in theory, remained there until 1964. There were, of course, interruptions following the annexation of Austria by Hitler and the Second World War. Rahner continued his study of Patristics and also of Anthropology. A course of lectures he delivered at Salzburg concerned the human spirit, which he saw as being both transcendent and historical. That course became his second published work, *Hearers of the Word.*

After 1938 there was a Nazi regime in Austria and the Innsbruck Theology Faculty was shut down. A Church theological institute continued to function, but their premises were commandeered and they transferred to Vienna, where teaching continued at the very limit of legal tolerance. Rahner now worked for a while in a pastoral setting but in 1944 was forced to leave Vienna and live in Bavaria. This was his first experience of country living and he had pastoral responsibilities for refugees there. He returned to Innsbruck in 1949 and resumed teaching Theology.

In 1950 he wrote a colossal study of the Doctrine of the Assumption of the Blessed Virgin Mary but encountered problems with the internal censors of the Society of Jesus. The matter was even referred to Rome. In 1954 he started publishing his *Theological Investigations*, which eventually grew to 23 volumes.

When, in 1959, Pope John XXIII announced he was going to call the Second Vatican Council, Rahner was consulted about certain preparations for it. However he was still having censorship difficulties in the Vatican and the German Chancellor Konrad Adenauer had to protest personally to the Pope who cleared the way for Rahner's full participation. After he had been named *peritus*, expert witness, to the Theological Commission, he co-operated with Henri de Lubac (1896–1990), Yves Congar (1904–1995), Hans Küng (b.1928) and Joseph Ratzinger (b.1927), later to become Pope Benedict XVI. It was about this time that he developed the idea of a fundamental course in the Christian faith which would be taught in the early years of seminary training. This became, in time, *Foundations of Christian Faith.*

**Ultramontane** The view that the Pope should have total authority in matters of doctrine.

**Transcendence** Above, independent of, surpassing the material universe.

**Metaphysics** is the study of being as being; speculation about the meaning of what is; the study of first principles and first causes; the rational knowledge of those realities that go beyond us; the rational study of things in themselves.

***A priori*** An *a priori* argument, statement, concept or judgement is not based on experience, on the five senses, but one which, following rigorous thought, is seen to be necessarily true or necessarily false. The term *valid* might be arrived at by *a priori* reasoning.

**Fathers** A restricted group of early church writers whose influence on doctrine was vital.

Rahner was now widely hailed as the greatest theologian of the twentieth century. In 1964 he was named to a professorial chair in Munich to teach Christian world vision and philosophy of religion. It was a chair which allowed him total freedom to lecture as he wanted and aimed at a wide audience, not just university undergraduates. He also, from 1967 on, lectured in dogmatics in Münster.

In 1969 Rahner was nominated by Pope Paul VI to the Roman Catholic Church's International Theological Commission, which had been set up to maintain the fertile co-operation between theologians and the Roman *magisterium* (the teaching authority of the Roman Catholic Church). However he did not feel comfortable there; the Curia (the government of the Church) was beginning to claw back influence it had lost in the aftermath of the council, and Rahner soon resigned.

In 1973 he retired, lived in a Jesuit philosophical institute in Munich and worked on his *Foundations of Christian Faith*. He was involved in controversy at this time. He criticized Hans Küng for certain views and was himself the subject of severe disparagement from his former friend, Hans Urs von Balthasar, particularly over his notion of the 'anonymous Christian'. In 1982 he returned to Innsbruck, where he died in 1984.

## Timeline

1904 Birth of Karl Rahner
1913 Henry Ford creates the first production line for mass-produced cars
1914–1918 First World War
1916 Einstein's Theory of Relativity
1920 Foundation of the League of Nations
1922 Creation of the Soviet Union
1923 Rahner enters the Society of Jesus
1928 Discovery of penicillin
1929 Wall Street Crash
1932 Rahner ordained priest
1933 Hitler in power in Germany
1934 Rahner prepares a doctoral thesis in Philosophy
1934–1935 Mao Zedong leads the Long March
1935 Gershwin's *Porgy and Bess*

1937 Rahner prepares a doctoral thesis in Theology
1938 Rahner starts teaching at Innsbruck
Anschluss of Austria
1939 Rahner's *Spirit in the World*
1939–1945 Second World War
1938–1949 Teaching at Innsbruck interrupted; Rahner engaged in pastoral activity
Rahner's *Hearers of the Word*
1945 Founding of the United Nations
1947 The Marshall Plan
1948 Beginning of the Cold War; Berlin blockade
1949 Simone de Beauvoir's *Second Sex*
1950 Rahner in trouble with the Roman censors
1950–1953 Korean War
1954 Rahner starts his *Theological Investigations*
1960s Many former African colonies become independent states
1962–1965 Second Vatican Council
1969 First man on the moon
1973 Rahner 'retires'
1976 Rahner's *Foundations of Christian Faith*
1978 Election of Pope John Paul II
First test tube baby
1984 Death of Karl Rahner
1985 Gorbachev First Secretary of the Communist party in the Soviet Union

## Thought

Rahner tried to discover and lay out the general principles underlying the doctrines of Roman Catholic faith. Aquinas was an early influence: the human capacity to know is rooted in the senses. But Rahner's vision of being human also involved being open to the infinite; human beings can think metaphysically because they can transcend particular being.

Rahner began with a phenomenology of being human. Although we are open to the infinite we only reach fulfilment in union with God (as revealed by Christian revelation). We will not be able to understand the world unless we understand this core relationship between the world and God. Rahner calls this key fact the 'supernatural existential'. We cannot proceed to any exploration of sin, grace or salvation unless we are aware of this principal reality.

**Phenomenology** A sustained and insightful description of how things appear.

### *The supernatural existential*

The word 'existential', as used by Rahner, is a term describing definite qualities of human existence. If something is a permanent, ever-present quality of human existence, and allows us to see that this feature makes humans different from all other forms of life, then that feature is a 'human existential'.

The word 'supernatural' describes whatever transcends nature. God's gracious self-communication to humans cannot be purely natural. It must come from beyond nature; it is therefore supernatural.

However Rahner wished to overcome or avoid a seeming contradiction in theological thought. He did not wish to give the idea that God's self-communication contradicts human nature. He did not wish to give the idea that God's self-communication is captive to human nature.

Consequently Rahner laid stress on the 'supernatural existential'. He held that humans are naturally open to God but that, in addition, they are supernaturally raised up by God, by means of that transcendental openness, so that they come to an actual experience of God in everyday life.

If every human is lit by the light that lights everyone in the world, as St John's Gospel states, then that light is not part of their natural composition but a divine gift. It is 'existential' but not natural; it is 'supernatural existential'.

'Supernatural existential' is what soaks into our entire existence because of God's free self-communication and, what is more, it is present even before we respond as free individuals to God's gracious self-offer. Humans are not only open to God's revelation; they actually receive God's self-communication.

## Spirit in the World

Human beings are, at one and the same time, both intelligence and body. We are in the world, which we know by means of our senses. How then can we come to know the truth absolutely? Rahner sought a description of how 'spirit', a faculty transcending the world (the reality immediately accessible to our experience), could be at work within the world.

Rahner starts by working with the problem as posed by St Thomas. There are two levels of knowledge. There is intellectual knowledge, dealing with ideas, and there is sensible knowledge, dealing with what we see, smell, hear and so on. Traditionally it was said that the first was superior and had no need of the second.

Aquinas did not agree. Intellectual knowledge arrives by means of abstraction from the message of the senses. Even when we are dealing with realities which have no material existence (God, eternity), we create images so that we can deal with them more effectively. So our knowledge is in the mind; it works by abstraction, but it is spirit in the world and cannot cope without using images.

In the second part of his book Rahner analyses how we develop metaphysical questions even though our starting point is our experience of the world. Rahner describes how we use the *a priori* structures of the senses (space and time) to trigger abstractions from the knowing subject and eventually work out concepts and ideas.

This is how our intellect moves into action and creates thought. It has its own structure; it does not invent itself afresh with every individual. It seeks to comprehend what is universal and what is necessary. Even though its supports are the gifts of finite being, intellect uses those senses in a movement of imagination to contemplate being itself.

The third part of the book defends the human capacity to arrive at what is true, even though it had started out from the promptings of the senses. Metaphysics is possible because it is the work of the creative imagination. This opens the way for a philosophy of religion. Because it is structured in this way, the human intellect allows us to be open to God's revelation. This in time would lead to the ideas of *Hearers of the Word.*

**Abstraction** The act of sorting out the intrinsic worth of something from its physical qualities.
**Word (The)** is a translation of the Greek word *Logos*, meaning word or reason. It was seen in the Old Testament and in Greek thought as referring to the universal reason which ordered everything in the cosmos. In Christianity it refers to the second person of the Trinity. Jesus was identified as The Word.

## Hearers of the Word

In *Hearers of the Word* Rahner is still in philosophical mode, but the core theological trend is becoming more obvious.

Rahner's central point is that human beings have the capacity to listen to the revelation of self that God makes to them. A human being is both spirit and a historic being. God's revelation is a Word event which human beings are capable of hearing. Rahner maintains a central link between the transcendental dimension and the historic dimension of human experience.

Rahner wants to describe what is meant by the human capacity to make a response in obedience to the free initiatives of God. The problem is how can the human spirit be open to God? The answer is that the human spirit is open to the totality of being (including God) and this clarifies our ability to identify what is an event of revelation.

Rahner goes on to explain the relationship between being and awareness. It is contradictory to talk of a being which is essentially incomprehensible in its being. The essence of every being is the capacity to know and be known. Ultimately knowledge is the lucidity of love. Human beings are thus in-dwelt by a transcendence that operates at every level of their being.

Human beings are therefore capable of opening themselves to God, even though God is still unknown. God is the 'free Unknown'; free to give a revelation of self or to withhold it. Human beings, who are also spirit and willpower, may freely decide to open themselves to God and to listen to what God says to them in love.

But what is the concrete instance where the free act of God's revelation can touch the free human awareness? If we can analyse what it is to be human in transcendental terms, we can prove *a priori* that divine revelation is neither pointless nor unthinkable. Being is lucidity; therefore, by definition, it is capable of being revealed. But it also remains unknown, waiting to be shown. The human spirit awaits and desires this revelation.

God is 'provisionally unknown' to human beings but is revealed by an act of God's personal freedom. To receive that truth, human beings need to do two things. First, they must position themselves so as to take full account, in freedom, of their being as humans. Secondly, they must take full account, in freedom, of their being before God. So the concrete instance of God's self-revelation can only be that of history.

## Foundations of Christian Faith

This quite difficult book was written as an introduction to Christian faith; it was not written as an introduction to Theology. Its aim is to help Christians, and those who want to be Christians, to understand how Christianity relates to the whole of existence.

The methodology used is to unite philosophy and theology in faith. Neither discipline was to be subordinated to the other. Philosophy asks questions about being human, about the goal and meaning of life. Theology is a measured, rational, reflective response, detailing how Christianity might answer such questions. The central argument and answer is that God wants to share divine life with all human beings and so offers divine life to them.

Rahner is concerned about how we can know ourselves and how we can know God. He talks about such subjects as the knowing person and Christian faith. He discusses how, as human beings, we are open to reality. He knows how limited our knowledge of reality is. He talks of what we know and how we organize it internally.

Spiritual knowledge is true knowledge leading to transcendence, yet rooted in history. Rahner never doubts the reliability of the bases of Christian faith.

## *Human transcendence*

Rahner considers human beings to be capable of hearing God's self-communication. When human beings hear this message they do not gather information about God, as one might accumulate facts. They hear the message in every experience of living. We are human because we have been created with the faculty of listening to God and listening for God. We have been created with an ability to meet the transcendent God. Thus the human being is defined as a being capable of a relationship with God; any question about what it is to be human is ultimately a theological question.

How does Rahner go about defining a 'person'? Hearing subjects, he says, cannot be reduced to a product of the forces that fashioned them. Subjects not only listen, but are capable of freely responding, what is more they stand back and reflect about themselves. This implies that they ask questions such as what is my true self.

Hearers know they are limited, but they also seek ways of going beyond and overcoming their limits. Human beings have a natural inclination towards surpassing limitations.

Transcendence presents limited human beings with choices. When they make 'better' choices they are acting freely and responsibly, and are thus agents of salvation. They are coming to be what God has called them to be.

Human beings make decisions; they choose freely. They then take responsibility for those choices. Human beings are responsible and free.

Nevertheless we exercise our freedom and responsibility as dependent beings. Our possibilities are those which history has placed at our disposal. We have a spiritual freedom; we can hear the message and respond to God's invitation to be what God wants us to be.

## *The Trinity*

Rahner makes use of two terms when discussing the Trinity: the 'essential' Trinity and the 'economic' Trinity. The essential Trinity tries to give expression to a notion of the Trinity outside of time and space.

The economic Trinity is how the Trinity comes to be known within the scheme of salvation.

The God shown to us in the scheme of salvation is the way God actually is. God's self-revelation corresponds to the way God essentially is.

We experience God in a certain way. Nevertheless that experience and reflection on salvation is a revelation of God's crucial and most intimate being.

This distinction concerns the way God is known to us (revelation and human history) and the way God actually has being.

The correct starting point for discussion of the Trinity is human experience of salvation. Father, Son and Holy Spirit are not just human ways of dividing up and making clear the experience of salvation.

Our creation, preservation and salvation are not three different functions carried out by three different persons. Rather they are all part of a single, united, shared work of love towards the human race. This is a very important idea to grasp, no matter how helpful it might be, on occasions, to give the most important role in one of those functions to one person of the godhead as opposed to another. However beneath that idea is the intermingling of each of the persons into the being of the other two, in order to be a community of being.

### *Christology*

Rahner wanted to demonstrate the identity between the historical Jesus and the eternal Word, the *Logos*, and to defend the unity between them. The Word demonstrates how God, from the very beginning, intended to reconcile humanity and divinity.

Rahner places himself within the evolutionary worldview of contemporary culture. But he lays down this refinement: human beings evolve and surpass themselves transcendentally in response to God's Word. Rahner asserts a 'transcendental' Christology: God's offer of salvation is absolute; God does not save from a distance; but does so by offering to human beings participation in the divine being.

Transcendental Christology presents Jesus Christ as the one who enables us to transcend ourselves. Jesus and the heavenly Father were completely and ultimately one. God affirmed Jesus' transcendence and offers that transcendence to us also.

In Jesus, the incarnate *Logos* caused human reality to be the reality of God. When the Word became flesh, human nature reached the goal towards which it had always reached out. Jesus is, and knew that he was, the incarnation of God's offer of salvation. The death of Jesus cannot be seen as propitiation for divine anger; it is the sacrament of God's saving will for us. It achieved what it revealed.

The death and resurrection of Jesus are an event in which all human beings may hope to participate. Here God gave total approval to the earthly life of Jesus. God always intended to reconcile all people through Jesus Christ. Through Jesus, the offer to share the very life of God is extended to all people. When people accept that offer, they show their hope that they will be validated by God in the same way as Jesus was.

**Christology** The study of the Person of Christ, particularly the union of the divine and human natures in Christ.

**Creation** The belief that everything that is was made by God. In some contexts the term is restricted to the notion that everything was made exactly as described in Genesis chapters 1 and 2.

**Preservation** The belief that everything that was created continues to be through the ongoing attention of God.

**Salvation** In negative terms, the saving of human beings from the influence of sin and from damnation. In positive terms, the destiny of human beings to be in the presence of God eternally.

**Incarnation** The Christian teaching that the Son of God became a human being as the historical Jesus, both fully God and fully man, permanently, without the integrity of the manhood or of the godhead being compromised.

**Propitiation** The belief that God is angry with human beings because of human sin and that Jesus Christ died on our behalf to take on himself the punishment that should rightfully be ours.

**Sacrament** A ritual action seen as being a special channel to God and a guarantee of God's grace.

**Expiation** When one puts things right, having committed a wrong.

### *The sacraments*

Christian life is not just one way of living life among others, but is life as it really is, open to the totality of reality, which includes the reality of God. This is not to say that death can be avoided, but that Christians can encounter death secure in the knowledge that they will have a share in God's future.

Rahner outlines his teaching on the Christian sacraments in the light of the basic sacrament of Christ which is the Church. It is in the sacraments that we see God's saving will operating in a concrete way throughout the process of history. Christians receive the sacraments so as to respond in a tangible way to God's offer of self and of life in God.

The Church is the sign of God's powerful and effective word. Here we see God's gracious self-communication become real. The Church is the salvation history of human life visible to all. It is the basic sacrament on which all others depend.

The sacraments can only be understood in terms of the relationship of transcendence established between humanity and God. The human essence has been divinized because of God's self-communication.

Just as Jesus Christ instituted the Church, so he instituted the sacraments, in order that God's grace might be perceptibly and evidently sacramental. The Church's sacramental action becomes effective when it meets humanity's openness and freedom.

Through Jesus Christ, the dialogue between God and humanity has entered into a phase which implies God's irreversible triumph. Whenever the finality and invincibility of God's self-offering becomes apparent both through the Church and in the concrete life of an individual, then that event is a sacrament. The Church is a sign of salvation; it is not salvation itself.

Every sacrament is a real word from God and a substantial response to God. Sacraments come both from God and from believing humanity; they are dialogue and partnership between God and humanity.

### *The 'anonymous Christian'*

When proposing this idea, Rahner was struggling with the traditional Catholic saying, *extra ecclesiam, nulla salus* (there is no salvation outside the Church). Rahner had to make sense of it in the contemporary world.

Salvation had traditionally been associated with belief in Christ and involvement in the Church. Nevertheless Rahner laid emphasis on God's will that all should be saved. This involved God's free giving of self and our free response to that gift. We are all oriented towards God.

Nevertheless we cannot forget that there are nominal Christians – Christians in name but not in outlook or behaviour. Rahner had little sympathy with such an attitude. He considered that there were individuals whose outward, explicit conviction was not Christian but who obviously had an inner commitment to living a life of love and service. He called these 'anonymous Christians'. Rahner did not hold the view that any type of belief or any standard of moral action could qualify for salvation under the notion of anonymous Christianity.

This did not involve delivering a judgement on which individuals will benefit from God's salvation. It is not our function to deliver such judgements; it was rather an attempt to understand.

Rahner develops his ideas of the 'anonymous Christian' by first maintaining that Christianity is the only valid religion founded on a unique event, which is the self-revelation of God in Jesus. Yet this event had a universal purpose: the desire that all should be saved. It took place at a specific point in time and place (Palestine, between 5 BC and 29 AD approximately). It had to take place in particular circumstances. We cannot avoid the specific place and time. Yet the fact that the event took place at a specific time and in a specific place did not exclude those who lived before the event or who were unable to receive the message.

Consequently Rahner recognizes that non-Christian religions can communicate the grace of God, until the Gospel is preached to their populations. So the faithful believer or practitioner of a non-Christian religion is recognized as an 'anonymous Christian'.

### *The quarrel with Hans Urs von Balthasar*

When stating their fundamental theological assumptions, Balthasar used a form of aesthetic reason; Rahner used a form of transcendental reason. When spelling out the relationship between God and human beings, Balthasar emphasized discontinuity; Rahner stressed continuity. Balthasar saw salvation in terms of deliverance; Rahner saw it in terms of divinization.

Balthasar feared that the style of thought used by Rahner and others would lead to an 'anthropological reductionism'. He was afraid the transcendental significance of revelation would be weakened and it would be reduced to human terms, rather than stated in divine terms.

Balthasar was sternly critical of Rahner's notion of the 'anonymous Christian'. He protested that it made the human being the decisive test for salvation rather than the cross of Christ. There is no such thing as an anonymous Christian. Only belief in Christ, openly confessed following personal decision, can turn somebody into a Christian.

Rahner had usually considered Christology in the framework of his discussion of what it is to be human (his anthropology). Balthasar objected to a notion of salvation depending on the incarnation and ignoring the decisive moment of the Cross. Rahner, he protested, lacked a theology of the Cross.

Throughout Christian history theologians have affirmed that we are saved through Jesus Christ. But there has never been a dogmatic statement of how redemption actually comes about. How can the work of Christ be applied to us in such a way that results in our salvation?

Several theories have been proposed, and the version of penal substitution has been popular. According to this theory, human beings deserve to die because of sin. But God, in love, sent Jesus into the world and Jesus died instead of us. We can now claim salvation through the sacrifice of Jesus in our place. However, no church body, with the possible exception of Bible fundamentalists, has ever declared one theory to be the correct one and that all others are to be excluded.

Balthasar held to the theory of substitutionary expiation. Rahner did not see the Cross as transforming an angry Father into a forgiving Father. He saw God as never changing; the Cross arose from the unchanging attitude of a forgiving God who kept bumping up against the sinful resistance of the human race. He saw the death of Jesus in terms of solidarity with us rather than as a substitution for us.

## Appraisal

Rahner's work is notoriously difficult to read; he seems to have delighted in dense and abstruse turns of phrase. Nevertheless he has become one of the inescapable presences in contemporary Roman Catholic theology.

He worked hard to prevent the Church taking refuge in Catholic fundamentalism, cocooning itself against the advance of contemporary modern culture, pretending that contemporary culture either does not exist or is of no consequence.

On the other hand, he tried to prevent any reduction of Christian thought which might come about when Theology adapts itself to modern thought because the thinker has been unduly influenced by a secular mindset.

Rahner wished his theology to be a dialogue: what was best in the long tradition of the Church in conversation with modern forms of thought and with the modern world.

In Rahner's thought, the self-communication of God has graced humanity, without raising humans to the status of God, without uniting them with God. In this theology, humanity still strives and yearns for more. That striving for more is the transcendent nature of the human which is capable of recognizing and receiving the gift.

Does this vision of God suggest that humanity and God are mutually interdependent?

Critics of Rahner ask if his distinction between openness to God and the 'supernatural existential' actually stands up. It is not a feature of Biblical revelation. How might it arise from Natural Theology? Does it really overcome the apparent contradiction in theological thought that Rahner wished to avoid?

Rahner's theological method reveals his belief that ordinary, everyday experience cannot be understood without transcendent holy mystery and that is what we call God. The holy mystery of God can only be experienced and known in the historical setting which is everyday life.

# 14 Rosemary Radford Ruether and Women-Church

Feminism is a key feature of contemporary, Western, technological culture. Christian feminist theology tries to express the Christian witness to Jesus Christ and to God from the viewpoint of women. Its distinctive feature is that believing women are expressing an evaluation of faith and of Church which is motivated by their awareness of being an oppressed group.

Feminist theologians complain that all Christian theology, up to now, has been done by men and for men. Consequently it has ignored women's experience or else has distorted it. This 'male' writing of Theology has had damaging consequences for women, who must now turn around and play a major role in reshaping theological expression. Many women now insist that women's experience, as they define it, must be the model for any future Christian Theology.

Rosemary Ruether has been a leading Christian feminist theologian, one of the most widely read in North America. In her writings she has undertaken a systematic feminist treatment of Christian symbols. But that is not the sum total of her achievements; she has an enormous range of interests and concerns. She is widely read in Patristics, the history and theology of anti-Semitism, the Israeli–Palestinian dilemma, the history of women in religion, Liberation Theology and Ecology.

## Life (1936– )

Ruether's mother was a Roman Catholic and her father an Episcopalian/Anglican. She was brought up in broadly ecumenical, open, Christian surroundings. Her father died when she was 12; she and her mother then moved to California. She attended Scripps College where she studied classics, being fascinated by the philosophy and history of classical antiquity. She was interested by the notion of an afterlife and wrote a thesis on how notions of a future life transformed into ideas of apocalypse in the Jewish literature of the inter-testamentary period.

She married Herman Ruether in 1958. This was a marriage of equals, and they continued their studies together. He was a political scientist, she a historian in the field of Christian thought. They had three children. She was awarded an MA in Roman history. She then proceeded to a doctorate in Classics and Patristics at the School of Theology at Claremont. The subject of her thesis was St Gregory of Nazianzus (329–389). Ruether used her knowledge of the classical world to understand Christianity. She was a supporter of the historical–critical method of Biblical interpretation.

Gradually Ruether became involved in the growing civil rights movement of the 1960s. She was particularly conscious of the injustices and racism suffered by the African American population in the United States. She then spent a number of years working in an African American theological college in Washington, DC, where she was exposed to the developing currents of thought expressed by Liberation Theology. She later taught at Garrett-Evangelical Seminary at Evanston in Illinois. She was becoming politically radicalized, often taking part in protest movements and spending periods of time in jail.

Ruether remained an active Roman Catholic, unlike some feminist theologians who abandoned the practice of Christianity altogether. She was friendly with Catholic campaigners and thinkers who were active during the heady and exciting Vatican II period. She was, however, critical and her first published book, *The Church against Itself* (1967), was a critique of the Roman Catholic doctrine of the Church. Catholic Theology was now being written by women; it was no longer an all-male preserve and these women frequently drew upon their experiences of motherhood to bring new ideas to bear on traditional church teachings on sexuality and the family.

**Historical–critical method** A way of understanding texts by trying to find out what they would have meant in their earliest forms and contexts.

**Anti-Semitism** Intolerance against Jews, often leading to aggression and persecution.

**Apocalyptic writings** Books claiming to reveal things normally hidden, often concerned with the end of the world and with human destiny.

From now on the rigorous scholar, well read in the Classics, Jewish Apocalyptic literature and historical–critical methodology was coming to grips with contemporary problems of race, political engagement, gender and ecology.

Ruether has had a consistent interest in Christian anti-Semitism. She recognizes that anti-Semitism is above all a Christian dilemma, rather than a national one. She has been equally critical of Israeli conduct towards the Palestinians and has intervened in many quarters in America and the Near East to seek greater justice for them.

### Timeline

1936 Birth of Rosemary Radford Ruether
1937 Japan invades northeastern China
1939–1945 Second World War
1947 The Marshall Plan and the rebuilding of Europe
1948 The Berlin Blockade
First Arab–Israeli War
1949 Simone de Beauvoir's *The Second Sex*
1950–1953 The Korean War
1952 The first H Bomb
1956 Second Arab–Israeli War
1957 The Treaty of Rome, gradual development of the European Union
1958 Election of Pope John XXIII
1959 Castro in power in Cuba
1960s African countries win independence
1962–1965 Second Vatican Council
1964 Increasing American involvement in Vietnam
1967 Third Arab–Israeli War
Ruether's *The Church against Itself*
1969 First human on the moon
1973 Fourth Arab–Israeli War, the Yom Kippur War
1976 Reunification of Vietnam
Death of Mao Zedong
1977 First *in vitro* fertilization and embryonic transfer
1978 Election of Pope John Paul II

1981 Ruether's *To Change the World*
1982–1983 Fifth Arab–Israeli War, invasion of southern Lebanon
1983 Ruether's *Sexism and God-talk: Towards a Feminist Theology*
1985 Gorbachev elected First Secretary of the Communist Party in the Soviet Union
1985 Ruether's *Women-Church: Theology and Practice of Feminist Liturgical Communities*
1987 First Intifada in Israel
1989 Fall of the Berlin Wall
1992 Ruether's *Gaia and God: An Ecofeminist Theology of Earth Healing*
1997 Birth of Dolly, the cloned sheep
1998 Ruether's *Women and Redemption: A Theological History*
2000 Second Intifada in Israel
2003 Europe experiences the hottest summer on record

## Thought

Before taking a look at the work of Rosemary Radford Ruether in particular, it might be a good idea to cast a broad, general glance at how feminists have viewed traditional, orthodox Christian Theology and how they have felt it to be problematic.

### *Is God masculine or even male?*

With very few exceptions (Isaiah 66.13 is one) the language used in the Bible to talk of God has a masculine focus. Grammatically speaking, the word used for God in most languages is masculine. The pictures used to give us a feel of what God might be like are pictures we normally associate with men: king, shepherd, father.

In addition we often use 'he', 'his' and 'him' for God. The linguistic problem is of course a result of the particular structures of English, where objects are referred to as 'it' and people as 'him' and 'her'.

These analogies never intended to say that God was actually male. The intention has always been to declare that the proper approach to God is made in terms of personal relationship rather than in terms of lifeless objects, and, moreover, that God's loving concern for the creation is something we can understand better if we look to the loving care and anxiety that parents bring to the nurturing of their children.

Classical orthodox Christian Theology has always stressed that God is neither male nor female, and that sexual differentiation on the basis of the analogies used was an error. The error, however, has taken root; the image has become skewed. The question now is how we correct it without falling into the opposite trap of appearing to suggest that God is not a person or that God is a female or has the sexual characteristics of both.

### *Feminism*

Feminism is now a worldwide movement promoting the emancipation of women. It is a liberation movement. It wants women to be the equals of men in society, in the workplace and in politics, so it is concerned to remove all barriers to their advancement. Many of the obstacles are, of course, quite hard to pin down and involve mindsets, values and beliefs – matters of ideology. These are often resistant to change, subtle in their expression and at times misleading.

Feminism has clashed with many religious traditions and Christianity is no exception. One is not born a woman, said Simone de Beauvoir; one becomes one. In other words, being a woman is not a natural state, it is a cultural construct; it is more than biology, it is mindset.

St Paul notoriously forbade women to open their mouths in church (1Cor.14.34, 35). Women feel treated as second-class persons where they are not allowed to become priests or ministers, and Christianity is accused of inbuilt bias against women. A number of feminist thinkers have decided that Christianity cannot overcome these objections and have left the Church.

Other Christian (mostly women) writers have set out to rediscover the huge role played by women within Christian history, to bring their leadership and skills to the fore and to revitalize awareness in this area of hidden history.

During the discussion there has been, and will continue to be, mention of women's experience. Women, it is said, experience their bodies differently from men; men's experience is distanced from the cycles of nature: men's involvement in the reproductive cycles is less intense. Women's experiences of socialization are different; they are culturally programmed to defer to men and to seek, by subtle measures, to be sexually attractive to them. Women are now teaching themselves, in a way that men are not, to be conscious of gender oppression and of subtle forms of injustice towards them in society. Men have never had to recover a 'lost history'; therefore their reading of the past is different. Women are, as a result of these forms of consciousness, more open to social and personal transformation. Women set greater store than men on relationships, intuitiveness and community bonding. All are agreed that every woman experiences oppression because of the patriarchal structures of society.

**Patriarchy** Social organization of families and communities where the organizing role is played by men. Within feminism it is seen as a form of oppression of women by men.

*The feminist agenda within theology*

The feminist agenda within theology has been concerned with language – the use of masculine pronouns for God and that God is frequently imaged or thought of as male. Then there is the figure of Jesus. Jesus was a man, so Christology is often expressed in masculine terms. This is often the reason given, in some traditions, why women are not allowed to become priests: only a male, it is claimed, may figure Christ.

More subtly, the notion has grown that the norm for humanity is to be male; to be female is to be second best. Aquinas (1225–1274) notoriously argued that men are more rational than women. Feminist thinkers have argued that the maleness of Christ is not the essential part of his identity or role. The essential part of Jesus' role is to announce God's loving concern for humanity and God's presence with them in the world. Above all, the role of such a person within the Christian tradition could not, in any case, be an excuse for the domination of one sex by another.

Feminist theologians agree that women's experience must be at the centre of theological reflection. They disagree about the role that other norms of Christian experience and other Christian sources must play in this project. Some see this programme as correlating Christian tradition with the questioning experience of women in the Church. The questions asked by contemporary culture, women's issues in particular, must be laid alongside the normal answers of the tradition and allowed to generate new, pioneering reflection.

It has been suggested that neither gender experience should be normative for the rewriting of theology and that the task of theology from now on is to construct a universalist and gender-neutral theology. Ruether, in particular, has rejected this on the grounds that theology has been too skewed in a male direction from the beginning. Men's experience has determined the forms and content of all theology. The role of feminist theology is to make that distortion visible.

### *Women-Church*

Some feminist thinkers consider classical theology to be so patriarchal that it is incapable of being sympathetic to women. Consequently they reject every aspect of traditional theology. Even Jesus is considered to be part of the anti-women power structures of his day and must be rejected.

Some such thinkers suggest that the answer to their dilemma is Women-Church. Women-Church supplies the normative community out of which God-talk can grow. Word of God has become, in that context, women who identify with other women to build community and together decide what is liberating for women.

### *Ruether's theological method*

We now turn to take a more particular look at the theology of Rosemary Radford Ruether. Ruether is not a systematic theologian; her investigations tend towards an analysis of the meaning and scope of symbols. Theological symbols are, for her, metaphors of human existence, and like all aspects of human living, they can be warped and impose distortions upon us by twisting our thinking out of shape.

Ruether talks of reading human contradictions as one might read archaeological layers of consciousness. In these layers of consciousness there is the evidence of evil at work. Human beings must therefore take responsibility for it and move to act against it.

So Ruether's theological method is a sustained social, cultural and ideological critique. She is trying to bring to light a lost layer of the Western consciousness. This lost, hidden layer and the dominant, visible layer are in serious tension, just as the world of classical antiquity, the original area of her academic training, is in tension with Biblical faith. But Ruether also wants to move beyond this dualism to a new accommodation of opposites.

**Proclamation** The 'telling out', the publicizing of the Christian Good News.
**Heresy** Teachings which cast doubt on or deny the official doctrines of the Church.
**Paradigm** A model or pattern or conceptual support within which theories are constructed.

Ruether sees the prophetic tradition within Biblical faith as the critical strand of the dualism. She includes Jesus in this prophetic tradition; he stands in opposition to the dominant forms of power. She has a simple test for discerning authentic proclamation: whatever fully defends and asserts women's humanity is authentic; anything else in bogus.

Ruether's method is to draw out elements of 'usable tradition' and she looks for it in five sources of Western culture. They are the Bible, the rejected heretical traditions, classical Christian theology, the pagan traditions of Antiquity and critical post-Christian liberalism.

All of these sources are contaminated by the very powerplay she condemns; so is contemporary feminism, as Ruether freely admits. But she is trying to recognize the shape of authentic feminist humanity. Ruether has found in what she calls the 'prophetic-liberating tradition' of the Bible, the source and inspiration of a 'feminist critical principle'. Anything that promotes the full humanity of women counts as word of God. Jesus, for her, remains the historical paradigm of that liberating tradition – the pointer to what, within that tradition, might count as word of God.

### *Christology*

Ruether's critique of Christology begins with what the Jews meant by 'Messiah' (in Greek, 'Christ'). She found quite a gap between the Jewish understanding and the Christian understanding of the term.

Her view is that Christians grant an old Jewish title to Jesus, but do not apply the same meaning to the term. Christians understand the title to mean 'saviour' and consider that the messianic hope has been fulfilled in Jesus. This was the foundation on which Christian dogmatic thought was built. Ruether sees it as a form of thought imperialism.

Because there was disagreement over the concept of Messiah, Christianity developed its Christological thinking in a way that was anti-Jewish. Christianity had to insist on its meaning of 'Messiah' as the correct one, in opposition to Jewish thought, which must be suppressed. In time, this turned into anti-Semitism.

Ruether went on to insist that the only way to cleanse Christian thought of this flaw was to reconstruct Christology in a radically different form. The Christian's faith in Jesus as the Christ must be re-expressed as something to look forward to, rather than as something fulfilled, and Christology must be understood as a pattern rather than as something exclusive.

Ruether's preliminary reflections concentrated on ideas of 'Messiah', but her thought soon moved to include feminist and ecological issues within this Christological critique. In her thought the three strands fused.

We shall first look at the distortions of *Logos* and Christology. We shall look at Ecology later.

Historically Christology had developed during the same period as the Church was establishing itself as the state religion of the Roman Empire. As this development took place, Theology took a new vocabulary on board. The *Logos* was seen as governing the universe in the same way as the Emperor governed the Empire, masters governed slaves, men governed women.

The church and Christology were becoming patriarchal. Theology in general and Christology in particular had become forms of powertalk. Ruether rejected this. She wished to peel all masculine imagery and all ruler imagery away from Christology. She saw such distortions arising out of pictures of Jesus as Messiah and as *Logos*.

When these distortions have been removed, the Jesus of the Synoptic Gospels emerges as a figure well-suited to feminism. Jesus is a revolutionary figure, breaking down social moulds and inaugurating a new reality in which notions of rule and dominance have no place. The word of Jesus is a liberating word which disturbs the traditional assumptions of the social order. She referred to Jesus as the 'kenosis of patriarchy'.

Jesus was the liberator. He did not come to proclaim himself but to preach something beyond himself, while rejecting all notions of power, status and privilege. He preached a new humanity freed of all dualisms and hierarchies.

**Christology** The study of the Person of Christ, particularly the union of the divine and human natures in Christ.
**Kenosis** A Greek word meaning 'self-emptying'. Often refers to the idea that Christ gave up divine characteristics during the period of his life on earth.
**Hierarchy** Any arrangement of elements where some are seen as more important than others. For example, bishops are considered more important than priests.
**Immanence** What is inherent in something's nature; what does not exceed the natural limits of that object.
**Transcendence** Above, independent of, surpassing the material universe.
**Dynamic** The physical and moral forces that produce change and interaction; the varying forces at work in interpersonal relationships.

### *What is God?*

Ruether saw that we tend to structure the way we look at the world into dualisms: good/bad, right/wrong, cooked/raw, male/female and so on. Things that should be together are set over against each other; there is a sense of hierarchy, one is better than the other. Men, she maintains, tend towards dualisms in a way women do not. As a result of this, female is identified with matter, creation, immanence, evil; male, on the other hand is identified with spirit, reason, transcendence, good.

Ruether is dissatisfied with the traditional way people picture God because it is conditioned by dualistic imagery. She is searching for a non-dualistic way of portraying God. The Father image of God is patriarchal; even the use of a word like 'parent' with a non-sexist loading is not enough and, what is more, it prolongs a sense of 'spiritual infantilism'.

She turns to the idea of God as the 'ground of our being' which had been promoted by Paul Tillich (1886–1965). God is not to be associated with spirit, transcendence, maleness or indeed body, immanence or femaleness. God embraces all dualistic divisions in a dynamic unity. Ruether rejects all images of God which affirm the power of God, the sovereignty of God or the freedom of God.

### *Ecology and feminism*

'Ecofeminism' is the union of the ecology movement and feminism. Basically ecology looks at how natural communities function to maintain a healthy network of life, for example the way plants and animals on the earth depend upon each other. Human interference is one of the chief disruptive forces to all community systems. The ecology movement often draws attention to the destruction which human activity causes to the natural environment.

#### The problem

Feminism is particularly worried about how male domination is at the heart of all society structures. It is also concerned with destructive tendencies in communities and blames it upon the ascendancy of one dominant class within those communities. Ecofeminism draws a parallel between the domination and destruction of nature by humans and the domination of human society, with destructive consequences, by men.

Ecofeminism asserts that all life, human and non-human, has intrinsic value. Richness and diversity are to be encouraged as valuable in themselves. Humans have no right to destroy any of this diversity, though they may satisfy basic needs.

However human beings interfere too much at present and the results are destructive and catastrophic. Human civilization would not be diminished by a reduction of the human population and the world now needs policies to reduce its population. There is a difference between maintaining a high quality of life and a high standard of living.

Ruether believes that the symbolic connection between domination of nature and domination of women stems from Mediterranean and Western culture where women are associated with nature and men with culture. This was originally because of women's childbearing role. All tasks involving food preparation and the work of the household belonged in the feminine sphere.

Men, on the other hand, concentrated on work demanding sudden bursts of energy: field-clearing, hunting, war. All of this allowed them more time for leisure; so culture became a male domain. Gradually all life and culture was defined by males and from a viewpoint of male advantage.

At the Reformation, particularly the Calvinist Reformation, the medieval sacramental sense of nature was abolished. Saving knowledge of God comes from God and is not found within nature. Only the Word was divine; everything human was fallen and women were the chief victims of this collapse. At the scientific revolution, nature was secularized; it was no longer where Christ and the Devil struggled. It was mere matter, subject to the laws discoverable by (male) intellect.

Scientific and technological control went hand in hand with colonial expansion. This involved huge new resources of land and labour out of which masses of wealth could be won by the application of technology. Over the course of the last three centuries this dream of an unlimited future and a technological, scientific answer to all human problems has begun to reveal itself as a nightmare.

Human progress, control over disease and longer life expectancy have not been matched by population control. The food supply has not kept pace with the population explosion. There is an increasing gap between rich and poor. The Western scientific enterprise has been built on the back of massively unjust work practices and, as this injustice grows more evident, the world has become more militarized to protect the advantages of privilege.

The problem is how to draw back from this disaster and remake the relationship between ourselves and the earth. This demand has to be made both on grounds of justice and of survival. Ruether calls for conversion to new sets of values, involving new ways of living on the earth.

THE TASK

Ruether suggests we reshape our dualistic concept of reality, which is currently split between soulless matter and transcendent male consciousness. Nature runs itself better without interference from human beings. We need to refocus our gifts so that we can harmonize our needs with those of the whole planet. This inevitably involves reshaping our concept of God.

The model for God must no longer be 'alienated male consciousness', which is apart from and dominates nature. God, in ecofeminist spirituality, must be seen as the immanent source of life sustaining the whole planet, the matrix that sustains the interdependent nature of all plants and animals.

**Matrix** The setting or mould in which anything is allowed to develop.
**Salvation** In negative terms, the saving of human beings from the influence of sin and from damnation. In positive terms, the destiny of human beings to be in the presence of God eternally.

Hierarchies of domination must be replaced by relationships between men and women, between human groups, between humans and other beings, which overcome all divisions of race, class, gender and species. There must be equitable sharing in work and in the fruits of labour. All patterns of interdependency have to be reshaped. There can no longer be a dominant side and a subjected side in any relationship.

There must be conversion of men to the work of women along with conversion of male consciousness to the earth. Such conversions will provide a new symbolic vision of salvation. Salvation will no longer be an escape to heaven but a continued conversion to the source out of which we build our relation to nature and our relation to each other.

Ruether calls on us to abandon the idea that we become free as we come to immortality. We are also asked to abandon a view of life which concentrates on disintegration in the processes of living. This is the notion that our death is the most important moment of our existence, because it is when we enter upon eternal life. Instead, we should be concentrating on the re-creative processes of living. These also involve seeing how we disintegrate back into the life process and arise again to new forms.

## Appraisal

Not all feminist theology is Christian. There is certainly Jewish feminist theology and there is no reason why critiques of other world faiths may not be written from feminist perspectives. Some forms of feminist theology have either abandoned Christianity or were never Christian in the first place.

Feminist theology in general, and Ruether's feminist theology in particular, is not necessarily content with restating Christian orthodoxy in words that are freed from sexist overtones, from the nuances of patriarchy. It frequently involves sweeping away much of the content of Christian theology and practice. Many people will have difficulty applying the label 'Christian' to this element of her thought.

This begs the question, what is Christian? Are there a few basic, fundamental characteristics that must be applied to all Christians to be worthy of the name? Can everybody agree on what they are?

A critical issue arising out of Ruether's discussion of the patriarchy of traditional Christology is the twin problem of ideology and revelation. Christianity is a faith of revelation and that revelation is expressed, first and foremost, in the person of Jesus Christ, in the witness given to him in the canonical scriptures and in the sacramental practice of believing communities. Those same canonical scriptures speak repeatedly of Jesus as Messiah and of Jesus as Logos.

How, on the basis of feminist ideology, can one declare what may or may not be accepted as revelation? How, on the basis of ideology, is it possible to revise the canon? How was the canon established in the first place, and what were the ideological issues that underpinned the decisions made at that juncture?

If the canon was established on the basis of ideology, can traditional teaching not be changed on the basis of ideologies which have arisen out of problems that only come to the forefront of awareness much later?

Does Ruether use the feminist critical principle to interpret Scripture and the tradition of the Church, or does that feminist critical principle over-ride them?

Many women now insist that women's experience, as defined by feminists, must be the standard for any future Christian theology. Is this is a demand to include women's experience, or a demand to exclude everything except women's experience?

If the prime task of feminist theology is to make the patriarchal distortion visible, does feminist theology only have a critical role? Where does its constructive focus lie? Is feminist theology open to the possibility of having its own critique of classical theology turned against it in the future?

Liberation movements of every sort often lead to new modes of oppression, also subtle in their functioning, as people rush uncritically to adopt the new dominant outlook. Is dominant discourse a good or a bad thing? What are its merits? What are its failures?

Feminist Theology is a Liberation movement. It also stresses the loving and pastoral concern of God. As such is it programmed to emphasize the immanence of God at the expense of divine transcendence?

# 15 Walter Brueggemann and the Biblical Imagination

Walter Brueggemann's specialized field of study is the Old Testament. In particular, he hopes that his writings may be of help to preachers, who must approach the Old Testament out of the experience of modern living and confront contemporary culture with the message of the Hebrew Scriptures.

Walter Brueggemann is an American Christian in whom Bible-based faith meets careful intellectual discipline. He is a scholar who reads the Old Testament in order to challenge the society in which he lives with Word of God. One of his constant themes is the way the chosen people in the Old Testament had to contend with the power of empire; an idea he likes to apply to contemporary America.

He confronts a confident, wealthy, industrial–military superpower with the destabilizing message of the Bible. He promotes new readings of Scripture; he considers postmodern culture to be a time of opportunity for faith and mission. He suggests different, creative, playful readings of the sacred text. He forces his readers to ask awkward questions. He presents a biblically informed engagement with the modern world.

## Life (1933–)

Walter Brueggemann was born in 1933 in Nebraska, in the United States of America, where the great central plain starts to rise towards the Rockies. His father was a German Evangelical pastor. He graduated from Elmhurst College in 1951 with a degree in Sociology. He continued his studies in Eden Theological Seminary in Missouri. He was awarded the Bachelor of Divinity in 1958, with a special interest in Old Testament. He was awarded a doctorate by the prestigious Union Theological Seminary in New York, where he studied from 1958 to 1961. Between 1971 and 1974, he worked for a further doctorate, this time in Education, from St Louis University.

He lectured at Eden Theological Seminary between 1961 and 1986. He then moved to take up a post teaching Old Testament at Columbia Theological Seminary at Decatur, Georgia.

He is an ordained minister of the United Church of Christ, a union between two church traditions in the United States. On the one hand there was the Evangelical and Reformed Church: descendents of immigrants from Germany, the Palatinate, Switzerland and Holland. The second strand of the union was from the Congregational tradition, which recognizes no hierarchy in church government but maintains that each local congregation is free to govern its own affairs under the headship of Christ. The union was negotiated between 1942 and 1957. Its members represent a variety of styles of worship and practice. They come from a wide variety of national and social backgrounds.

Walter Brueggemann has been honoured by many of the principal theological schools and been a guest lecturer at many of the leading universities of America. He retired in 2003. He is married and his wife is also an ordained minister of the United Church of Christ. They are parents and grandparents.

## Timeline

1931 Empire State Building opens in New York
1932 Huxley's *Brave New World*
1933 Birth of Walter Brueggemann
Adolph Hitler comes to power in Germany
1934 The 'Dust Bowl' disaster in the United States
1941 Attack on Pearl Harbour
Manhattan project to build an atomic weapon
1942 Camus' *Outsider*
1945 Atomic bombs dropped on Hiroshima and Nagasaki
Founding of the United Nations
1954 McCarthyism at its height in the United States
1955 Supreme Court orders end to racial segregation in American public schools
1957 Soviet Union launches first Sputnik
1958–1961 Brueggemann at Union Theological Seminary

| | |
|---|---|
| 1961 | Soviet cosmonaut Yuri Gagarin orbits the earth |
| | Brueggemann teaching at Eden Theological Seminary |
| 1963 | Martin Luther King leads Civil Rights march to Washington, DC |
| | President Kennedy assassinated |
| 1972 | Anthony Burgess' *A Clockwork Orange* |
| 1977 | Brueggemann's *The Land* |
| 1978 | Brueggemann's *The Prophetic Imagination* |
| 1981 | AIDS identified |
| 1983 | The 'Star Wars' project |
| 1986 | Brueggemann teaching at Columbia Theological Seminary |
| 1990 | Hubble space telescope |
| 1991 | Strategic Arms Reduction Talks limit US and USSR nuclear arsenals |
| 1992 | Soviet Union dissolved |
| 1993 | First genetically engineered vegetable |
| | Brueggemann's *Texts under Negotiation* |
| 1997 | Dolly the sheep, the first cloned animal |
| | Brueggemann's *Theology of the Old Testament: Testimony, Dispute, Advocacy* |
| | Brueggemann's *Cadences of Home: Preaching among Exiles* |
| 1999 | Serb atrocities in Kosovo |
| 2001 | Terrorists pilot aircraft in the 9/11 attack on the United States |
| 2003 | America and its allies invade Iraq |
| | Brueggemann retires |

## Thought

### *The Old Testament and the contemporary world*

Brueggemann looks back to the way life was lived in Old Testament times and at the same time criticizes vestiges of that model still remaining in contemporary culture. He reflects on the Jerusalem establishment (temple and monarchy) at the centre of the way of life portrayed in some of the Hebrew Scriptures. He then wonders how models like this dominate our thinking in the modern world. He uses the Old Testament as a means of reading contemporary culture.

That convergence of State and Church represented by the Jerusalem establishment occupies only a small period of the Old Testament history. But we think of it as the norm. He points out that such a model really only promotes the interests of an 'established, culturally legitimated church'. These institutions were established and well financed. The king provided civil and military leadership. King and priesthood tended to agree. What was good for one was good for the other. There was both cross-fertilization and cross-criticism.

The people of those Jewish kingdoms were served by a church intelligentsia; their role was to act as both civil service and higher education service. All assumed the rule of the Lord God, Lord of the universe. They believed there was a single moral rule for all: good and evil were not matters of cultural relativism. Nevertheless Brueggemann sees this intelligentsia as having self-sufficient, secularizing tendencies and as being advocates of state ideology.

At the same time, but outside the circles of self-satisfaction and power, were the ardent, critical voices of the prophets; that criticism was harsh, troubling and far reaching. This critical, prophetic tradition seems only to have existed during the period of centralized monarchy.

This fourfold package of stable temple institution, acceptable civil leadership, secularizing intellectuals and passionate prophecy were not unlike models of state and church institutions in the contemporary United States and they work well in times of political, cultural and economic stability. Brueggemann points out that historically, in the Old Testament context, they were swept away in a 'geo-political upheaval' in 587 BC, the period of the Exile when the nation had to seek new models of life and faith. He further points out that we live today in an unsettling period of upheaval where we wonder if the models we have received at both personal and institutional level can really serve our needs.

Brueggemann turns to the time before the monarchy was established, when Israel operated with a different model of 'church' and government. Here the central figure was the memory of Moses. Self-awareness and identity were expressed in what he calls the 'the exodus liturgy', where the people retold the story of deliverance from slavery in Egypt, where God is seen as calling for moral separation from the power structures of Egypt and, later, of the Canaanite states.

Here the voice of God did not operate out of a culturally dominant structure, but came from a marginalized people. The community can only be its true self if it has operated a costly break from its comfort zone represented by the 'flesh pots of Egypt' (Exod. 16.3).

This break is also an experience of freedom and, once they had received the Law at Sinai, the people are constantly challenged to express and live that faith in the light of that ethical call. This situation demanded constant arbitration and negotiation between conflicting opinions. It was not stable but in constant flux.

There was a continuous attempt to discern the mind of God. This is a community aware of a covenant relationship between itself and God, a community freed by God for God's service, and refusing the comfortable temptation of conformity to dominant culture. In such a situation nothing is permanent; nothing is settled.

Brueggemann paints a picture of a people called to unsettling insecurity, to constant improvization, to daring decisions. Its only central institution was a remembered story of unsettlement, freedom and risk. Out of this, it built its story which was new and fresh every day. It was a community of the socially and economically marginalized. But its speciality was concern for the neighbour and out of those circumstances it moulded different forms of community, vision and power.

In the earlier period, the believing community lived in a setting where it had little influence. It did not belong to the power structures which surrounded it. In later days there may have been conflicts between faith and power, but they tended to be short-lived and minor. Once the believing community had got its hands on power, it became indifferent to faith and grew so apathetic that it was innocuous.

There was always a temptation to abandon identity, to become indifferent to faith. Both the religious and civil institutions were at one time so much in concord that, while they supported the identity of the nation, apathy was widespread.

But in the Greek period after the Exile (late fourth to early second centuries BCE), Jewish political identity had been lost, was now almost irrelevant; it needed an upheaval to awaken the people to concern.

That identity survived because, in the first place, the faithful worked to recover memory. It survived secondly because they worked to promote hope. They are dependent, not on themselves, but on the promise of God.

Thirdly, and most importantly, that identity survived because the people became a community of the book, the text where the histories, the laws and the promises were written.

Brueggemann reminds us that the period after the Exile was the period of canon formation: when it was decided what was authoritative text of the Old Testament and what was not. But more importantly, it was also the period of the 'imaginative construal of the text', when they allowed the old story to work on their imagination with positive results for living in the present. He believes that faith calls us, in our generation, to a similar task. This was not, he points out, a controlled activity; such an act, in a context of marginal existence, did not, and does not, need a controlled outcome. Here, we note a distinctly Protestant voice.

Brueggemann makes the point again and again that the purpose of sustained textual study is not erudition or knowledge; it is the task of entering into a tradition of speech, reflection, discernment and imagination that empowers individuals and communities in the face of superior social, economic and political power.

The story offered by dominant habits of speech, dominant power, dominant ways of viewing the world, is no story at all; it is powerless to engage, to empower, to enthuse or to involve. Passionate involvement with one's own story, with renewed memory and with renewed hope, allows one to dare to imagine one's own story as the voice of God and to develop a new and vibrant confidence. We need a shift from a culture of cohering, dominant institutions to a text culture which promotes the imagination to engage with more creative models of reality and often in a thoroughly subversive mode.

Brueggemann sees the collapse of modernity as calling us to reconsider a vision of church which was built for modernity; conventional 'theological speech' is not understood by a contemporary audience. Finally, he asks us to consider what we intend when we embark upon the journey of faith. Why do it?

He wants us to move from being a temple community to being a text community. He suggests that wilderness and exile models of community are demanded. Does God, he asks, 'cringe at the prospect of this community being one of wilderness and exile'? God, he points out, actually resisted the temple (2 Sam. 7.6–7). The text calls us to an alternative imagination and new strategies in an out-of-the-ordinary community.

### The Old Testament Story: A Timeline

| | |
|---|---|
| 1900 BCE approx. | Ur of the Chaldees: stories of Abraham, Isaac and Jacob |
| 1700 BCE approx. | Egypt: stories of Joseph |
| 1300 BCE approx. | Stories of Moses, the Exodus from Egypt<br>The desert wandering: the people receive the Law |
| 1200 BCE approx. | Stories of Joshua and settlement in Canaan |
| 1200–1000 BCE approx. | The period of the Judges |
| 1000 BCE approx. | David establishes a united kingdom |
| 950 BCE approx. | The two Israelite kingdoms; the time of the prophets |
| 722 BCE | The Northern Kingdom destroyed by the Assyrians |
| 605–586 BCE | The Southern Kingdom defeated and finally abolished by the Babylonians; a series of deportations when Jewish citizens are exiled to Babylon |
| 538 BCE | Collapse of the Babylonian Empire, rise of the Persian Empire; first exiles return to Jerusalem from captivity |
| 333 BCE | Alexander the Great defeats Darius III; end of the Persian Empire; beginning of Greek period |
| 167 BCE | Jews revolt, led by the Maccabees |
| 63 BCE | Romans take Jerusalem |
| 5 BCE approx. | Birth of Jesus |
| 38 CE approx. | Conversion of Paul |

Note: The 'traditional' story is outlined above; it raises critical problems. Its historicity has been questioned. Its dramatic, teaching power has always been valued.

*The radical consequences of praise*

In his book *Israel's Praise: Doxology against Idolatry and Ideology*, Brueggemann declares praise to be the duty and delight of the human being and, indeed, of all creation. Every one of us has the urge to move beyond self and return our energy to its source, the creator God. This is a study of the Psalms as the vehicle of praise, but it is also an attempt to move the study of these texts in the direction of social interaction and function. He suggests that the function of a psalm is never focused along a purely transcendent axis. That is to say in a vertical direction, one aimed at God. A psalm also expresses, establishes and legitimates social power; it feels out along a horizontal axis.

Brueggemann, of course, never looses sight of the pastoral aspect of Bible study. The duty of pastors is to encourage a communal, intentional and alternative vision in their flock. The Psalms play a vital role in the 'doing' of liturgy, which is the recitation and repetition and the re-organizing of symbols in order to present an alternative vision of the world; an outlook to which ordinary men and women can aspire in the contemporary, post-industrial, post-Christian world.

Each of us acts out of a life world, a framework for understanding life, created by self and by community. We participate in other life worlds through the power of advertising, propaganda, education, nurture. These are frameworks created for us, and we create more of them for ourselves. As it worships, the worshipping community is engaged in an act of world creation: the building of an alternative, an ideal world against the grain of modern living. Praise sings songs to create this world and against all other false worlds.

In the 'doing' of liturgy, Christian ministers define reality as they offer a new way of looking at the world they have been given and of ordering that given world in the direction of ethical values, along the transcendental, vertical axis.

As Israel worships God, it celebrates a world over which God rules and, in so doing, Israel accepts and legitimates God's justice, revealing the demands that sovereign justice addresses to each of us. Worship expresses, calls into being, the claims of the social, horizontal axis.

**Doxology** Expressing praise for God.

**Transcendence** Above, independent of, surpassing the material universe.

**Pastoral** Aspects of the clergy's work in offering help, care, advice and guidance.

**Ethics** Concerning the principles of right and wrong.

**Ideology** The characteristic convictions, preferences, prejudices and ways of reasoning of a group.

That praise, then, offers a world of promise, compassion, mercy, justice and truth. The world of praise is consequently a threat to all vested interests and all forms of self-sufficiency, all advertising, big conglomerates, financial institutions and development corporations, which are the realizations of idolatry and ideology.

The creation is as it is. How do we act upon it? And as we act upon it, what sort of world do we make of it? This is where the ethical demand comes in. This is where we are asked to re-examine our values, the ones that have shaped the world. We are invited to substitute new values and re-shape the world.

This time we are asked to shape the world, not in order to favour self, but in a way that carries truth and justice to all. Doxology, praise of God, invokes power, but a power that will not be contained in sectional aims. It will refuse to be domesticated by aims which favour me, or my company, or my political party or any system of government. It is power that insists on being heard afresh.

This is not a reasoned or calculating stance; there is 'nothing in it for me'. It is an outlook driven by amazement and gratitude. It dares to recognize great power in the holiness of God; it is not content to submit to a dull conventionality of 'the way things are' or 'reasonable' assumptions.

This faith is revolutionary in its possibilities. It announces a God who does not respect persons, institutions or conventions. Brueggemann talks of a move from reason to summons. We are moved away from the calm assumption of practicality and reason, and not rocking the boat, and confidence that we can manage all of creation. Even while admitting that the world does need managers, we are called to abandon our self-sufficient view of a world where amazing transformations cannot happen and enter a world of God's reign, not ours.

The dominant ideology of the world is an ideology which does not recognize this new, raw and unregulated energy of possibility. We tend to prefer a world where we expect nothing from God; we live in a system which cannot be changed. But that is a system where individuals are not allowed a voice and where hurts cannot be given expression; it is a world without passion or hope.

Against the dominant ideology, Brueggemann asserts that liturgy does make a world, that there is a dramatic, dynamic reality in the 'doing' of worship. Everything in worship is subversive of dominant idolatry and ideology. It is subversive because it proclaims the possibility of justice in the face of injustice and of hope in the face of the present order. Brueggemann refers to it as pain-informed, subversive praise.

It allows us to glimpse a living God; it holds out the possibility of a world of truth and justice. It calls us to be authentic, committed persons rather than self-sufficient, uncritical followers. It urges the creation of a compassionate community towards the voiceless and despairing.

### *Gift, temptation and task*

Walter Brueggemann's study, *The Land* is a study in gift, in temptation and in task. It proposes how a sense of place can be recognized as gift, as promise and as challenge in Biblical faith. He views Israel's story as a history of promise into the land, followed by a history of management into exile followed by a new history of promise into kingdom. That pattern grew out of his growing awareness of how Israel's story was remembered and told.

Brueggemann's aim has been to tell the stories and let them impact on the consciousness of community. He has grown tired of the superficial dichotomies of culture such as scientific/mythological or technology/mysticism; the story allows us to understand more easily a vision of a human future which is historical but also involves covenant and promise.

**Dichotomy** Division or separation into two groups which are sharply opposed and contrasted.

**Mythology** Old stories which are often used to explain some natural occurrence or cultural understanding.

**Mysticism** Having direct communication with God through prayer and meditation.

**Covenant** Originally an agreement between two parties; it came to be seen as the faithfulness of God towards Israel in return for the inner righteousness of the people before God. Jesus restated it as humanity receiving a gracious gift from God by which their desire to serve God was made perfect. It requires a response. It has its highest expression in the example of the life and death of Jesus.

The sense of place in the story is where one is with God. Biblical faith is about the life of a people with God. Even when Israel is without a place, it survives and marks its special identity as a people being led to a place. An important idea here is the 'sojourner' or resident alien, to be where one is, but to be an outsider. Even though marked by a promise, this is a people marked by precariousness. Even in exile, although not abused or enslaved, their existence was marked by a sense of discontinuity; their trust in their traditions and institutions was no longer well founded.

In periods of its story when it had land, both in Egypt and later in Palestine, Israel's story is one of problem and temptation. That possession could be marked by slavery, oppression and exploitation. When they had returned from exile the sense of land was the experience of living in a place controlled by another, to continue to live a problematic existence. The story is of being in, and belonging to, a land which was never fully given. The faith of Israel focuses around a journeying in and out of land.

Nevertheless the hold the people had on the land came as a gift from God. To be a people under gift is to be rare and new, and Israel had to face the demands of that newness: the land was *demand*.

If one keeps the consciousness of gift as gift, one is addressed by the giver: addressed by God. The first temptation is to be satisfied by the land and enjoy it without covenant, without demand and without mystery. Therefore Israel was asked to remember, to reflect on the difference between what was then and what is now. The second temptation is to pretend that things are as they are because Israel, not God, made them so; this is the temptation to be seduced by other gods.

Land with God brings responsibility; to be in a free society is to have responsibility. To live in a coercive society is to see that those in control, those who have made the situation what it is, need not obey. So Israel must both manage and obey. Israel's appreciation of land is first to live under Torah, under divine demand. It is secondly to keep Sabbath.

Brueggemann points out that Sabbath was originally a radical ethical demand. It was for freeing slaves, for resting land and for cancelling debt. Sabbath is itself the challenging voice of gift in a coercive world. That challenge asks if I can give as freely and as boldly as the way the gift was given to me.

But Brueggemann also points out that in order to enter into the land one must live daringly, live up to mighty expectation when it might be more comfortable to settle for far less than the promise. It is to be like grasshoppers challenging giants (Num. 12.32–34).

Finally, we are led to consider that the movement which gathered around Jesus was, in a similar way, a people grasping for courage and waiting for gift, expecting a breaking of patterns. This situation throws up at least two responses which are in tension with each other: that of daring waiting which allows the great Giver to work, and that of overconfidence in one's ability to manage history oneself.

In Christian awareness the theme of land as promise, gift, demand, task and challenge has been replaced by the same themes around the person of Jesus Christ. The new image is that of the kingdom of God. It is an image which is both present and awaiting realization. It contrasts what is with what might be. It proclaims a daring break with the unimportance of our expectations. It calls us to value once more a world of gifts and to work for the rehabilitation of the rejected who are the bearers of promise.

### *Being a prophet today*

*The Prophetic Imagination* is a study in the meaning of prophecy in the late twentieth century, an attempt to understand what prophets are doing. Brueggemann is persuaded that prophets understand best how change works in society, how change is related to the emotional fringes of experience and how public certainty and private longing often clash. They recognize the power of language to call newness into being. This book is particularly directed towards the new prophetic vision and ministry which women bring to the Church.

The 'task of prophetic ministry is to nurture, nourish, and evoke a consciousness and perception of the dominant culture around us'. This does not mean that the task of prophecy is to understand dominant culture; Brueggemann takes it as given that Christianity is an alternative culture, a counter-culture. The task of prophecy is to understand how dominant culture tries to domesticate, tame and use for its own purposes any prophetic voice.

Alternative voices and awareness criticize dominant power, even as that power attempts to dismantle and disarm them. How does one construct any alternative voice that will resist being domesticated by dominant power? Alternative voices go one step further; they also function in order to energize, to promote action.

Brueggemann studies several versions of dominant power and several versions of the alternative voice in the Old Testament, before turning to the example of Jesus of Nazareth.

The first voice studied is that of Moses in opposition to Pharaoh. Moses gives expression to a radical break from triumphalism, oppression and exploitation but the vision of Moses was more than mere protest. It was the mission to counter empire with the politics of justice and the social reality of compassion.

Real criticism, says Brueggemann, begins with the capacity to grieve. This grief is more than resignation, for it institutes the first energizing step which allows a new theological and social reality to emerge. The last energizing step is doxology: praise which redefines the way we see social reality and asserts the reality of God – a reality which empire cannot tolerate if it is to survive.

Historically however few revolutions have ever survived long and old habits of domination and empire return, often in new forms. Brueggemann uses the example of Solomon. Here the radical quality of Moses' vision is undermined by new social developments. Brueggemann uses the term 'temple' to symbolize all these changes in the direction of what we now call modernity.

What were those new, 'modern' social developments? First there was a harem which is a sign of concern for the self-securing of power. There were tax districts which indicate the eradication of tribal identity in the interests of mass identity. Then there was a standing bureaucracy and army who could often act as if they were above all notions of justice and compassion. The writings of the day stress wisdom, where global reality is managed, indeed conveniently packaged.

Solomon's temple successfully undermined the radical quality of Moses' revolution because now Solomon could seduce by affluence, he could pressurize by high-handed policy and he could appear to domesticate God within the confines of a controlled state religion.

Brueggemann allows us to see the contemporary management mentality functioning in the ancient story. All policy must, after all, be expressed in language and Brueggemann maintains that managed prose cannot invent new ways and does not wish to permit them. Radical alternatives can only be envisioned by lyrical, poetic utterance.

He is further concerned that managed, apathetic everydayness is not just created when we are confronted by the great affairs of state. It is deeply rooted in the everyday conditions of every home, family and marriage where people unthinkingly and numbly accept the bland and controlled choices offered to them by bank, supermarket, High Street fashion gurus or social convention.

The task of prophetic imagination is as follows:

- to penetrate self-deception;
- to offer symbols adequate to the horror of experiences which evoke numbness;
- to reactivate symbols that have been means of redemptive honesty;
- to bring fears that have long been denied to public expression;
- to speak concretely about the alienation and loss of heritage involved in mass-packaged living.

If one denies this pain and grief there can be no new movement from God or towards God. Grief permits newness, because it acknowledges loss.

Brueggemann says that the 'royal consciousness leads people to despair about power to new life. It is the task of prophetic imagination and ministry to engage the promise of newness that is at work in our history with God'. The task is to cut through despair and penetrate the dissatisfied coping involved in the everydayness of living: to offer symbols that none can think imaginable.

This involves penetrating the memory of people to allow them to use the tools of hope and to offer them language that reshapes consciousness, redefines hope and contradicts the 'world of kings' – to bring to consciousness hopes that have long been denied.

Finally, Brueggemann sees, in Jesus, decisive criticism of dominant consciousness. Luke's account talks of solidarity with the poor, while Matthew's depicts the murderous reaction that his birth drew from the power of Herod.

Jesus spoke to the oppressed, but there are no oppressed people without oppressors. He forgave sin and he healed on the Sabbath; he threatened the priestly forms of social control. He ate with outcasts, challenging accepted norms of morality. He was highly critical of the morality of the traditional Jewish ritual law.

Jesus expressed compassion which is a radical form of criticism. The crucifixion of Jesus is the decisive criticism of royal awareness. Jesus announces the end of the world of death by taking death into his own person. The Cross signals the end of the king's freedom, justice and power. It expresses a religion of God's freedom, a just society with an economics of sharing and power to engage in the politics of justice.

In all these events in the life of Jesus, Jesus himself announced an energizing word and the possibility of praise arising out of amazement. This prophetic word of energy is addressed to a minority community of marginal people. The criticism is addressed to a dominant community, where it may not be heard.

### *The opportunities of the postmodern imagination*

Modernism refuses to accept any assertion that cannot be empirically tested. That is the core 'truth', the foundational story on which it rests. Postmodernism is the experience of living according to a foundational story which is in the course of disintegrating.

In the postmodern universe, the autonomy of the individual is doubted and scientific objectivity is questioned. Moreover, the promotion of social well-being is treated with suspicion. This is the case of the 'nanny-state' in which ignorance still flourishes, poverty has not be eradicated, disease increases and war has not been made obsolete. A culture of confidence is in decline; the white, male, Western, colonial mindset is collapsing.

It is being replaced with a pluralistic, multilayered outlook; viewpoints are provisional in character. There is little coherence between the various components of this outlook, which easily fracture and pass away. This is a condition described as a suspicion of metanarratives, of all foundational, explanatory stories.

Modernism has long been seen as a main stumbling block to Christian belief. Postmodern thinking is suspicious of metanarratives, and Christianity is a metanarrative. But postmodernism does not rule metanarratives out; it can at one and the same time accept several contradictory ones. However, the features of modernity have not gone away; it is possible for institutions and individuals to show characteristics of both.

Brueggemann develops his ideas in *Texts under Negotiation*. He considers the old interpretation formed by historical criticism as no longer adequate. The intellectual, cultural and political promise of the Enlightenment has led to tyranny supported by ideology. Salvation history is not now understood; after all, the Enlightenment project took shape in opposition to the Hebrew and Christian stories. Most people now have some exposure to other world religions; Christianity's claims of monopoly do not convince. This situation, says Brueggemann, establishes a new interpretive situation.

Brueggemann's view is that this shift creates new and creative opportunities for Christian ministry. The desire to achieve mastery of the text and the quest for objective, standard readings had been important concerns up to now. But they had eliminated daring, testing speech and subversive text. Speech was used only to describe reality. This was dull and conventional. But in a new interpretive context, imagination has been freed up to picture, perceive, portray and practise the world in ways that are different from what might seem possible at first glace.

The task of the new Christian imagination is how to *fund* the new situation. Where and how can we find materials and resources out of which to imagine a new world? We are looking for materials that authorize a *counter-imagination* of the world: a dogged imagining against the grain.

In a world riddled with the fruits of modernism, consumerism and positivism, we must construct an evangelical counter-culture that makes a different communal life possible. Where modernism makes the present absolute, Biblical faith is ordered into past – present – future, with a life created by God and also consummated by God.

First, Brueggemann reminds us that this new evangelical outlook operates with a memory that we originate in a past created for us and kept for us by a faithful, sovereign God. Creation explains nothing; creation is an attitude of praise, a praise-filled response to the world and all its wonder.

Here we note the total lopsidedness between God's generosity and our fragility. Modernism and the individual seduced by it have worked hard to hide that fragility from themselves.

Secondly, Brueggemann is not trying to accommodate scientific learning. The good news is that God has ordered the world as a 'life-giving, joy-producing system of generativity'. The world does not depend on us and is not available for us.

Lastly, we are asked to ponder the origin of the believing community. The Church is an alternative community within the world, not an accident of human preference. Church is an 'odd community' grounded in God's love; it raises questions of justice and enacts answers of love and care.

Turning from past to future, an evangelical infrastructure invites to an act of 'futuring': a notion of newness, discontinuous with the present. The hope, the conviction that God will bring things to a full, glorious completion is, once again, not an explanation of anything. Modernism expects nothing of God; evangelical hope hands over our existence to God. An evangelical proclamation must require the regular proclamation of 'the most extravagant and outrageous promises of God'.

These promises concern self which is not a fixed identity. The believing self turns to God, asking God to do what we cannot do for ourselves. We give voice to this pastoral eschatology in our prayerful petitions. All we can say is that we are deformed and hope to be reformed. The hoped-for self will thus seek to live in full communion with God, safe, at peace, at home in God's presence. Modernism has almost talked us out of this hope.

**Metanarrative** An important story that both establishes and explains a particular worldview and mindset.
**Eschatology** Concerned with the last things: death, judgement, heaven and hell. It is concerned with the final destiny and hope both of the individual and of humanity.

These promises concern the world as a life-giving, food-producing system of interrelations which is as yet unfinished. What we actually see is 'the political–economic–military capacity to brutalize humanity and to terrorize the earth . . . the dysfunction of the ecosystem, dominated by greed and fear . . . the world as we know it is not the one called "good," not the one that God intended.'

It is not easy to say such things in a technological society. An evangelical proclamation will announce that the world has the potential to be harmonious, productive and at peace, as God intended. It cannot tell us how or when but it does tell us who. This is the 'Holy Who' whom modernism tries to eliminate from all its calculations.

These promises concern a finished church. The Church is not the goal of God's creation but God's chosen means – that portion of humanity committed to, and participating in, God's resolve for a new world. The gospel claims are imprecise; they are acts of hope and trust affirming that what God intended is possible.

We are being shown a community that, first, yields its past to a memory of generous origins in God's power and, secondly, hands its future over to the intentionality of God's promises. Brueggemann asserts that such a community must live differently in the present.

In the first place, we are called upon to imagine a self which is free of consumer advertising and the unending efforts of self-security. We are to be open only to the proclamation of presence. We are to imagine a reframed, reshaped self, where obedience to the Law of God is joy rather than burden.

In the second place, we are asked to imagine a world where creatures, under God's presence, no longer hurt or destroy. Here anxious fears are unnecessary and brutal selfishness is inappropriate.

In the third place, we imagine a community of faith where the exile of loss and abandonment is renovated by act of God. The present, still in exile, is transformed.

Brueggemann's call to live differently in the present is a call to live by an act of creative imagination. He demands that Christians free themselves from consumerism and the rat race. The enemy remains amnesia, forgetting our origins as people of God and the values which that point of generation installs in the world. Modernism talks us out of this hope, replacing it with a protective shell of our own self-constructed safety.

Brueggemann's suggestion is that Christians should climb out of the protective shell of self-constructed safety and live faith as a doxological response to God which arises out of the self's fragilities.

### *The pastoral task of theology post 9/11*

In a text written the day after the 9/11 outrage and published on the internet, Brueggemann considers the pastoral role of theology and theologians in the wake of the shock. The first point to take from his reflections is that doing theology is not the reserve of professional theologians; Brueggemann suggests it is the work of all Christian pastors, something they do for and with their communities. In fact it is the work of all the people of God, helped by their pastors and theologians.

The first task of the Church concerns grief and comfort over loss of life. Meaningless violence drives the Church to texts of sadness it has not 'needed' for a long time. The lament psalms provide a powerful resource. He notes the loss as a systemic shattering, a new public sense of vulnerability. The shared sense that the United States were immune from the rage of the world has now been sabotaged.

He draws attention to 'communal laments' (such as Psalms 74 and 79) that communicate the shattering of the most basic public symbol of meaning in the Old Testament: the Jerusalem temple. This public dimension of grief is deep underneath personal loss and not easily spoken. But grief, he feels, will not be articulated adequately until attention goes underneath the personal to the public and communal.

The full voice of grief is to be matched by the enactment of comfort that seeks to meet grief. That begins in bodily contact; but eventually we must speak about the God of all comfort beyond feeble personal offers of comfort. The Easter claim has been ignored and undermined in late twentieth century self-confidence and self-sufficiency. Now the Church is driven back to and must rediscover Easter seriousness. This is the claim that 'the last enemy' (death) has been rendered ineffective by the God of the gospel. That 'last enemy' can no longer rob us of life with God.

If the sense of the tragedy is a coming face to face with evil, theologians must sense that the term 'evil' involves more than particular sins enacted by human individuals. 'Evil' draws us beyond 'bad deeds' to cosmic questions. In the Hebrew Bible, 'evil' is a cosmic force but is not contained in or reduced to visible acts. Evil persists in a powerful way in defiance of the will of the creator.

Americans are a protected and privileged nation which may need to be delivered from innocence. They are forced to recognize that they live in a profoundly contested world, between God's goodwill and the deathliness of evil. In Christian commitment, individuals join the contest as followers of the Vulnerable One. They are called to assume a vulnerable vocation. Being vulnerable is the God-willed future of the world.

Brueggemann has long seen that the temptation for 'Christian America' is to imagine that the United States is a righteous empire doing good around the world. It often refuses to think systemically about how the United States embodies the 'Christian West' against non-Christian societies. When doing this it is often seen to act as an international bully with its huge economic leverage and immense military power.

The old texts claim that God does criticize and move against God's own chosen people. That simple prophetic statement by itself is too raw. It must be accompanied by patient education in systemic analysis of power – an analysis known in the prophetic texts but seldom made explicit.

That is a raw, pressing task for Theology. All Christian thinkers who face such questions will be engaged in deep questions of their own faith. As they engage in that raw questioning, they will suffer, because a triumphant society does not relish truth-telling.

### *Biblical authority*

Brueggemann has always revealed a deep desire for Christian unity and not just amongst Evangelicals; he has an intense sense of compassion and justice for the underprivileged and marginalized and a thoughtful love for the divine character of Holy Scripture. He talks of the Bible as an imaginative narrative of God's care for the world – an account that encourages obedience, builds community and respects the freedom of individual Christians.

He reads the Bible aware of two realities. The first is that all of us do so out of our own unique backgrounds which are compounded of family, friends and personal culture: our socialization process. The second is the fact of our development in faith. The interpretation and the authority of the Bible are not matters of intellectual argument but well up within us from sources that are deep, unrecognized and often embedded in distress, rage and worry. The way we read the Bible is the fruit of habit and conviction, and these often take shape long before we may be conscious of them.

When he writes, a number of aspects of recognition and interpretation, both positive and negative, always appear to be at work:

- God's word is not fixed, it is live and it comes to life in the text of Scripture, speaking through authors who speak their faith out of given backgrounds and circumstances. They transmit but also warp the voice of God. The divine voice is within the text but may not be easy to locate.
- God's spirit blows through the text, allowing it to suggest a resonance of something which is not ourselves. We identify it using the discipline of prayer and meditation in concert with scholarship.
- The Bible needs to be interpreted, but that explanation will be subjective; so there will be disagreement. All such interpretation must be tentative.
- We need a degree of imagination to convert ancient voices into word for the present time. We use subjective freedom here; it cannot claim the seal of certainty.
- Our unique experiences and histories cause us to read all texts with a degree of bias. This refers to both individual and group experiences. These act as filters determining how we read the text. There is no such thing as an interpretation without 'vested interest'.
- We do not interpret the Bible in order to control the Church, but to bring the world into contact with Word of God. We cannot reduce that Word to polished technique or slick formula. We cannot allow any form of trivialization.

## Appraisal

Brueggemann's theology is contextualized. It is ripped from ancient texts and forced into cotemporary settings.

In Brueggemann's view, with the capture of Jerusalem, the destruction of the temple and the end of the house of King David, the nation's long tradition of theological confidence was crushed. However this ruin produced new ways of looking at the nation's relationship with God and the community was re-invigorated.

Out of the diverse elements of Old Testament theology, Brueggemann has forged a Christian response to the experience of the secular, managed society. Spiritual health is the awareness of being loved and receiving the Creator's gifts as surprise. Dominant culture, perpetually forgetful of God, seeks denial and despair. God's alternative must be grasped in faith and made one's own.

Brueggemann repeatedly emphasizes the duty of Theology to address the contemporary world. He also emphasizes the duty of Theology to work with imagination – to test new ways of envisioning faith. And the responses he suggests are never definitive but always provisional. He challenges us to live both with and without certainties.

Other theologians, particularly Liberal ones, have talked of how necessary it is to restate the Christian message in order to make it understood by the contemporary imagination. Brueggemann seems to regard contemporary culture as a sort of filter through which the message must pass. He does not talk about 'restating' the message; he talks of daring, subversive speech and text by means of which the message can either grasp the hearers or be grasped by them.

Brueggemann's theology is about (counterfeit) worlds that are created for us by vested interests such as banks, big business, governments and mass media. It is also about the power of liberating imagination which denies any limitation on divine power. This theology is how ordinary human beings may come to see what is being kept from them by a tamed, domesticated imagination and receive power to break those limitations and have access to the infinite possibilities of God.

Brueggemann's vision of false living is composed of two pictures. On the one hand we see free and responsible individuals who make up their own world, investigate their own problems, fashion their own responses and are self-sufficient. On the other we see mass-produced individuals who live in a pre-packaged world, with limited control over their own conditions of living: residing in residences that all look alike, their income regulated, their tax deducted at source. Both are inauthentic. What are they both lacking?

Brueggemann's work is a revalidation of the capacity of the Bible, in particular of the Old Testament, to *fund*, to provide raw material for, the task of constructing an alternative Evangelical imagination.

But Evangelical faith is often held with great certainty and lived with great intensity. So there is a danger of an uncritical response to his proposition.

The proposal of an evangelical counter-imagination resonates differently in post-Christian Europe where God is largely absent from any self-understanding which individuals and communities articulate. It may be necessary to proclaim an evangelical counter-imagination, but proclamation is not enough. Absoluteness of conviction and intensity of religious emotion are not good decision-making tools. The teasing, probing, playful, imaginative building of an alternative mindset based on Scripture is necessary, but it must be a reasoned proclamation.

Brueggemann does not outline how the task of holding together the free, imaginative play of renewal and the equally creative criticism of discipline might be accomplished. He does not explicitly acknowledge the problem.

If the dominant discourse of modernism is portrayed as an imaginative construal in need of subversion, any evangelical counter-drama which in turn becomes dominant must obviously be undermined in the same way. Brueggemann maintains his project as a dogged imaging against the grain as he warns against Christians relying on a dominant consumerism.

So we are not faced with an 'either-or', rather with a dialectical 'both-and': with the tensions of daring and caution, of imagination and criticism, the tension of an innovative openness and the brake of reason and generosity. Maybe this discipline is already inherent in Brueggemann's proposal that we hold a de-absolutized present between a past tied to the faithfulness of God and a future liberated to the extravagant, outrageous promises of God. The search for an Evangelical counter-imagination is to be a 'faithful practice of imagination'.

Brueggemann's work is a powerful social criticism, yet it never relies on purely human remedies; it constantly remembers the incisive intervening possibilities of the power of God.

What is wrong with bourgeois self-sufficiency? What is right with it? Can one only respond to God's gracious call if living in economic precariousness? Is this really what Brueggemann means?

What hopes are denied in the dissatisfied coping with twenty-first century everyday life? What might one grieve for? How might one be amazed and what would be expressed in praise?

# 16 Don Cupitt and Being Adrift

Don Cupitt's theological thought has gone through a number of developments. He first tried to defend orthodox theology and to restate and reinterpret central ideas in new ways. At this early stage he discussed the possibility of objectivity in faith. The notion of transcendence was still for him an important idea. He thought it was necessary in order to advance in theological and ethical thinking.

He wished to avoid saying that the believer creates the religious meaning he believes in. He was particularly critical of projection theory in religion. This is the idea that religious belief is merely an expression of our deepest desires rather than a coming to terms with something actually there.

Nevertheless he did develop objections to certain accepted dogmas and he came to believe that much of church life and outlook had a repressive quality. This stage marks a shift in his search. Formerly he was looking for religious meaning *from above*; now he looks for religious meaning *from within.*

If human beings are to come to genuine moral choices, then they cannot be adopted in obedience to a God who imposes them (heteronomous faith); they must be freely accepted. Cupitt now thinks that religious language is losing its objective quality and becoming more symbolic.

The aim of Cupitt's religious–ethical thought is to allow human beings to become fully independent, self-regulating individuals. An objective God who imposes divine will cannot allow fully autonomous human beings. Cupitt's thought is now turning to what can or cannot be meaningfully said about God.

**Objective** Having actual existence, independent of a person's thoughts, feelings or prejudices.
**Transcendence** Above, independent of, surpassing, the material universe.
**Ethics** Concerning the principles of right and wrong.
**Orthodox** Adhering to accepted, established religious faith.
**Dogma** A system of religious teaching authoritatively considered to be absolute truth.
**Autonomy** Self-governing; freedom from outside influence.

## Life (1934– )

Don Cupitt was born in Lancashire in the north of England in 1934. He was educated at Charterhouse and later at Trinity Hall in Cambridge. He studied Natural Sciences, Theology and the Philosophy of Religion. He prepared for ordination at Westcott House, Cambridge, a college for training clergy of the Church of England.

He was ordained priest in 1960 and had a brief spell as a curate in the north of England. He then quickly became vice principal of Westcott House and was later made a member of the academic staff at Emmanuel College, Cambridge. He remained at Emmanuel College. He was appointed a university teacher in the Philosophy of Religion in 1968. He retired from that post for health reasons in 1996.

Don Cupitt is widely known for his many writings and because he is a controversial religious thinker. He has made gifted use of television to reach a wide audience. His programmes, some of which have been published as books, have included *The Great Debate, Who was Jesus?* and *The Sea of Faith.*

Cupitt has tried to state a philosophical system which reconciles a scientific view of the world with the artistic-mythological view of the world expressed by religious thought. To this end he has tried to make metaphysics meaningful again. He does not believe in seeking to escape this world in order to achieve salvation. For him the religious ideal consists of trying to add joy and value to life. Cupitt also challenges traditional views of the 'afterlife'. He maintains that true Christianity is about living productively and rewardingly in this life.

His hobbies include art, walking and the study of butterflies. His wife is a potter. They have three children and are grandparents.

He ceased to officiate at services of public worship in the 1990s. His writings are valued by 'liberals' in the church.

### Timeline

1933 Hitler becomes German Chancellor
1934 Birth of Don Cupitt
1939–1945 Second World War

1948 Beginning of the Cold War
1949 Simone de Beauvoir's *The Second Sex*
1950–1953 Korean War
1952 Samuel Beckett's *Waiting for Godot*
1953 The structure of DNA
1956 The contraceptive pill
1957 Jack Kerouac's *On the Road*
The Soviet Union launches the first artificial satellite
1960 Don Cupitt ordained priest
1966 The Cultural Revolution in China
1969 First man on the moon
1971 Cupitt's *Christ and the Hiddenness of God*
1973 Cupitt's television programme *The Great Debate*
1976 Cupitt's *The Leap of Reason*; Cupitt's television programme *Who was Jesus?*
1978 First test tube baby
1980 Cupitt's *Taking Leave of God*
1984 Cupitt's television programme *The Sea of Faith*
1988 Cupitt's *The New Christian Ethics*
1989 Fall of the Berlin Wall
1990 Cupitt's *Creation out of Nothing*
1991 Abolition of apartheid in South Africa
1994 Cupitt's *After All: Religion without Alienation*
1999 Cupitt's *The New Religion of Life in Everyday Speech*
2001 9/11 attack on America
2003 American and British troops invade Iraq
2005 Cupitt's *Way to Happiness: A Theory of Religion*

## Thought

Cupitt developed his early theological thought around the idea of *via negativa*: we can only say what God is *not*; we cannot say what God is. He quickly came to the conclusion that all language about God is anthropocentric, always related to an understanding of what humans are. We create this language, we use it to talk about God; so then God must be, through language, a human creation. Nothing exists outside language.

If you try to think of something outside language, you will be using language to think of it.

## The Sea of Faith *(1984)*

Cupitt's television programme grabbed headlines when it seemed that a religious programme was being introduced by a Church of England clergyman who did not believe in God. In fact Cupitt believes passionately that we need a new way of understanding what it means to believe in God.

Faith, for Cupitt, is a cultural event. It takes different forms at different times. God is the sum of our values, their unity, the demands they make of us and their creative power. We cannot hold the same type of faith as early, or even medieval, Christians. The way we view the world changed with Galileo and the sixteenth-century scientific revolution. How we view ourselves changed once we adopted the insights of Darwin and Freud. Theology could never be the same again following Kierkegaard, Nietzsche and Wittgenstein. *The Sea of Faith* is an interesting, but polemical, view of the evolution of Western Christianity.

**Polemic** Controversial, one-sided attack upon, or defence of, a given opinion or doctrine.

## The Last Philosophy *(1995)*

Cupitt argues that God does not exist independently, 'out there'. God is the personification of our religious values. He seeks a new form of Christianity, often called a Christian Buddhism, which allows us to investigate this new idea of God. His aim is personal development and social change.

He wants to present his thinking in ordinary, easily understood terms without jargon – in what he calls 'democratic terms'.

If we try to sit quietly and observe our consciousness, what we become aware of is that we have to express it in language: what is deepest inside us generates language. Life is fundamentally a constant flow of energy.

Cupitt's good news, or gospel, is that this is all that there is. We become enlightened when we realize that there was never a time when we were not enlightened.

What Cupitt fails to explain satisfactorily is where the notion that we are not enlightened came from. It is a cultural construct? Is it a power game a priestly class has played upon the entire human race, in every culture, since time began? Is such a notion credible? Does the original impulse towards religious feeling flow from lack, from imperfection or from an urge to go beyond, to stretch out towards what cannot be said?

### *The experience of being adrift*

Cupitt was once critical about the language we use about God. He has since changed his stance. What we say about God is not really what we mean. Language is an inadequate tool for talking about God. He now argues that there is no objective God. When we talk about God we are really talking about ourselves.

Cupitt's thinks of humanity as adrift from any tie to realism; by this he means God as an objective entity. We have now become the Creator. From that position Cupitt sets out to explore the fundamental nature of humanity and the world and wonders what that involves in practical or ethical terms.

Traditional religions state that humans are imperfect, sinful and in need of salvation. This can only be offered by God. But what if there is no God, no heaven and no mind or language apart from what we, the human race, has created? In that case our earthly lives cannot be a preparation for eternity. Cupitt consequently rejects all such notions. There is no 'outside'.

We must turn attention away from the invisible to the visible. Morality has developed within the bounds of our needs and experience. It is not a 'given' from outside. We have our most immediate access to what exists through language. Language provides the concepts, ideas and notions which allow us to analyse the world, to use and control it.

Here we are approaching the notion of 'projection theory'. We see the world the way we do because we project our desires and needs onto it. We 'construct' the world because of our needs and desires.

Traditional projection theory talks of the mind projecting our desires onto what is there and, by this means, giving it a shape in accordance with that interpretation. Cupitt wants to discard the notion of mind or 'inner space'. Kant had claimed that time and space were essential categories of the mind. We could not think or speak or operate without them because our minds are pre-programmed in such a way that we cannot understand anything without them.

Cupitt abandons such notions; the world is being played out in front of us. The only thing that gives form to such experience is language.

If there is no invisible realm of the mind there can be no *orthodoxy* and the only thing that can concern us is *praxis*: what we do. The world of quietness, stillness, reflection, meditation, prayer and praise does not exist.

The world and language are relative and impermanent. Meaning is simply what is agreed among members of the human community. We are in a world of constant rootless change; it is not even a process. Process would suggest purpose.

The old system was just a form of slavery. Whoever had power imposed meaning on those who had no power and did so for their own purposes. We now enter a world of free choice and free values. We are totally free, there is no pre-determined truth. We are whatever it is that we are becoming.

## Solar Ethics *(1995)*

How should we live with this situation? Cupitt uses the image of the sun to explain his point. The sun integrates both living and dying perfectly. It is giving itself to our world and to other planets of the solar system, thus allowing them to live. At the same time, it is dying. The sun is not essence; it is just act.

We also are performance. There is no chance to practise, to repeat or to correct. We are not limited by any ideal to which we should correspond. We are free and in the course of becoming.

There is no fixed moral law. The only demand is to express ourselves fully. The only sin is not to do so. Nobody is bound in any way. All that exists is language and time. The only mechanism to avoid anarchy is the fact of language. If pure anarchy were the only principle of order, there could be no language.

Cupitt's philosophy is an attempt to free people from the belief that there is something wrong with us and the way we live. The function of philosophy is to help us to understand what we already know; its role is to be descriptive, not prescriptive.

We should, however, be cautious of freely accepting the reductionism in Cupitt's description of the human condition. If there is no 'outside', notions such as continuity, meaning and personality are all meaningless. Language cannot be reduced to a mere set of agreed mechanisms which came from nowhere. There are problems in understanding how language functions. But it does function, in spite of the appearance of having no deep meaning. The correspondence between an idea intended and the sound used may be arbitrary, but it is there, it is necessary and is very subtle.

**Personification** When inanimate objects or ideas are represented as having human form or human qualities.
**Anarchy** Disorder, confusion, absence of any form of authority.

### The Religion of Being *(1998)*

Cupitt argues that once we abandon belief in a Supreme Being we need a new theory of Being and for that he turns to the philosopher Martin Heidegger (1889–1976). Cupitt argues that we should turn our attention to human beings in time and how they relate to Being. Being is both 'letting be' and 'letting go'. Nothing physical underpins us in time. We are the products of a transient contingency.

Being is not another word for God. Being is not substance or form or nature or force or power or any of the standard words of traditional metaphysics. Being is finite, contingent and limited in time.

For Cupitt, God was, at times, an idea with violent overtones. We have abandoned it and must wait before we can accept a more gentle and mild notion such as Being. Everything is contingent; it just happens to be as it is. Nothing is necessary. Being is near and evident; it energizes us and comes to expression in language. To come to some realization of this truth, our reflection should attend to the here-and-now quality of the world. Even if dreadful events occur, we cannot blame some all-powerful being, we can only say 'yes' to what is. This contingency can only be innocent, not evil.

Cupitt turns to a number of contemporary philosophers to find a vocabulary to replace the Super-Male controlling power of the traditional, transcendent God who rules by decree. Being has feminine qualities – is 'inturning', womb, matrix of possibilities, self-giving.

Throughout Western intellectual history the 'wise' have believed in the possibility of order, and when order failed, they have fallen into pessimism. The common people have seen reality as 'trickster', breaking the rules, upsetting the applecart, getting away with it, and they have loved that chancy, fickle disorder. Cupitt believes we should set out to rediscover that lightness of meaning.

As we delve down into language, all we find at each level is another veil of language; decisive meaning always dodges away from us. Meaning presupposes being; being presupposes meaning. We must learn to see a void, a chaotic world rather than an intelligible one filled with order. Meaningful views of the world are short-lived creations of language.

Religious experience is possible when we allow Being to creep forth into individuals. Human beings are not naturally and fundamentally rational creatures. We are creatures of desire and need; reason and reflection were late developments.

As we became more technologically skilled, and gradually possessed enough wealth to realize dreams, we forgot the fundamental qualities of Being which were limited, contingent and ephemeral. We deceived ourselves into thinking we could realize theological hopes. Cupitt thinks of such theological hopes in terms of knowledge, control, power, pleasure and the sublime.

So we need to turn the values we have received upside down. We ought to imitate the trickster and the fool, to take our example from the mad prophet Ezekiel or the cynic Diogenes and concentrate on what 'rationality' ignores. We should turn to the uncertainty of life; should seek the elusiveness we shall never master, the slipperiness and contingency of Being. We must abandon our desire for meaning in the face of meaninglessness. When we come to understand that point, when we realize the emptiness of Being and the death of the Self, then we are on the road to a new awareness of salvation. Religion is not about belief; it is about practice. It is not a question of accepting a set of propositions with our minds and our reason; it is an affirmation of being. In cultural terms, at the present moment, we are in transition from God to Being.

**Transient** Passing away with time, not permanent.
**Contingent** That which can happen or can exist, yet need not.
**Substance** Nowadays the word means a form of material, like earth or lead. In metaphysics it means the essence or form that makes something what it is. The substance of the stool makes the wood a stool rather than a walking stick.
**Metaphysics** is the study of being as being; speculation about the meaning of what is; the study of first principles and first causes; the rational knowledge of those realities that go beyond us; the rational study of things in themselves.
**Necessary** What has to be. Without which some other thing cannot be or some other event cannot take place.
**Ephemeral** Lasting for a brief time, short-lived.
**Hierarchy** Any arrangement of elements where some are seen as more important than others. For example, bishops are considered more important than priests.
**Absolute** Perfect in quality, complete, not limited by restrictions or conditions, something considered to be the ultimate basis for all thought and being.
**Ineffable** Unable to be described in words, either because it is beyond our understanding or too sacred.

### *Thought in transition*

Early in his career, Cupitt took the view that theological statements are regulative: they guide our actions. He tried to state theological insights in new ways. He later came to criticize what he called 'realism', the view that God existed 'out there'. He moved to the view that God was the embodiment of our religious values. He has since moved to seeing religion as rather like artistic activity, we express ourselves by creative action. Religion is the affirmation of Being, a cultural activity.

So is Cupitt a Christian or an atheist, a prophet or a heretic? He has certainly argued that the Church must get rid of its supernatural beliefs. They were being gradually eroded anyway. We no longer blame God if a hurricane blows; we no longer assume we have sinned if we fall ill. We live in a world governed by rational, discoverable scientific laws and are able to control and predict many events. It is, however, a long leap to infer from this that God is a human creation.

We have always created ethics; we must now redefine our metaphysical vocabulary and our mental outlook. There can be no final definition of Christianity. The strange thing is that, in fact, there never was; but the obsession with orthodoxy often blinded us to that fact.

In addition, the idea that we can no longer talk about an objective God or ethical absolutes is not new. It has been at the heart of debate, since the theological adventure began.

The history of Theology has been a constant redefining of concepts, a sorting out of nasty ideas. Nevertheless, if human beings have notions of transcendence and wish to find ways of expressing the ineffable, the theological enterprise will continue to be valid.

## Appraisal

Is Cupitt's 'solar ethics' really religious?

Christian theologies had largely underpinned the 'modern' mindset. On the other hand they had also been obliged to turn around and criticize the drift towards secularism which was one of the outcomes of modernity.

All knowing, says Cupitt, is done by a subject. All the stimuli received by the knower are taken, categorized and interpreted by the same knowing subject. There is no objective knowledge, only knowledge as it appears to us. All knowing is relative to the knowing subject and created by the same knowing subject. We therefore cannot find absolutes outside of ourselves. We make, rather than discover, the world. Religion is completely human – a product of history, of culture and the stories and values they create.

If we use language to refer to something outside language, then does that really mean that language has created it? In what way might it be said that language has created it? Would that something still exist if there were nobody there to talk about it?

In Cupitt's view, Christianity did not allow for human creativity, since God was considered to be in control. Christian morality was just an effort to please this dominant, frightening God.

Cupitt's new ethics are an effort to affirm the self and the self's creativity, to accept them joyfully. Religion becomes ethics. The task is not to give metaphysical explanations of how things are but to shape and direct the way we live.

Does an objective God who is unlimited and supreme have to be a tyrannical God who imposes his will? Can such a God be gentle or loving, where necessary chiding, but nurturing rather than compelling?

How might some one who thinks like Don Cupitt view the Bible? Would such a person need the idea of revelation? How would he use sacraments? What might they mean? Why might this form of thinking do without them? What use are they? Is Theology nothing more than metaphysical speculation?

In Cupitt's view, is salvation the work of God or the work of human beings? Can Christianity be Christian without 'resurrection faith'?

Why has the Christian view of Trinity become such a stumbling block to acceptance of Christian faith in the late twentieth and early twenty-first centuries? Has the Christian Church been so obsessed with 'correct dogma' that it has become repressive rather than pastoral?

Are we pure act without values? Are we content that all should live in this fashion? Are the rules of language the only restriction on us? Do we, and ought we, demand that others should conform to a standard of life? And are they right to make similar demands on us?

If others rob or kill me, should I accept it as part of their expression of who they really are? Or have I the right to demand a brake on that self-expression? And where do the agreed communal values, that together we accept and impose, come from?

Do ethics depend on the values (positive and negative) we give to certain words? 'Murder', 'rape', 'cheat' all have negative values. 'Help', 'gentleness', 'solidarity' all have positive values. Are these purely linguistic?

What is linguistic meaning? Words have always subtly created their meanings, suggestions and connotations in relation to other words, in a sophisticated complex that is always shifting. Does this mean they have no external reference?

# Conclusion

I hope you have found our short meander along the course of Western Christian Theology interesting.

We have emphasized here that Theology is something that is done by everybody. The theological questions we all ask are reflected in the concerns of these and many other thinkers.

We started with writers who are not often thought of as theologians. Revelation was in Christ and these authors were among the first to record their reaction to that self-disclosure of God. We then took a jump of a few hundred years and looked at St Augustine, one of the most influential thinkers of the Western Latin tradition.

He was followed by St Thomas Aquinas, whose systematized thought would, in time, become the standard expression of Western Christian orthodoxy.

The sixteenth century saw a major upheaval in the Latin Church and one which eventually resulted in the personal freedoms of Western liberal civilization. The notion of 'authority' has become a much less forensic concept; it has become a word which one must now approach more tentatively, more humbly.

The sixteenth century reformations are represented here by Luther, Calvin and Loyola. Ultimately arguments between Christians were not played out along the faultline of that cataclysm which divided 'Protestants' from 'Catholics'. They were increasingly played out along lines of objective and subject authority, as standards such as Bible, Church, 'magisterium', reason, Natural Theology, dogma, individual experience and feeling came into play. These divergences frequently appeared on both sides of the more visible, historical and institutional divide. Wesley played an obvious role in the drama of religious feeling. So did Schleiermacher, more urbanely. So too, quite subtly, did Newman.

The liberal tradition wished Theology to speak directly to the specific thought patterns and concerns of contemporary culture. Here God becomes less personal and more of an abstraction. With Cupitt, however, God fades from consciousness and appears to dissolve into ethics.

Liberation theologies are also theologies of Immanence. The term had not been invented in Bonhoeffer's time, yet he occupied a unique position, crushed between creeping secularization and rampant, political aggression. The feminist thought of Rosemary Radford Ruether represents a different form of Liberation Theology. Other varieties have flourished in the late twentieth and early twenty-first centuries.

In case you thought that Theology had become a new form of humanism, there have been powerful influences stressing the otherness, the awesomeness, the majesty and transcendence of God. Barth's has probably been the fiercest and most passionate voice. Rahner, with his emphasis on the transcendence of the human, occupies an interesting and nuanced position. Brueggemann's finely crafted Biblical imagination brings yet another form of fine shading to these theologies of Transcendence.

Over half of the theological thinkers outlined in this book belong to the modern period: from Schleiermacher onwards.

Religion is a bit like aviation: wonderful when saving lives and deadly when bombing cities. As in every sphere of human experience, religious activists can do and have done great good; they have also sinned grievously. The writer to the *First Epistle of John* wants us to 'test the spirits to see whether they are from God . . . Every spirit that acknowledges that Jesus Christ has come in the flesh is from God' (1 Jn 4.1–2). Obviously this writer does not wish us to accept everything at face value. Ideas must be probed and examined; reason and experience must be brought into play. Particular elements of understanding, familiarity and memory must be reconciled within a cohering whole. One can leave things at the level of wonderful but nice story or one can move to the level of deeper and more universal significance. That is the task of Theology.

Theology is a form of deliberation which takes place within each one of us and it is simultaneously a thoughtfulness which marks a wider community of faith and interchange, as we all develop the ability to create a space where faith and reason may dialogue.

Thankfully, we no longer live in a society where we must swallow everything dished up by the 'elders of the tribe'. Within Theology, as within all forms of social order and tradition, there are elements which are agents of alienation, outdated custom and convention which have been raised to mythical status. Religion and politics often become confused; hostility and violence are visited upon the weak and vulnerable in the name of truth. This is as obvious within the Christian tradition as it is elsewhere. And it is actual; it is with us today.

As we ponder theologically, our rational side is always conscious of problems, questions and arguments; our prayerful side dwells on the deep and silent unity of the universe. That awareness of Being, the Holy, God, the profound necessity to sit and contemplate, can only be eradicated by stunting our growth.

We are more than flesh, blood and electrical impulses. The human beings who make machines and tools also invent stories and create works of art, construct the great scaffolding of the human imagination, searching for meaning and creating value, ever expanding the bounds of human possibility. These too are the tasks of Theology. We subsist by economic activity and material gain; we live by poetry, love, enthusiasm, communion and the search for truth.

Theology is the intellectual, rational, disciplined approach to revelation, to a summons, in Jesus Christ. Therefore Theology must move between three poles of influence, hold three forms of abstraction in tension. They are the rational and speculative, the mystical and imaginative and the Biblical Gospel revealed in Scripture and in the tradition of the Church of God. How this threefold pondering has been accomplished in the past is the subject of this short book.

# Further Reading

We start with two general single-volume histories of Theology which you may find helpful. Alister McGrath's *Christian Theology: An Introduction* (Oxford: Blackwell Publishing, 2001) is a sober survey of both the historical development and the subject matter of (mostly) Western Christian Theology. S.J. Grenz and R.E. Olson's *20th Century Theology: God and the World in a Transitional Age* (Downer's Grove, IL: IVP, 1992) is written from an American, Evangelical perspective. A more weighty series is entitled *The Great Theologians.* It is being published by Blackwell Publishing. Volumes dealing with *The First Christian Theologians, The Medieval Theologians, The Reformation Theologians, The Pietist Theologians* and *The Modern Theologians* have all been published. At the time of writing we await a volume on nineteenth century theologians. Each theologian is presented by a world renowned scholar.

On the subject of Western civilization, one might try R. Osborne's *Civilization: A New History of the Western World* (London: Pimlico, 2007) and R. Tarnas's *The Passion of the Western Mind* (London: Pimlico, 1991).

The following is a list covering each of the individual chapters mentioned in this work:


Armstrong, K., *The First Christian: St Paul's Impact on Christianity* (London: Macmillan, 1983).

Brueggemann, W., *A Theological Handbook of Old Testament Themes* (Louisville, KY: John Knox Press, 2002).

Dauphinais, M. and Levering, M., *Knowing the Love of Christ: An Introduction to the Theology of St Thomas Aquinas* (Notre Dame, IN: University of Notre Dame Press, 2002).

Dramm, S., *Dietrich Bonhoeffer: An Introduction to His Thought* (Peabody, MA: Hendrickson, 2007).

Dulles, A., *John Henry Newman* (Outstanding Christian Thinkers) (London: Continuum, 2005).

Kilby, K., *The SPCK Introduction to Karl Rahner: A Brief Introduction* (London: SPCK, 2007).

Leaves, N., *Surfing on the Sea of Faith: The Ethics and Religion of Don Cupitt* (Santa Rosa, CA: Polebridge Press, 2005).

O'Donnell, J.J., *St Augustine: Sinner and Saint* (London: Profile Books, 2006).

Parker, T.H.L., *John Calvin* (Oxford: Lion Hudson, 2006).

Rack, H.D. *Reasonable Enthusiast: John Wesley and the Rise of Methodism* (London: Epworth, 2002).

Ruether, R.R., *Sexism and God-Talk* (SCM Classics) (London: SCM, 2002).

Sklar, P.A., *St Ignatius of Loyola: In God's Service* (Mahwah, NJ: Paulist Press International, 2001).

Stanton, G., *The Gospels and Jesus* (Oxford: OUP, 2002).

Tice, T.N., *Schleiermacher* (Abingdon Pillars of Theology) (Nashville, TN: Abingdon Press, 2006).

Walker, J., *Karl Barth* (Outstanding Christian Thinkers) (London: Continuum, 2000).

Wilson, D., *Out of the Storm: The Life and Legacy of Martin Luther* (London: Hutchinson, 2007).

# Index